Introduction to Alcoholism Counseling

Second Edition

Introduction to Alcoholism Counseling
A Bio-Psycho-Social Approach

Second Edition

Jerome David Levin
New School for Social Research
New York, New York

Taylor & Francis
Publishers since 1798

USA	Publishing Office:	Taylor & Francis
		1101 Vermont Avenue, N.W., Suite 200
		Washington, D.C. 20005-3521
		Tel: (202) 289-2174
		Fax: (202) 289-3665
	Distribution Center:	Taylor & Francis
		1900 Frost Road, Suite 101
		Bristol, PA 19007-1598
		Tel: (215) 785-5800
		Fax: (215) 785-5515
UK		Taylor & Francis, Ltd.
		4 John St.
		London WC1N 2ET
		Tel: 071 405 2237
		Fax: 071 831 2035

INTRODUCTION TO ALCOHOLISM COUNSELING:
A Bio-Psycho-Social Approach, Second Edition

1 2 3 4 5 6 7 8 9 0   B R B R   9 8 7 6 5

This book was set in Times Roman by Sandra F. Watts. The editors were Christine E. Williams and Alice S. M. Rowan. Cover design by Michelle Fleitz. Printing and binding by Braun-Brumfield, Inc.

A CIP catalog record for this book is available from the British Library.
∞ The paper in this publication meets the requirements of the ANSI Standard Z39.48-1984 (Permanence of Paper).

Library of Congress Cataloging-in-Publication Data

Levin, Jerome D. (Jerome David)
    Introduction to alcoholism counseling: a bio-psycho-social
approach / Jerome David Levin.—2nd ed.
      p. cm.
    Includes bibliographical references and index.

    1. Alcoholism. 2. Alcoholism—Treatment. 3. Alcoholism
counseling. I. Title.
    RC565.L4333   1995   94-44764
    362.29'2—dc20   CIP

ISBN 1-56032-355-8 (cloth)
ISBN 1-56032-358-2 (paper)

For Melissa, Bernadette, and Spooky

Contents

Chapter 5   **What Is Alcoholism?**   87

Chapter 6   **What Do We Know About Alcoholism?**   111

PART 2: THEORETICAL

PART 3: CLINICAL

Preface

The use and abuse of mood altering substances is a ubiquitous concomitant of human life. Yet times change and the ways and extent to which a culture uses such mood changers including alcohol also change. There have been some attitudinal changes in the American, and Western industrial, attitude toward alcohol during the past five years and I have striven to reflect these changes in this Second Edition of *An Introduction to Alcoholism Counseling: A Bio-Psycho-Social Approach*. The growing social disapproval of heavy drinking and of drunkenness has simultaneously and paradoxically deepened alcoholic shame, guilt, and denial and made recovery from alcoholism easier. The growing acceptance of alcoholism as a disease in the popular mind, at a time of growing scientific criticism of the disease concept, has made for conceptual confusion, but has probably also made it easier to recover. So the counselor works in a different climate, a climate that in some ways facilitates his or her work and in other ways impedes it.

There has also been an explosion of research on alcoholism, an explosion so voluminous and so complex that its assimilation and evaluation is extremely difficult. It is my allover impression that this research has advanced our knowledge of alcoholism, but that that advance is extremely modest. I have found surprisingly little that significantly illuminates our vexed subject. I think part of the problem is an overemphasis on technique—on methodology—resulting in multiauthored, multivariate studies in which the statistical analyses become so arcane, and the conclusions so observation distant, that their interpretation becomes problematic. One often gets the feeling that we are learning more and more about less and less. Although I respect the thrust for scientific rigor and share the newer researchers' distrust of constructs without empirical support and of overly broad generalizations, I do think that boldness of speculation has a place in science. Additionally, the research methodology now in vogue has a strongly behavioristic (when it is not neurochemical) bias, making it difficult for more psychodynamic formulations to get a hearing. Alcoholics, like everyone else, have inner worlds as well as neurotransmitters and operant conditioning mechanisms. The experiential, the unconscious, and the relational have as much reality as anything else, but exist and need to be explained on a different conceptual level. Hence, the necessity of the alcoholism counselor having multiple models with which to organize and comprehend the data of the consulting room. I have tried to provide these models by expanding and updating both the empirical psychological and psychodynamic sessions in this edition. In doing so, I tried to be just to the contributions of theorists with whom I do not have an overwhelming sympathy. In summarizing the newer psychological literature, I have not always cited individual studies, although I have provided enough references for the reader to pursue any of a wide variety of approaches to alcohol abuse. In response to the virtual ubiquity of cross addiction, I have added a chapter on other drugs of abuse.

Apart from updating psychological, sociological, and pharmacological findings and demographics, the main change in the Second Edition is a broadening and deepening of the clinical sections including discussions of such new approaches to treatment as the use of acupuncture and network therapy. Here I have tried to be comprehensive. So although this book remains primarily informational rather than being a text on alcoholism counseling technique, it focuses much more on clinical implications and strategies. The careful reader will be in a position to inform his or her counseling with the latest scientific knowledge and will have a broad understanding of how the various treatment modalities work and what they do best.

This book starts with the chemical and pharmacological, proceeding to the medical; and only then dealing with the social, anthropological, and psychological. Some readers may wish to reverse this order and since the psycho-social chapters are self contained, there is no reason not to do so. The clinical material, on the other hand, does assume familiarity with the empirical and theoretical.

The Second Edition continues to assume no prior knowledge of any of the areas it discusses, so it is accessible to the general reader, the recovering person, and the family and friends of the alcoholic, active or recovering, as well as being a text for alcoholism counseling students. Agreeing with Aristotle that "Man by his nature desires to know" and with Francis Bacon that "Knowledge is power," it is my hope that this edition finds, and is of help to, that broader audience.

Jerome David Levin

Preface to the First Edition

Alcoholism counseling is an art and a science; it involves both intuition and reason. Integration of the intuitive and the rational aspects of alcoholism counseling is not an easy task and cannot be approached without knowledge of what is known about alcohol and alcoholism. A careful reading of this book will provide such a knowledge base. The book is comprehensive, summarizing biochemical, pharmacological, physiological, anthropological, sociological, epidemiological, historical, and psychological findings on alcohol and its use and abuse. The book concludes by discussing the principles of alcoholism treatment. Although primarily addressed to counseling students, the information on alcohol and alcoholism in this book is presented in accessible language, which makes it useful to a wide variety of other readers.

This book is the fruit of many years of experience teaching alcoholism counseling at Marymount Manhattan College and the New School for Social Research as well as teaching psychoanalytic candidates at the American Institute for Psychotherapy and Psychoanalysis and the Post-Graduate Center for Mental Health. All of these institutions are located in New York City. I am very grateful to my students for their patience in learning from a work in progress and their feedback, without which this book would not have been possible.

I wish to thank Jason Aronson, M.D., of Jason Aronson, Inc., for giving me permission to modify and use material from chapters 2 and 3 of my 1987 book, *Treatment of Alcoholism and Other Addictions: A Self-Psychology Approach.*

I owe a special debt of gratitude to Robert Maslansky, M.D., of the Bellevue Hospital-New York University Medical Center for his consultation so freely given, in spite of his heavy schedule, on all matters medical and biochemical. Bob also teaches in my alcoholism counseling program at the New School for Social Research. I also thank one of my students, Shelden Pisani, for compiling the biological marker literature.

Jerome David Levin

Part One

Factual

Chapter 1

Alcohol: Chemical, Beverage, and Drug

One reason the study of alcoholism is so fascinating is its complexity. The physical sciences, the biological sciences, and the social sciences are needed to help illuminate the strange and baffling phenomenon—the slow, relentless self-poisoning of a human being—that we call alcoholism. Alcohol is a chemical and a drug; it is contained in a vast range of fermented fluids; it is consumed by people; it affects their bodies and their minds, in ways not fully understood. People who drink have personalities, are members of families, live in societies, and are influenced by cultures. To understand the phenomenon of alcoholism, we will need to look at the chemical and drug; its physical and psychological effects; the people who drink it; and the families, societies, and cultures those people live in. This book begins with an examination of the chemical and drug, with alcohol itself.

ALCOHOL AS A CHEMICAL

Alcohol is a chemical. When swallowed, it has pharmacological properties; that is, it acts as a drug, powerfully modifying the functioning of the nervous system. To provide an understanding of the kind of chemical alcohol is and how it works, this chapter begins with a review of some elementary chemistry.

All matter is composed of chemical *elements*. There are 106 of these elements. They vary in the complexity of their structures. These elements are the building blocks of the universe. The qualities of the substances we encounter daily depend on their chemical composition—that is, on the kind and arrangement of elements they contain.

Elements consist of *atoms*. Atoms are basic in that they cannot be further subdivided without losing the very qualities that make an element distinct. Each element consists of atoms that differ in their structure from the atoms of other elements. Atoms consist of a nucleus containing particles called *protons*, which carry positive charges, and rings of *electrons*, which carry negative charges. The nucleus may also contain electrically neutral particles called *neutrons*. Atoms as a whole are electrically neutral. The simplest of the elements is hydrogen; its chemical symbol is H. Its atom consists of one proton and one electron (Figure 1.1). The other elements have progressively more complex atomic structures, but the idea remains the same. In each case there is a nucleus with protons and perhaps neutrons and one or more rings of electrons. The *periodic table* arranges the elements according to their atomic structure.

In nature, atoms are usually combined into larger units called *molecules*. The number of electrons in the outer ring of an atom determines how readily and with which other atoms it will combine. Atoms are said to seek a stable configuration of electrons in their outermost rings and to enter into chemical reactions to achieve this. Of course, to attribute a desire for stability to an atom is to *anthropomorphize* it—to attribute to it human qualities—but "motivation" aside, that is the way an atom behaves. When two or more atoms combine, the resulting entity is called a molecule.

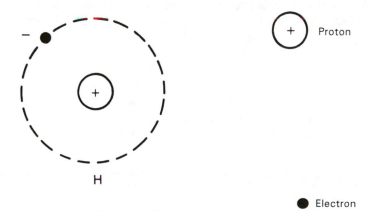

Figure 1.1 Hydrogen atom.

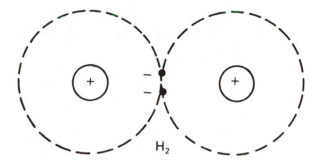

Figure 1.2 Hydrogen molecule.

In the hydrogen molecule, shown in Figure 1.2, each atom's outer ring—which in this case is its only ring—contains two electrons. This is a stable configuration for this ring, or shell. The hydrogen atom's ring can hold only two electrons, and as part of a hydrogen molecule it has them.

If the atoms forming a molecule are atoms of different elements, the result is a chemical *compound* with a definite molecular structure. Just as an element cannot be divided into more ultimate units than atoms without it ceasing to be that element, a compound cannot be divided into more ultimate units than molecules without it ceasing to be that compound.

Atoms combine into molecules in two basic ways. They can share one or more electrons, forming what is called a *covalent bond*, or one of the atoms forming the bond can "donate" one or more electrons to the other atom forming the bond. Thus, one atom becomes positively charged and the other negatively charged. Such bonds are called *ionic bonds*. The hydrogen molecule, illustrated in Figure 1.2, is an example of a covalent bond. One of the most familiar examples of a compound formed by ionic bonding is ordinary table salt, which consists of one atom of sodium and one atom of chlorine and is symbolized as NaCl. When an atom or a molecule either has more or fewer electrons than it has protons, it has an electrical charge and is called an *ion*. If salt (sodium chloride) is dissolved in water, it forms sodium ions (Na^+) and chloride (Cl^-) ions—charged particles in solution.

Alcohol Is a Compound

The substances known as chemicals are *compounds* of elements or mixtures of compounds. Alcohol belongs to a class of chemicals called *organic compounds*. Organic compounds contain carbon (C), a unique element that plays an essential role in the chemistry of living things, or organisms—hence the name organic. Carbon is unique because its atomic structure includes an outer ring that can form four bonds with other atoms. The way chemists express this is to say that carbon has a *valence* of four. These bonds are covalent bonds in which the four electrons in carbon's outer shell become linked with four electrons from other atoms. These atoms may be either other atoms of carbon or atoms of other elements that will bond with carbon. Thus, by "sharing" electrons, the carbon atom obtains the use of four additional electrons, allowing it to reach the stable configuration of eight electrons in its outer shell. This allows carbon to combine in variegated and complex ways into an extraordinary range of substances, including the principal components of all living things.

Alcohol, then, is an organic compound. Actually, there are many alcohols. The alcohol we drink is called *ethyl alcohol* or *ethanol*. A group of chemicals that share certain characteristics and a common structure is called a *family* or *class*. What do the members of the alcohol family have in common? They are organic compounds that contain a certain kind of charged particle, called a *hydroxyl group*. A hydroxyl group consists of an oxygen atom combined with a hydrogen atom. It carries a negative charge and is symbolized as OH⁻. In an alcohol, the hydroxyl group, also called the hydroxyl *radical*, is combined with a chain of one or more carbon atoms. The number of carbon atoms determines the type of alcohol. Since carbon "requires" four bonds to complete its outer shell, something must bond with the "unused" positions. In the case of the alcohols, these positions are filled by hydrogen atoms.

Methyl Alcohol   The simplest of the alcohols is *methyl alcohol*, or *methanol*. It consists of one carbon atom (C), three hydrogen atoms (H_3), and one hydroxyl group (OH). This can be written as CH_3OH. This is known as its *empirical formula*. It is also possible to draw a picture of the methyl alcohol molecule. Such a picture is called a *structural formula*. Methyl alcohol's structural formula is shown in Figure 1.3. As can be seen in the figure, the methyl alcohol molecule is built around a carbon atom that forms bonds of shared electrons with the hydrogen atoms and

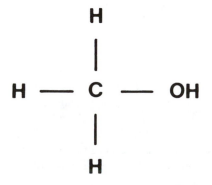

Figure 1.3   Methyl alcohol molecule. The lines represent covalent bonds between atoms. These bonds consist of shared electrons.

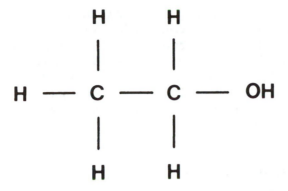

Figure 1.4 Ethyl alcohol molecule.

the hydroxyl ion. Methyl alcohol is also called *wood alcohol*. Because it is a poison, it is sometimes added to products containing beverage alcohol to "denature" them, thereby making them undrinkable. Methyl alcohol was the ingredient in the bad hooch of prohibition that caused blindness and death.

Ethyl Alcohol The alcohol that interests people most—the kind that we drink—is *ethyl alcohol*, or *ethanol*. It is more complex than methanol. The ethanol molecule consists of one hydroxyl ion joined to a chain of two carbon atoms with their associated hydrogen atoms. The empirical formula for ethyl alcohol is C_2H_5OH. Its structural formula is shown in Figure 1.4. It is with the ethanol molecule and its physiological and subjective effects that we will be concerned in the rest of this chapter.

The ethanol molecule is small as organic molecules go, and it is perfectly miscible in water and fairly soluble in fat. Beverage alcohol consists of ethanol, various by-products of fermentation known as *congeners*, flavorings, colorings, and water. Although congeners probably have some biological effects, ethyl alcohol is the active ingredient in beer, wine, and distilled spirits.

Higher Alcohols The "higher" alcohols are simply modifications of methyl or ethyl alcohol in which the hydroxyl ion is combined with longer carbon chains. The next two in the series are propyl and isopropyl alcohol, both of which have the empirical formula C_3H_7OH. Their structural formulas differ, however, in the position of the hydroxyl group. These alternate forms are called *isomers*. Propyl alcohols are used as rubbing alcohol. Alcohols with four carbon atoms are called *butanols* and are used as industrial solvents. Alcohols with 13 or more carbon atoms are solid at room temperature. The higher alcohols need not concern us further.

We now know something about the *chemical* ethyl alcohol: It is a member of a class of organic compounds called alcohols, which are characterized by carbon chains linked to hydroxyl ions; its empirical formula is C_2H_5OH; and it is a relatively small molecule, perfectly soluble in water and significantly soluble in fat. What about the *drug* ethyl alcohol? Before the chemical can become the drug, it must be present in a beverage, be ingested and absorbed, and then assert its effects on the body. The next section traces this process.

FERMENTATION AND PRODUCTION OF ALCOHOLIC BEVERAGES

Fermentation

Alcohol[1] is produced by the *fermentation* of substances containing sugar by enzymes that are produced by a microorganism yeast. Fermentation is a process of *partial oxidation* in which part of the energy in sugar is released by combining it with oxygen, converting the sugar to alcohol. The alcohol retains some of the chemical energy that was stored in the sugar, and it can be released by further oxidation.

Yeast spores are present in the air. A sugar solution left a few days at room temperature will *ferment*, that is, turn into alcohol and carbon dioxide. Yeast is a *fungus*—a small living plant-like organism[2]—that secretes a substance that forms a wall around the yeast cell. Yeast cells multiply by cell division into units of four to eight cells, which form the yeast spore. When yeast spores come in contact with a nutrient solution, such as a sugar solution, the wall breaks down and the yeast cells become metabolically active. As a result of this metabolic activity, the yeast cells grow and multiply and in the process secrete substances known as *enzymes*. An enzyme is a catalyst produced by a living organism. A *catalyst* is a chemical that changes the rate of a chemical reaction. For all practical purposes the reaction will not take place without the catalyst. Enzymes work by entering into intermediary chemical reactions that facilitate the primary reaction without the enzymes themselves being permanently changed. The primary reaction thereby proceeds to completion, producing the end products of the reaction.

Put more simply, enzymes are biological agents that facilitate chemical reactions. In the case of yeast and sugar solutions, the enzymes involved include *zymase*, *invertase*, and *maltase*. Each enzyme is specific in

---

[1]Henceforth the word *alcohol*, unless otherwise noted, will be used to mean ethyl alcohol.

[2]Some biologists classify the fungi as a phylum of plants, others consider the fungi a separate "kingdom."

its action. Invertase and maltase facilitate the conversion of the complex sugars sucrose (cane sugar) and maltose (malt sugar) into, respectively, the simple sugars glucose and fructose. These simple sugars are in turn acted on by the enzyme zymase in such a way that the glucose or fructose is converted into alcohol, carbon dioxide, and heat. The chemical equation for this reaction is as follows:

$$C_6H_{12}O_6 \xrightarrow{\text{Zymase}} 2C_2H_5OH + 2CO_2 + 20 \text{ kg/cal}$$

$C_6H_{12}O_6$		$2C_2H_5OH$	$2CO_2$	20 kg/cal
Glucose		Alcohol	Carbon	Heat
or fructose			dioxide	

Thus, if the juice of grapes or another sweet solution is kept at room temperature, it will change into wine as yeast spores settle into the juice and begin to produce their enzymes. Bubbles of gas (carbon dioxide) will rise to the surface, and a scum of yeast will collect. Primitive peoples probably discovered this by accident, and in this sense man's use of alcohol is serendipitous. However, this serendipity soon resulted in planned production. The development of reliable and replicable techniques for the production of beverage alcohol is one of man's earliest technological achievements. Almost every known culture discovered or developed a form of alcohol production, and every substance that can be fermented has been made into a beverage. Perhaps this early development of techniques for the production of alcohol, with its inherent potential for both beneficent and malignant consequences, is emblematic of the double-edged nature of all subsequent technological advance. From this point of view, human ambivalence toward alcohol is a manifestation of ambivalence toward technology.

Distillation

Distillation, which became popular in the fifteenth century, is a way of removing water from the fermented product, thereby increasing the concentration of alcohol. Put simply, alcohol boils at a lower temperature than water; therefore, heating a fermented product will result in the alcohol boiling off first. This gaseous alcohol is then cooled as it passes through coiled tubes. The cooling produces condensation, and the resulting distillate is collected. Brandy is the distillate from fermented grapes; bourbon is the distillate from fermented corn; rye whiskey is the distillate from fermented rye; vodka is the distillate from fermented potatoes; and sake is the distillate from fermented rice. The concentration of alcohol in distilled products is measured in *proof*. A proof is half a percent by volume. Pure or absolute alcohol is 200 proof. The alcohol content of beer and wine is generally reported as a percentage of alcohol by volume.

By-Products of Fermentation

Fermentation results not only in alcohol but also in a variety of by-products known as *congeners*. Congeners give a particular form of beverage alcohol its unique quality. Chemically, congeners mostly fall into three groups: alcohols other than ethanol, members of a class of chemicals known as *aldehydes*, and members of a class of chemicals known as *esters*. Aldehydes differ from alcohols in that their hydroxyl group is replaced by a double bond to an oxygen atom. As we will see, one of these aldehydes is produced by the metabolism of alcohol in the body. Esters have two carbon chains separated by an oxygen atom. Esters give a beverage its characteristic aroma. The chemical structure of aldehydes and esters is illustrated in Figure 1.5. Although some researchers believe that congeners contribute to a hangover and may have long-term effects, congeners are present in very small amounts and do not play a major role in the effects of alcoholic beverages on people. They will not be considered further here.

Now we know what is in the bottle and how it got there: ethyl alcohol; other alcohols; aldehydes; esters; possibly flavorings, as in the case of juniper berries added to gin; possibly colorings; possibly carbon dioxide, as in the bubbles of beer; and water. The next section looks at what happens when the contents of the bottle are ingested.

INGESTION AND ABSORPTION OF ALCOHOL

Ingestion

From the bottle, alcohol usually goes into the glass, although "serious" drinkers may omit this step. From the glass, alcohol goes into the mouth and is swallowed. Although alcohol can be absorbed by the mucous membranes of the mouth, it is rarely retained there long enough for this route of absorption to be of much practical importance. Nonetheless, part of the enjoyment drinkers derive from drinking comes from the gustatory and

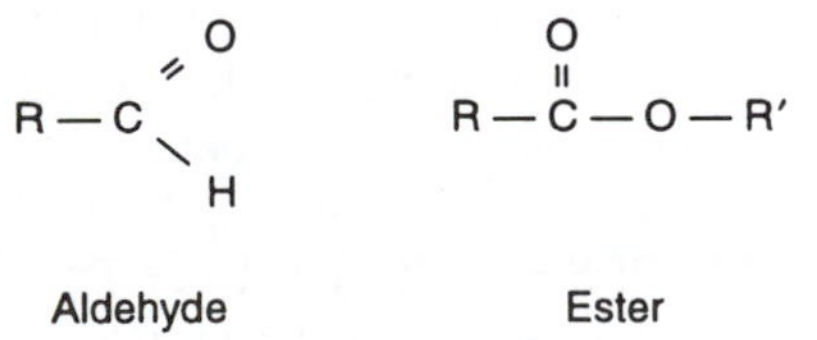

Figure 1.5 Structure of by-product molecules. R and R' are carbon chains.

olfactory sensations that accompany the passage of alcohol past the lips and through the mouth. Alcohol can also be absorbed by the lungs, but this too is of little practical importance. From the mouth alcohol passes through the pharynx, is swallowed, descends the esophagus, and enters the stomach. It is important to note that alcohol irritates the tissues with which it comes in contact. This may also be true of congeners. Prolonged, heavy, particularly abusive alcohol consumption is associated with an increased risk of disease in these tissues. It is believed that prolonged, heavy drinking may be an etiological—that is, causal—factor in cancers of the lips, mouth, pharynx, esophagus, and stomach.

Absorption

Alcohol requires no digestion; that is, no physical or chemical processes need intervene between the ingestion of alcohol and its absorption from the digestive tract. It is absorbed into the body and asserts its influence there without undergoing any change. Along with its small molecular size, this makes alcohol readily and rapidly absorbable. The actual rate of absorption depends on the concentration of alcohol in the stomach and bloodstream and on the contents of the stomach. Drinking on an empty stomach "hits" the drinker much harder than drinking with a meal or after eating.

Absorption begins when the differential concentration of alcohol in the stomach and bloodstream sets up a pressure gradient that moves the alcohol across the *gastric mucosa* (the lining of the stomach). This diffusion across a membrane is called *osmosis*. Most nutrients are not so readily absorbed. It has recently been discovered that the enzymes that metabolize alcohol are present in the stomach and that they are capable of breaking down low concentrations of alcohol before it can be absorbed into the bloodstream. It is believed that heavy drinking exhausts these enzymes, so the liver must metabolize all the alcohol consumed. The remaining alcohol passes through the *pyloric valve* at the bottom of the stomach and enters the small intestine, where it is then absorbed. Approximately 20% of the alcohol consumed is absorbed by the stomach. The remaining 80% is absorbed by the small intestine, whose mucosa is specialized for the task of absorption by the presence of tiny tubes called *villi*. Little, if any, alcohol normally descends lower in the digestive tract than the *duodenum* (the first part of the small intestine). Thus, alcohol rapidly enters the bloodstream from the stomach and small intestine.

Once alcohol enters the bloodstream it is transported throughout the body. The distribution of alcohol to various organs and tissues is understood, but for our purposes it is sufficient to know that it is distributed to and affects every cell in the body. Alcohol's small molecule and its solubility make it readily transportable across cell membranes, and its resulting ubiquity in the body is the reason that alcohol abuse can harm so many different organs.

Of all the actions of alcohol on cells and tissues, its action on the nervous system is by far the most important. Alcohol's effect on nerve tissue produces both the objective, observable changes in behavior that follow its consumption and the inward, subjective changes in thought and feeling that the drinker experiences. It is the action of alcohol on the nervous system that makes one "high."

EFFECT OF ALCOHOL ON THE NERVOUS SYSTEM: WHAT PRODUCES THE HIGH

The Neuron

In order to understand the effects of alcohol on the nervous system, it is necessary to have some understanding of how that system works. The nervous system is composed of specialized cells called *neurons*, which conduct electrical impulses. The information that it is the business of the nervous system to transmit is encoded in the pattern and frequency of these impulses. The typical neuron consists of a cell body, called the *soma*, which contains the nucleus of the cell; the *dendrites*, which are projections that receive impulses from other neurons; and the *axon*, which transmits the impulse to the next neuron. The neuron, like all cells, is separated from the surrounding extracellular fluid by a semipermeable barrier known as the *cell membrane*. This membrane's semipermeability allows some, but not other, molecules and ions to cross it.

Neurons do not quite touch each other, and the gap between them—between the axon of one neuron and the dendrites of the next—is the *synapse*. Two neurons and their synapse, or junction, are shown in Figure 1.6. The electrical impulses in the *presynaptic* neuron are transmitted across the *synaptic cleft*, by chemicals known as *neurotransmitters*. Neurotransmitters induce an electrical impulse in the *postsynaptic* neuron. Thus the electrical impulse travels from neuron to neuron. A neuron may junction with many other neurons, thereby being *polysynaptic*. Further, synaptic transmissions, which can be either *excitatory* or *inhibitory*, can be combined or *summed* either spatially or temporally by the receiving neuron. Excitatory neurons do just that—they excite, or increase the activity of, the neurons with which they communicate. Inhibitory neurons inhibit the nerve cells to which they send messages. *Spatial summation* means that a given neuron may receive impulses from two or more contiguous neurons

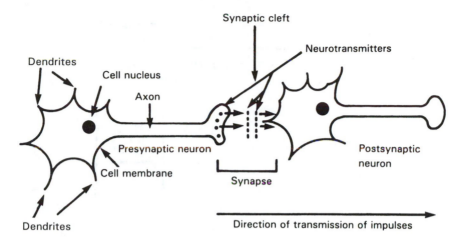

Figure 1.6 Neurons.

simultaneously and combine their messages into one. Nerve impulses arriving sequentially can be combined in the same way; this is *temporal summation.* This arrangement allows the nervous system to encode and fine tune highly complex information and provides for exquisite control of the functions of the organism.

The electrical activity of the neuron is called an *action potential.* In the neuron, as in all cells, there is an electrical charge, a difference in potential, across the cell membrane. This electrical potential is caused by differences in the type and concentration of ions within the cell and without the cell. Normally there is a greater concentration of negatively charged ions within the cell, intracellularly. More explicitly, large negatively charged organic ions (A^-) are found inside the cell, while positively charged sodium ions (Na^+) are found in greater concentration in the extracellular fluid, that is, outside the cells. Potassium ions (K^+) are found in greater concentration intracellularly, and chloride ions (Cl^-) are found in greater concentration extracellularly. This results in a *negative voltage differential* between the inside and outside of the cell. The uniqueness of the neuron consists in the ability of its cell membrane to undergo a sudden change in permeability, which allows the sodium ions to cross the membrane and enter the cell. As the sodium ions move in, some of the potassium ions move out. This sudden influx of sodium ions results in an abrupt change in the electrical potential of the cell from approximately 70 millivolts of negativity to a slight positivity. This change is the action potential. We speak of the neuron "firing." This is an all or none phenomenon; it has no degrees; it occurs or it does not. The number and pattern of these action potentials encode the information that is transmitted. The process is illustrated in Figure 1.7.

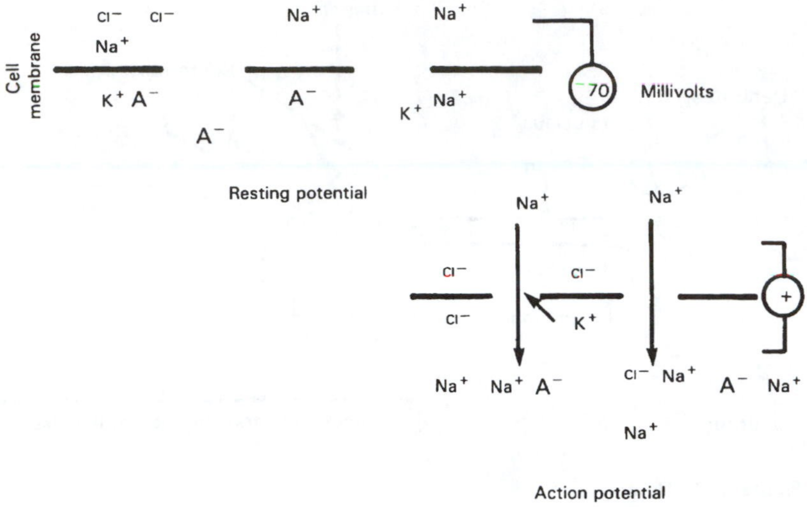

Figure 1.7 Firing of a neuron.

Alcohol and the Neuron

Before the neuron can fire again, the *resting potential*—the negative voltage differential across the cell membrane—must be restored. The gun must be cocked, so to speak, before it can be fired again. The resting potential is reestablished by an active metabolic (living chemical) process within the cell membrane, which transports the sodium ions outward across the membrane and the potassium ions inward across the membrane, reestablishing a negative potential between the intra- and extracellular fluids, restoring the ionic status quo ante, and permitting the neuron to fire again. It is postulated that alcohol interferes with this active transport of sodium ions by disrupting the membrane. In other words, alcohol slows, or depresses the functioning of the neuron by interfering with the reestablishment of its resting potential.

Ethanol not only interferes with the active transport of sodium ions across the neuron membrane but also *disturbs membrane phenomena* in general and retards the transport of numerous, variable metabolites—the products of metabolism—through the cell membrane. Cell membranes consist of lipids (fats) and proteins. Because it is soluble in fat, ethanol penetrates the neuronal membrane, swelling it and disrupting the lipids. This in turn alters the function of the membrane proteins, contributing to the depression of neural activity.

Ethanol is a "dirty little molecule" (R. Maslansky, personal communication, 1988) that not only penetrates every system, organ, tissue, and cell in the body but also, once it penetrates the cell, intrudes on and disrupts a wide variety of biochemical reactions on the molecular level. Unlike a drug such as morphine, which reacts with a specific receptor at a definite site in particular cells, ethanol's dirty little molecule has no one specific receptor upon which it acts. Instead, it becomes involved in numerous pharmacological actions, which is one reason it is so toxic. Thus, ethanol's action is *multimodal*, that is, it asserts its pharmacological action through a variety of mechanisms. It is likely that further research will establish the primacy of one or two of these effects, but at present all are considered significant.

The current "hot" biochemical research focus is ethanol's effect on the *second messenger system*. Once metabolites such as amino acids and proteins cross the cell membrane, they not only perfuse the *cytoplasm*—the fluid part of the cell—and *organelles*—substructures within the cell—by diffusion but they are also directed and transported—sort of piggybacked—to the sites of their metabolic actions by second messengers, the most prominent of which is *cyclic adenosine monophosphate* (cAMP). cAMP tells the neuron to engage in various metabolic processes, including the synthesis of proteins from amino acids that enter the cytoplasm. Alcohol's dirty little molecule gets into the neuron and disrupts the interaction of cAMP with various proteins. This depresses cell activity. Calcium ions (Ca^{2+}), for example, open and close channels to receptor sites used by second messengers as well as carrying information and signaling by modifying the microelectrical environment of various biochemical transactions. Researchers believe that ethanol acts on the calcium–second messenger system and that disruption of the second messenger system by ethanol is one of the primary ways that alcohol affects the central nervous system. The hypothesized mechanism of this action is complex. Neurons contain receptors for the various neurotransmitters in a sort of lock and key arrangement. One of these receptors is *N methyl D aspartate* (NMDA), which is the receptor site for the amino acid neurotransmitter *glutamate*. When glutamate binds to the NMDA receptor, it activates a system that permits CA^{2+} to enter the cell turning on cellular processes, some of which involve cAMP, and thereby exciting the neuron. If ethanol binds to the NMDA site, as hypothesized, then it acts as a glutamate *agonist* (an imitator that blocks an action), slowing the flow of Ca^{2+} and thereby decreasing neural activity.

The neuron is constructed so that the action potential travels rapidly down the axon to the synapse. Here it brings about the release of a neurotransmitter, which diffuses across the synaptic cleft and changes the permeability of the postsynaptic membrane. If the transmitter is excitatory, the postsynaptic neuron will fire. It is believed that alcohol interferes, in unclear but complex ways, with this process. Thus, alcohol decreases the frequency of the action potential by disturbing the membrane, slowing the active transport of sodium ions and retarding the transmission of impulses across the synapse. The higher the dose of alcohol, the greater the retardation. The net effect of alcohol on the nervous system, and its primary physiological effect, is this *graded depression of synaptic transmission*. Graded depression means that parts of the central nervous system are more sensitive to the effects of alcohol than others, and their rates of synaptic transmission will become depressed at lower doses. It is the parts of the nervous system with the most synapses—the greatest number of junctions—that are the most easily affected by alcohol.

The pharmacology of ethanol is extremely complex and at present only partly understood. Some researchers (Cloninger, 1987b) believe that in very low doses ethanol has an excitatory rather than an inhibitory effect on neurons in the tegmental area of the midbrain and that this stimulation is pleasurable to some people. Cloninger also postulates that such an individual difference in reaction to ethanol may help account for some forms of predisposition to alcoholism. Wise (1987) goes further and postulates a common excitatory (reward-center stimulating) mechanism for all addicting drugs, including alcohol, mediated through the action of these drugs on a part of the midbrain called the *nucleus accumbens*. In his view, the main pharmacological effect of alcohol, its stimulation of the pleasure center, is masked by its overwhelming "side effect," sedation. This has interesting clinical implications suggesting that while some people may become addicted to alcohol because of their strong attraction to its stimulating effects, others become addicted because of their attraction to alcohol's sedating effects.

Be this as it may, alcohol's usual pharmacological action is inhibitory. Although the mechanism of this inhibition remains unclear, one additional possibility is that ethanol facilitates the action of an inhibitory neurotransmitter called *gamma aminobutyric acid* (GABA). Most neurotransmitters are excitatory in their actions; they increase the rate of firing of the postsynaptic neuron. The family of neurotransmitters called the *catecholamines*, which includes *epinephrine* (adrenaline) and the neurotransmitter *acetylcholine*, which plays an important role in muscle contraction, are excitatory; GABA is not. It is, so to speak, the nervous system's "brake"; it decreases the rate of firing in the postsynaptic neuron. The *anxiolytics* ("minor" tranquilizers) Librium and Valium, which are also central nervous system depressants, work primarily by helping GABA do its work, facilitating its action on the neuron by enabling GABA's bonding to its receptor. Ethanol may do the same. Prolonged heavy drinking depresses the level of GABA in the brain, seriously disturbing the normal balance of neurotransmitters required for optimal functioning of the central nervous system. It apparently does this by reducing the number of GABA receptor sites, which may be the mechanism of seizure vulnerability during withdrawal.

In summary, apart from its possible action as a psychomotor stimulant of parts of the mid-brain, alcohol's primary pharmacological action is depression of the central nervous system. It apparently brings about this depression through three mechanisms: (1) disruption of membrane phenomena; (2) blocking of the NMDA receptor, thereby depressing the flow of the second-messenger calcium ions; and (3) potentiating—that is, augmenting—the action of the inhibitory neurotransmitter GABA.

Alcohol as a Sedative-Hypnotic Drug

Chemically, the classification of ethanol as an alcohol is based on its molecular structure. Pharmacologically, ethanol belongs to the class of *sedative-hypnotics*. This classification is based on its effect on the nervous system. Sedative-hypnotics are central nervous system depressants; they are not necessarily similar in chemical structure, but rather in their pharmacological function. As their dosage increases, their sedative effects progress. The sedative-hypnotics family includes barbiturates, the so-called minor tranquilizers such as Valium, and general anesthetics.

The initial effect of sedative-hypnotics, including alcohol, is to depress the inhibitory synapses of the brain. Since the negation of a negative is a positive, the depression of the inhibitory synapses is excitatory. This is one reason why alcohol is sometimes misclassified as a stimulant, rather than as a depressant. Behaviorally, this disinhibition may manifest itself in high spirits and a "devil may care" attitude. Subjectively, it may be experienced as euphoria. There is often a concomitant reduction in anxiety, especially in inhibited people. It is for this reason that the superego—Freud's term for the conscience—has been defined as that part of the psyche that is soluble in alcohol. The sensation of euphoria and feeling carefree are what many drinkers seek. However, excitatory synapses are soon depressed, and the behavioral and experiential effects of alcohol catch up with its pharmacological effect, which has been primarily depressive all along. The progressive effects of sedative-hypnotics, including alcohol, are depicted in Figure 1.8. There is another, not quite as scientific, way to conceptualize the effect of progressively greater doses of ethanol on the drinker: jocose, bellicose, lachrymose, comatose!

As will be discussed in more detail later, alcohol is addictive in that the drinker develops a tolerance to it, requiring more and more to get the same effect, and in that withdrawal symptoms are experienced after cessation of heavy and/or prolonged drinking.

METABOLISM OF ALCOHOL

Metabolism is the sum total of the chemical processes and energy exchanges that take place within an organism. Metabolic processes include

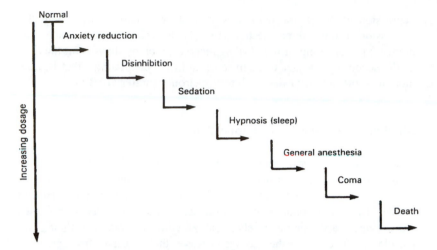

Figure 1.8 Progressive effects of sedative-hypnotics.

the *anabolic*, in which more complex substances are built from simpler ones (as when the constituents of protoplasm are built from the amino acids derived from ingested proteins) and the *catabolic*, in which more complex substances are converted into simpler ones, usually with the liberation of energy (as when the glucose derived from ingested carbohydrates is converted into carbon dioxide, water, and energy). Life is dynamic; building up and tearing down, construction and destruction, anabolism and catabolism ebb and flow ceaselessly.

Metabolic processes usually either require or release energy. Metabolic processes take place in every cell and tissue of the human body, but the liver is a specialized organ designed to do metabolic work. The liver performs most specialty metabolic processes, such as the metabolism of drugs and of some hormones. It is, among other things, a very complex and efficient "chemical factory." Since the liver has a uniquely arranged blood supply, the *hepatoportal circulatory system*, that conveys substances absorbed by the gastrointestinal tract directly to and through it, any substance that is absorbed from the gut and enters the bloodstream can be readily acted on by the liver. This is true of alcohol, which is largely metabolized by the liver. The metabolism of alcohol entails its chemical conversion into metabolites and energy. The metabolites, or breakdown products, are then eliminated from the body.

The metabolism of alcohol—its conversion into waste products and energy—is to be distinguished from its pharmacological effects, discussed earlier. The metabolism of alcohol is a process by which it is changed and eliminated from the body; its pharmacological action is the result of the effects of the intact alcohol molecule on the functioning of the neuron. The two are often confused.

The Normal Pathway

The metabolism of alcohol by the liver takes places in several steps. These steps occur in the individual liver cells, the *hepatocytes*, which contain the "ingredients" necessary for these metabolic transactions to take place. Essentially, there must be (1) something with which the alcohol can react and (2) an enzyme to facilitate that reaction. The hepatocyte has both, dissolved in its cytoplasm. The first is *nicotinamide adenine dinucleotide* (NAD), and the second is *alcohol dehydrogenase* (ADH). The first is a *cofactor*; the second is an enzyme. The first "reacts" with alcohol; the second facilitates that reaction. In the reaction, alcohol "loses" a hydrogen ion, which is "gained" by the NAD. Thus, the cofactor, or *coenzyme*, serves as a *hydrogen receptor*. In this reaction alcohol is converted into an aldehyde, *acetaldehyde*. This is illustrated by structural formulas in Figure 1.9.

When alcohol is converted into acetaldehyde, the hydrogen ion circled in the figure is split off and transferred to the NAD, with which it combines to form NADH. Simultaneously, the carbon attached to the hydroxyl radical (OH$^-$) of the alcohol molecule forms a double bond with the oxygen. The alcohol has now become acetaldehyde. This process takes place only in the presence of a specific enzyme. Since this enzyme facilitates the removal of a hydrogen atom from the alcohol molecule, it is called alcohol dehydrogenase. It is primarily found in the hepatocytes. This is why alcohol metabolism is almost entirely a liver function. The kidney and stomach contain some ADH, so they too have a role in the metabolism of alcohol, but it is a minor one. The amount of ADH, which is fixed, sets the maximum rate at which alcohol is normally metabolized. This rate is independent of the concentration of alcohol in the blood and is approximately the alcohol contained in one drink per hour. This first step in the metabolism of alcohol can be symbolized as follows:

Ethanol   Acetaldehyde
$$C_2H_5OH + NAD \xrightarrow{\text{ADH}} C_2H_4O + NADH$$

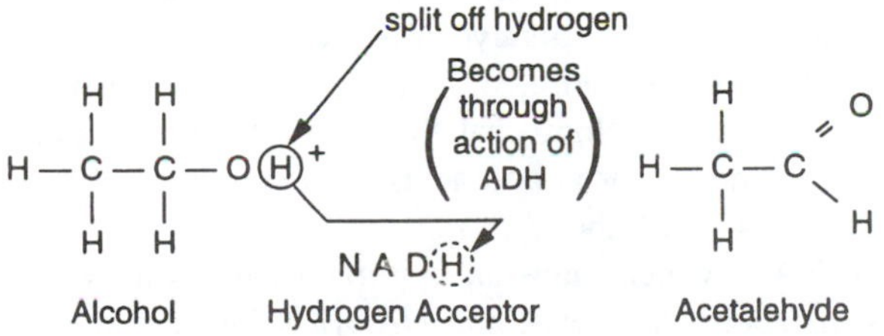

Figure 1.9 Alcohol is metabolized to acetaldehyde.

Acetaldehyde is then converted by the enzyme *aldehyde dehydrogenase* (AldDH) into acetate. NAD again acts as a hydrogen acceptor. The reaction is as follows:

Acetaldehyde
$$C_2H_4O + NAD \xrightarrow{\text{AldDH}} \text{Active acetate} + NADH$$

The drug *disulfiram*, sold under the trade name *Antabuse*, blocks the conversion of acetaldehyde to acetate, leading to accumulation of acetaldehyde, which is highly toxic, in the body. This property of disulfiram has led to its use in the treatment of alcoholism. The Antabuse user cannot drink alcohol without becoming acutely and severely ill. Depending on the dosage of Antabuse, its reaction with alcohol ranges from unpleasant to potentially lethal.

Acetaldehyde can react with a number of neurotransmitters, including *dopamine*—which plays a vital role in both normal and pathological brain function—to produce a class of chemicals known as *tetrahydrosioquinolines* (TIQs). TIQs are similar in structure to opiates, such as morphine, and have similar effects. Morphine is, of course, addictive. When TIQs are injected into certain parts of animal brains, the animals develop an addiction to alcohol. It is speculated that a similar mechanism, the production of TIQs from the reaction of acetaldehyde with various neurotransmitters in chronic heavy drinkers, is implicated in alcohol addiction in humans. In animals, addictive drinking continues whenever they have access to alcohol, once their brains have been exposed to TIQs. If this animal model has relevance to humans, it would have important implications for the treatment of alcoholism—namely, that total abstinence from alcohol would necessarily be the treatment of choice for neurochemical reasons, quite apart from psychological factors. However, this is a theory and not a fact about the development of alcohol addiction.

Acetate, which is the end product of the second stage of alcohol metabolism, in turn undergoes a complex series of metabolic reactions known as the *Krebs cycle*, or *tricarboxylic acid cycle*. The Krebs cycle is the final common pathway for the conversion of sugars, fatty acids, and amino acids into energy. Thus, it is not unique to the metabolism of alcohol. The Krebs cycle is the means by which energy is derived from alcohol. The acetate is burned, so to speak, in this cycle. Since energy is derived from it, alcohol is, in this limited sense, a food—one that consists of empty calories. Alcohol provides nothing that the body can use to build new tissue—no vitamins, minerals, or amino acids; it is simply used as a fuel in the series of steps described above.

The conversion of NAD, which plays an important role as a hydrogen acceptor in many metabolic processes, into NADH during the metabolism of alcohol significantly changes the chemical environment of the

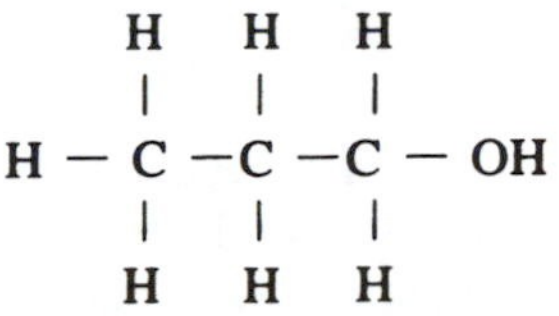

```
    H   H   H
    |   |   |
H — C —C —C — OH
    |   |   |
    H   H   H
```

Figure 1.10 Structural formula of pro-pyl alcohol.

liver. There is now less NAD available for the other work of the liver. NADH is ultimately changed back to NAD by the *mitochondria*, an organelle in the cell that does specialized metabolic work; however, this process requires both time and the expenditure of energy. When alcohol consumption is heavy, the mitochondria cannot keep up and the NAD/NADH ratio remains altered. These changes in hepatocyte chemistry impair the normal biochemical activities of the liver, which can result in a variety of disease processes. Explicitly, the metabolism of both carbohydrates and fats in the liver is affected by the altered NAD/NADH ratio, with its resultant reduction in the availability of a basic hydrogen acceptor. These processes and their resulting pathologies will be discussed in more detail in the next chapter.

ADH and AldDH, like all enzymes, have complex molecular structures involving many constituent atoms and ionic groups. These atoms and groups can be put together in more than one way. Variations in the structure of the constituents of a molecule are called isomers. An example we have already encountered is propyl alcohol, the alcohol that contains three carbon atoms. Its empirical formula is C_3H_7OH, but it can have different forms depending on where the OH group is attached. Propyl alcohol is shown in Figure 1.10 and its isomer, isopropyl alcohol is shown in Figure 1.11. In the case of enzymes whose molecules are far bigger and more complex than alcohol molecules, the structural variants are called *isoenzymes*. Isoenzymes are also known as *atypical* enzymes. Both ADH and AldDH have isoenzymes. The amount of atypical ADH and atypical AldDH is genetically determined and is an individual variation. The presence or absence of atypical forms of these liver enzymes affects alcohol metabolism. Some researchers postulate that such variations in liver enzymes affect susceptibility to alcoholism and may be a predisposing factor. Being a genetically determined trait, this lends credence to theories of the heritability of alcoholism. The precise mechanisms by which the atypical enzymes would predispose to alcoholism, if this is indeed the case, are unknown.

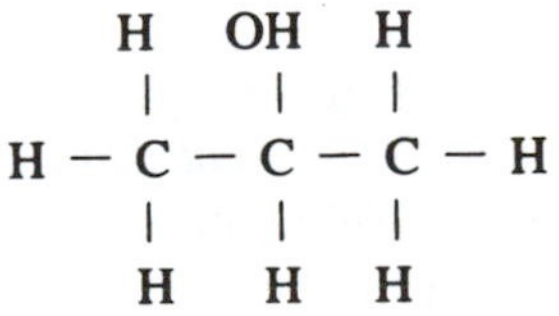

```
    H   OH  H
    |   |   |
H — C — C — C — H
    |   |   |
    H   H   H
```

Figure 1.11 Structural formula of iso-propyl alcohol.

Other Pathways

There are other enzymes in the hepatocytes that can facilitate conversion of alcohol to acetaldehyde. They normally play a minor role in the metabolism of alcohol. However, with prolonged heavy drinking, these "alternate pathways" come to play a more significant role. They are "overflow valves," called into play when the primary valve, metabolism by ADH, is overburdened. There are two alternate pathways: the metabolism of alcohol by the enzyme *catalase*, in which the cofactor is hydrogen peroxide, and metabolism by the *microsomal ethanol oxidizing system* (MEOS). Both change alcohol to acetaldehyde. Microsomes are organelles that have explicit metabolic functions. The MEOS is involved in the metabolism of many drugs as well as various naturally occurring substances, including some hormones. Repeated heavy drinking "induces" (that is, produces more of) the enzymes involved in the MEOS. This is not true of ADH. The buildup of microsomes, thread-like particles in the cytoplasm of the hepatocytes, can be seen under the microscope. This induction of the MEOS means that alcohol is metabolized more rapidly by a heavy drinker, and this is one of the bases of the development of tolerance for alcohol by the heavy drinker. The other is accommodation of the neurons themselves to alcohol. Since the MEOS also metabolizes other drugs, *cross-tolerance* is built, and more of these other drugs become necessary for them to achieve the same effect. *Cross-addiction* and cross-tolerance are terms that are often confused. Cross-addiction means addiction to more than one drug—alcohol and cocaine, for example. Cross-tolerance means that the tolerance a person has acquired for a given drug, so that more of that drug is needed to get the same effect, makes that person more tolerant of other drugs in the same pharmacological class. For example, increased tolerance for one sedative-hypnotic drug, such as alcohol, results in increased tolerance for other such drugs (such as Quaalude). Barbiturates and general anesthetics are among the drugs to which cross-tolerance is built by heavy drinking. This can be of considerable practical importance, as when an active alcoholic requires emergency surgery and normal levels of anesthetics are ineffective because of cross-tolerance.

ELIMINATION OF ALCOHOL

Approximately 95% of the alcohol ingested is absorbed and metabolized as described above. What is eliminated are the end products of that metabolic process: carbon dioxide and water. Carbon dioxide is eliminated by the lungs and water by the kidneys. The increased urinary frequency observed after drinking is due partly to fluid intake, partly to the direct effect of alcohol on the kidneys, and partly to alcohol's suppression of the antidiuretic hormone produced by the pituitary gland. Five percent of the alcohol is eliminated unmetabolized, primarily in the urine and respired air. (This active exhalation of unchanged alcohol is the reason breath mints do little to conceal alcohol consumption.) If alcohol consumption has been heavy and prolonged, some of the alcohol will be excreted in the sweat.

Chapter 2

Other "Recreational" Drugs

Today it is rare to encounter a problem drinker or alcoholic who has not at least experimented with other drugs. Many alcohol counseling clients/ patients do more than dabble with psychoactive substances. They either are or have been seriously involved with addictive drugs of various sorts. Cross-addiction is increasingly common, and the counselor must deal with the client's total drug involvement. To do so effectively, it is necessary to know what those drugs are, how they work, and what they do. The following section conveys that information. It is a summation of many years of reading diverse sources not individually cited here and of extensive clinical experience. It provides a working knowledge of the chief substances of abuse. Readers interested in a more in-depth discussion of the modes of action and the effects of these drugs than that provided here are referred to Julien's (1991) monograph or to Gilman, Goodman, and Gilman's (1985) pharmacology text.

It is generally held that persons once addicted to any psychoactive substance cannot safely use any of the others. Although some dispute this, and I have occasionally met the exception that proves the rule, my clinical experience strongly supports this view.

The so-called *recreational drugs* fall into a few major categories: marijuana and hashish, central nervous system depressants (sedative-hypnotics), central system stimulants, opiates and other narcotics, and psychedelics (hallucinogens). Central nervous system depressants are called *downers* on the street; central nervous system stimulants are called *uppers*. Alcohol is a downer, although we usually don't think of it that way.

MARIJUANA AND HASHISH

Marijuana is the second most popular recreational drug after alcohol. Marijuana and hashish contain *tetrahydrocannabinol* (THC), a *psychoactive agent*. A psychoactive agent changes how people think and feel. Marijuana is illegal, although this does not seem to stop people from using it. Many people smoke marijuana without becoming dependent on it. However, this is far from always the case and psychological addiction to THC in its various forms is quite common.

Marijuana and hashish are prepared from the *hemp* plant, *Cannabis sativa*. Marijuana is a mixture of the crushed leaves, stems, and flowers of male and female Cannabis plants; hashish is the resin obtained from the flowering tops of the female plant. Hashish is considerably more potent than marijuana. The pharmacological and psychological effects of marijuana and hashish are almost entirely due to the action of THC. Marijuana and hashish are usually smoked, although some people bake hashish and marijuana into cookies or brownies and eat them.

Marijuana has many pet names, including *reefer*, *grass*, and *pot*. It is usually rolled into a cigarette called a *joint*. Hashish is usually smoked in a pipe. Their psychological effects vary a good deal with set and setting, that is, expectations and the environment partly determine how one experiences the drug. In low doses, THC is a sedative-hypnotic. It induces feelings of relaxation, drowsiness, and well-being. Smokers seem to enter an anxiety-free drifting stage resembling a pleasant daydream. Marijuana, unlike alcohol, does not disinhibit or provoke aggression, and violence while high on pot is rare. Many users report intensified perceptions and enhancement of sensory experiences. They report that food tastes better, that music is more acutely experienced, and that sex is more enjoyable. In large doses, THC is a psychedelic, inducing hallucinations and changes in body image. Prolonged heavy use can result in toxic psychosis. "Losing it" in this way is terrifying and usually profoundly shakes the smoker. The marijuana sold today is two or three times as potent as the pot used in the sixties and this makes pot smoking far more dangerous than it used to be. THC increases pulse rate and reddens the eyes. The mechanism by which THC asserts its effects is not known. THC is metabolized by the liver and the metabolites are excreted in the urine and feces.

Frequent heavy marijuana use leads to psychological dependency. Smoking it on a regular basis risks addiction. Whether or not physiological dependency develops is controversial; however, abrupt cessation of prolonged heavy marijuana smoking results in withdrawal symptoms. Chronic marijuana usage is associated with respiratory illness including bronchitis and asthma, with suppression of the body's immunological system, and with reduced levels of testosterone. Heavy marijuana or hashish smoking leaves residues in the lungs. Recent research suggests that this residue may be carcinogenic. THC, like all psychoactive drugs, crosses the placental barrier and enters fetal tissues. Its effects on the fetus are unknown. Therefore, it is unwise to smoke pot during pregnancy.

Chronic pot use results in apathy, social withdrawal, and impairment of goal-directed behavior. Impairment of short-term memory also results from chronic use. Being hooked on pot is no bargain. As in any addiction, life gets narrower and emptier as the smoker loses interest in everything else.

CENTRAL NERVOUS SYSTEM DEPRESSANTS OTHER THAN ALCOHOL

All central nervous system depressants disinhibit and relax in low doses and induce sleep in high doses. They assert their pharmacological effects by depressing synaptic transmission in the central nervous system. They slow the information flow in the wires of the nervous system and retard release of the neurotransmitters that convey that information across the gaps between the wires. Sedative-hypnotics come in pill form and are usually taken orally. Their effect in low doses is a feeling of euphoria and well-being. As dosage increases, they assert their hypnotic effects and sleep results. In still higher doses, they act as anesthetics and can cause death. There are several types of downers; they all do pretty much the same thing.

The Barbiturates

The barbiturates are a class of chemical compounds derived from barbituric acid. The most common are pentobarbital (Nembutal), secobarbital (Seconal), amobarbital (Amytal), phenobarbital (Luminal), and thiopental (Pentothal). The primary medical use of the barbiturates is to induce sleep. People sometimes get hooked on sleeping pills and become barbiturate dependent without realizing it.

Sleep is complex and has many stages. Sleep induced by barbiturates is not normal sleep. It is deficient in REM, the stage of sleep in which dreaming takes place. Those who have access to downers and are anxiety-prone are prone to addiction. Barbiturates are addictive both psychologically and physiologically. Severe, even life-threatening, withdrawal effects result from suddenly stopping prolonged heavy use of barbiturates. This is not a drug to go off "cold turkey" without medical advice.

The combined effect of more than one sedative-hypnotic drug is much greater than the sum of the effects of each drug. Each drug potentiates the other resulting in a *synergistic reaction*. This is the reason that consuming barbiturates and alcohol is so dangerous.

The effects of barbiturate abuse are very similar to those of alcohol abuse. As dosage increases, signs akin to drunkenness appear, including cognitive and motor impairment. Both thinking and walking become sloppy. Psychological dependency followed by physiological dependency develops with protracted use, and life becomes progressively impoverished as obtaining and using the drug becomes all-important. People who would be horrified at the thought of becoming alcoholic sometimes become barbiturate addicts.

Cross-tolerance develops between central nervous system depressants, and cross-addiction is extremely common. Cross-addiction may be to various kinds of downers or to alcohol and downers. AA speaks of *sedativism*, the use of down drugs of whatever sort to alleviate or mask psychological pain. AA calls such pill use "taking a martini in powdered form."

Nonbarbiturate Downers

The nonbarbiturate central nervous system depressants include Miltown, Librium, Valium, Dalmane, Tranxene, Xanax, Ativan, and Quaaludes. Miltown is a trade name for a drug called *meprobamate*. Librium, Valium, Dalmane, Tranxene, Xanax, and Ativan all belong to a class of drugs called *benzodiazepines*. The drug *methaqualone* is marketed under the trade name Quaalude.

Meprobamate   Meprobamate was introduced in the fifties as a tranquilizer. Under the trade names Miltown and Equanil, it became a best-seller. Miltown and Equanil were introduced to replace the barbiturates and were supposedly safer. Experience has shown this not to be the case. Sedativists will take any downer, and Miltown abuse is certainly not unknown. People who buy drugs on the street often take meprobamate without knowing it.

Benzodiazepines   The benzodiazepines are a class of sedative-hypnotic drugs in very widespread use. They are "minor" tranquilizers. That is, they have sedating effects and are anxiolytic (antianxiety) agents, but they do not have antipsychotic properties like the major tranquilizers.

The distinction between the minor and major tranquilizers is extremely important. The minor tranquilizers, Librium, Valium, and Xanax, are sedative-hypnotics that are used as antianxiety agents. They build tolerance and have withdrawal symptoms. The major tranquilizers are not tranquilizing in this sense; they are correctly called *neuroleptics*. They are *antipsychotic* drugs. They work quite differently than the benzodiazepines. They block receptor sites for the neurotransmitter *dopamine*. Their ability to do this makes them extremely valuable in treating serious mental illness. They eliminate or reduce hallucinations and delusions. They do not build tolerance, have withdrawal symptoms, or get people high. They are not martinis in pill form. Thorazine, Stelazine, Mellaril, and Haldol are some brand names of neuroleptics. (Another class of psychotropic medication—drugs that change thought, feeling, or mood—are called *antidepressants*. Elavil, Tofranil, and Prozac are examples. They also do not build tolerance, have withdrawal symptoms, or get you high, and are extremely useful in treating some forms of depression.)

The first of the anxiolytics, Librium, was introduced in 1960. The chemical structure of the benzodiazepines is quite different from that of the barbiturates, but pharmacologically they are quite similar. They are more specific as antianxiety agents and they are less hypnotic; that is, less sleep-inducing. Their primary site of action is the *hypothalamus*, a part of the brain concerned with emotionality. They depress the respiratory center of the brain less than the barbiturates and are, therefore, less likely to result in a fatality if an overdose is taken. They potentiate the inhibitory neurotransmitter GABA, by helping GABA bind to its receptor site. In low doses, they produce the same feelings of disinhibition, euphoria, release from anxiety, and feelings of well-being as do the other sedative-hypnotics. In higher doses, the same impairments in memory, judgment, cognitive functioning, and motor coordination occur. Contrary to early reports, prolonged use does result in tolerance and physiological addiction. Withdrawal from these drugs, especially Valium, is particularly severe. They can definitely be drugs of abuse. Cross-addiction to alcohol and benzodiazepines is very common. Like other prescription drugs, Valium and Librium are abused by people who abhor drug addicts. Dalmane and Halcyon are central nervous system depressants prescribed as sleeping medicines. They too mix poorly with alcohol.

Methaqualone   Methaqualone, marketed as Quaalude, enjoyed a vogue as a "love drug." Actually it is a sedative-hypnotic of average strength that has no aphrodisiacal qualities. It is strikingly similar to the barbiturates in its psychological and behavioral effects. It has been taken off the market but is still available on the street, where it is known as "lude." People usually drink when they take ludes. All that does is get them down faster.

CENTRAL NERVOUS SYSTEM (CNS) STIMULANTS

The central nervous system (CNS) stimulants are among the most frequently used drugs. The amphetamines and cocaine are wildly popular. They are used by dieters to reduce appetite, by students to stay up to study for exams, by the depressed to self-medicate their emotional pain, and by party goers to get high. The recreational use of these drugs is risky. A considerable percentage of recreational users become hooked.

In low doses, CNS stimulants elevate mood, produce euphoria, increase alertness, and reduce fatigue. In high doses, they produce irritability, tension, anxiety, psychotic behavior, and convulsions (Spitz & Rosecan, 1987).

Like a vast majority of psychoactive drugs, CNS stimulants assert their effects in the synapses. Neurotransmitters carry nerve impulses across the synapses. There are many different neurotransmitters in the brain. Among the most important are a class called *catecholamines*. Adrenaline and its relatives are members of this group of neurotransmitters. CNS stimulants act by increasing the amount of available adrenaline-like substances in the synapses of the brain. Amphetamine and its derivatives do this by increasing the release of these substances into the synapse. Amphetamine also mimics these neurotransmitters by directly stimulating the neurons. Cocaine blocks the reuptake of adrenaline-type neurotransmitters.

Both amphetamine and cocaine make more of these neurotransmitters available to stimulate nerve cells and the system gets hopped up. Once a neurotransmitter is in a synapse it would go on acting forever unless something happened to it. Two things happen to it: (1) it is actively pulled back into the neuron that released it, which is called *reuptake*, and (2) it is destroyed by enzymes in the synapse. Cocaine acts by blocking reuptake, but this leaves the transmitter that remains in the synapse subject to enzymatic destruction. The enzymatic destruction of these vital brain chemicals is responsible for the crash, the intense depression that follows a cocaine spree, and, in part, for the craving for the drug, which can be highly persistent.

The Amphetamines

Amphetamine is widely used. It has legitimate medical uses in the treatment of narcolepsy (sleeping sickness) and some forms of epilepsy. Its relative, Ritalin, is used in the treatment of hyperactivity in children. Why a stimulant should be an effective treatment for hyperactivity is something of a mystery. One theory that has been put forward to explain this paradox is that these children are depressed and that their hyperactivity is a desperate attempt to ward off their depression.

Amphetamines also have been widely used as diet pills because they suppress appetite. Unfortunately the body very quickly develops tolerance to the appetite-suppressant effects of amphetamine. The dosage must then be increased to achieve the same degree of appetite suppression. Many people have been hooked on uppers in this way. There is no medically sound reason to use amphetamine for weight reduction. In the (not very) long run, they are ineffective and they have very real potential for abuse.

Amphetamines used to be used for the medical treatment of depression. They no longer are. However, they are widely used as a *euphoriant*, both recreationally and in the self-medication of depression. Amphetamine in low doses improves psychomotor, intellectual, and athletic performance to a slight extent. Many people use it for this purpose. Unfortunately, they soon have to increase the dosage, and fine motor control is lost and performance goes down.

Benzedrine (Bennies) is the mildest of the amphetamines. The amphetamine derivative *dextroamphetamine* (Dexedrine, Dexamyl, or dexies) is more potent, and *methamphetamine* (Methedrine or Speed) is even more potent.

Amphetamines mobilize the fight/flight/fright reaction, the body's response to threat, resulting in increased blood sugar, decreased blood flow to internal organs, increased blood flow to muscles, increased respiration, and dilated pupils. Speed prepares the body to meet an emergency, even though there isn't one. Amphetamines also increase mental alertness and elevate mood. Subjectively, this is experienced as sharpness and euphoria. No wonder uppers so easily generate a craving to repeat the experience and are so notoriously psychologically addicting.

At high dosages, amphetamines produce tremors, restlessness, agitation, and sleeplessness. Tolerance quickly develops and more and more is needed to get the same sensations. "Speed freaks" inject amphetamine into their veins. They experience a rush said to be like a whole-body orgasm. Unfortunately, tolerance soon builds to this effect also and "mainliners," as they are called, engage in a futile search to reexperience the quintessential high that they so vividly remember. Heart palpitations, extreme anxiety, and drug-induced psychosis are some of the "benefits" of shooting amphetamine.

Amphetamine withdrawal results in prolonged sleep, radically increased appetite, and profound depression. The depression following a prolonged amphetamine run, or spree, can be intolerable, and the user feels impelled to take more of the drug.

Speed and alcohol is a popular combination. It quickly becomes a merry-go-round. Drinking to come down and using uppers to recover from hangovers is a setup for getting hooked.

Cocaine and Crack

Cocaine, or coke, is strikingly similar to amphetamine in its physiological and psychological effects, although far more powerful and far more dangerous. It is a white powder that can be introduced into the body in several ways. It may be sniffed and absorbed by the vessels of the nasal passages, a practice known as "snorting"; it may be treated with an alkali, usually sodium bicarbonate, and smoked, a practice known as "freebasing"; or it may be dissolved and injected directly into a vein, a practice known as "shooting" or "mainlining." Crack is a form of relatively cheap cocaine that is smoked. It is coke that has already been cooked (freebased) and is ready to be smoked. It is rapidly addicting and not what it's "cracked up" to be. Before the passage of the Harris Law (the Federal Food and Drug Act) in 1914, cocaine was present in Coca Cola, where its stimulant effect helped make Coke extremely popular. Cocaine is a potent local anesthetic and has been used for that purpose in ophthalmology.

Freud (1974) discovered the euphoric properties of cocaine and wrote about them both in his correspondence with his fiancee, Martha Bernays, and in professional journals. He wrote about it as a "wonder drug," uncritically praising its ability to alleviate low spirits. He used the drug for many years. Freud also discovered the anesthetic effects of cocaine, but his friend Carl Koller published first and received the credit (Gay, 1988). It is interesting that Freud was misled by ambition, by the need for self-aggrandizement, in his erroneous judgment of cocaine. Freud's ambivalent feelings about cocaine play a large role in his masterpiece, *The Interpretation of Dreams* (1900).

Freud was not alone in his enthusiasm for cocaine. Europeans had long known of South American Indians chewing coca leaves and being stimulated to great feats of strength and endurance. They had particularly noted that the coca chewing natives could work almost indefinitely without eating. The Spanish conquerors had at first tried to suppress the chewing of coca leaves, but soon realized that the Indians could work harder, especially in the mines, and would be easier to exploit if they were allowed to chew their precious leaves. So the Spanish came to encourage the habit, while Jesuits and Spanish physicians wrote unrestrained praise of cocaine's marvelous effect of combating hunger and fatigue.

By Freud's time, an Italian physician had written a manual on the therapeutic uses of cocaine and a Viennese chemist had extracted pure alkaloid cocaine from the leaves. The American medical literature, which kindled Freud's interest in cocaine, was effusive in praising it. William Hammond, who had been Lincoln's surgeon general, was one of its strongest advocates, ultimately becoming addicted as did William Halsted, one of the founders of Johns Hopkins Medical School. The drug companies were not slow in jumping on the bandwagon, and Parke-Davis asked Freud to certify that their cocaine was just as psychoactive as that manufactured by Merck. In spite of his later bias against all things American, Freud endorsed the cheaper American product. Reading the nineteenth century claims for cocaine, one is ineluctably drawn to the parallel with the present day enthusiasm for Prozac. In both cases, a "cure all" had been discovered and recommended for the treatment of depression, low spirits, eating disorders, alcoholism, and other addictions. One hopes that the latest mind elevator proves, in the long term, to be as innocuous as cocaine was claimed to be. Freud was merely joining a growing chorus when he recommended cocaine therapy in the treatment of alcoholism and morphine addiction, although warning voices were soon enough heard. Besides, he had the support of one of his heroes, Sherlock Holmes, who, brushing off Dr. Watson's admonitions, alleviated his "boredom," that is, listless depression, with shots of cocaine. Ultimately, cooler heads prevailed and Freud was pilloried for introducing the "third scourge of mankind."

Cocaine is an extraordinarily potent CNS stimulant especially when freebased or injected. It does all the things that amphetamine does, only more so. High doses of cocaine can produce convulsions. I once treated a man who reported that he *enjoyed* the convulsions he sometimes had when he shot cocaine. In fact, he looked forward to them as a kind of grand climax of his drug experience, and mainlined coke in the hope of having one. He worked as an operator of a Van de Graff generator, an apparatus that generates very high voltage electricity. His whole life was an attempt to reach maximum voltage. He did not remain in treatment and I don't know what became of him.

Drug-induced psychoses occur at far lower doses of cocaine than amphetamine. Cocaine is metabolized by the liver much more quickly than amphetamine and its effects last only a short time. Short-acting drugs call for more and that makes them highly addictive. Psychological habituation occurs readily, tolerance develops rapidly, the crash is extremely painful, and craving lasts weeks and even months after the last "run."

Some researchers believe heavy cocaine usage results in permanent changes in brain chemistry. Cocaine devotees frequently use alcohol to come down then they get too high. Alcohol is also used to medicate cocaine-withdrawal "crashes." Alcohol actually makes the depression worse, but it masks it for the moment. This is soon followed by a new round of freebasing or mainlining, and the cycle starts again. The cocaine-alcohol user thus attempts to fine-tune moods and feelings through the use of drug technology.

Cocaine was an "in" drug, extremely popular with the yuppies. Its status as a glamor drug made it attractive to the upwardly mobile. Less "fashionable" now, it is still considered by some a "glamour" drug. The glamor is all glitter. The truth is that people who are into stimulants are warding off feelings of inner deadness and emptiness.

THE OPIATES (NARCOTICS)

Opium is a naturally occurring substance that is obtained from a plant, the poppy, *Papaver somniferum*. It is a *narcotic*. Narcotics have both a sleep-inducing (sedative) and a pain-relieving (analgesic) effect.

Opium has been used since antiquity for the relief of pain and the treatment of cough and diarrhea. It has also been used recreationally, and addiction to it was well known in classical times. Wars have been fought over it. Opium is a crude extract that contains many pharmacologically inert substances. Opium was used in patent medicines until the Harris Act (1914) put these substances under strict control. In its original form, Lydia Pinkham's Remedy for "female complaints" was alcohol laced with opium. Needless to say, it was wildly popular.

Opium contains many biologically inert compounds. The biologically active portion consists of two substances: *morphine* and *codeine*. Morphine is a powerful pain reliever and a potent anti-diarrhetic agent. Codeine shares its basic chemical structure with morphine, but it is much less potent. It is used mostly as a cough suppressant. Heroin is a synthetic derivative of morphine. It was originally developed to treat morphine addiction.

The opiates are used in a variety of ways. The resin may be smoked or, like cocaine, its derivatives may be finely powdered and snorted. This is the usual introduction to the drug. The opiates may also be injected under the skin (skin popping) or into the veins. Some people mix heroin and coke and shoot it. This is called a *speedball*, and it is not recommended for those who wish to live a full life span.

Citing the prevalence of tattoos among mainlining addicts, Henry Jay Richards (1993) hypothesized that in addition to psychosexual (oral and phallic) and sadomasochistic dynamics, intravenous (IV) drug users are driven to use the needle by boundary and identity problems. He postulated that they need to repeatedly pierce the skin to affirm a boundary they are not sure exists, and that a similar dynamic may drive some forms of self-mutilation.

Although the reaction varies, most people experience a sense of euphoria and well-being, feelings of warmth and contentment, and feelings of great power when they take opiates. These feelings are followed by an enjoyable dreamlike state and by sleep. Some experience a rush similar to, but more powerful than, an orgasm. Although opiates are used medically to manage physical pain, they also make people indifferent to psychological pain, which explains much of their appeal.

Opiates act by binding with specific receptor sites in the brain and in the intestinal tract. These receptors appear to be designed to receive opiates. This seemed strange before the discovery of naturally occurring opiatelike substances, the *endorphins*, in the body. Exercise releases endorphins and can give a natural high.

Morphine and heroin are rapidly metabolized by the liver and ex-creted by the kidneys. They disappear from the body in four to five hours, which means that a narcotics addict must constantly renew his supply. Tolerance to the analgesic, euphoric, and sedative effects develops. Tolerance can be incredibly great, so the user needs ridiculous amounts to get high.

Withdrawal from opiates is painful, although not dangerous in the way that withdrawal from alcohol is. Withdrawal symptoms include agitation, restlessness, craving, intense anxiety, fever, vomiting, fluid-like pains, rapid breathing, chills, and violent diarrhea. They last about a week. Because they bind to receptor sites, opiates do much less damage to the body than alcohol.

PSYCHEDELIC DRUGS (HALLUCINOGENS)

Psychedelic drugs are drugs that alter sensory experience and consciousness. The experience induced by these drugs is called a *trip*. They induce hallucinations, alter the perception of time, and change the conception of the self. They may cause what psychiatrists call "derealization" and "depersonalization." That is, they put the reality of both self and world into question. Chemically, they differ widely, but all of them either mimic or modify the action of a neurotransmitter. Their effects are primarily psychological. They are not physiologically addicting, but they do produce tolerance and they may induce psychological dependence in susceptible individuals. Their long-term effects are unknown. Some researchers believe that repeated use may cause brain damage. Heavy users sometimes experience *flashbacks*, involuntary trips that occur months or years after their last dose of the drug.

Addiction to these drugs is rare. Their use tends to be self-limiting and most users return to alcohol, pot, or uppers as their drug of choice. Bill Wilson, the co-founder of AA, experimented with psychedelic drugs toward the end of his life, but he neither became addicted to them nor returned to alcohol. The use of these drugs may lead to psychotic episodes in vulnerable individuals. Although psychedelic drugs are less popular than they were in the sixties and seventies, "bad trips" still account for a significant number of psychiatric hospital admissions.

The use of psychedelic drugs has a long history. They occur naturally in a variety of plants and herbs that have been used medically, recreationally, and ritually. They have been used to induce ecstatic or mystical states as part of religious rituals. The best known of these naturally occurring substances are the mystical mushrooms of Mexico and the *peyote* cactus of the American southwest. The mushrooms contain *psilocybin* and *psilocin*, both of which have been synthesized and are available on the street. The "buttons" of the peyote cactus are chewed to obtain its active principle, *mescaline*, which has also been synthesized and which is also available on the street. In the late fifties, the novelist and student of mysticism Aldous Huxley wrote a book called *The Doors of Perception* (1954), which reported his experience with mescaline. He regarded mescaline as a shortcut to mystical insight. The book was widely read and the drug enjoyed a vogue among rebellious youth. Mescaline is structurally similar to the neurotransmitter norepinephrine (NE). Mescaline, like NE, induces behavioral arousal, but unlike NE, it also alters perception, changes the experience of time, and induces hallucinations.

Lysergic acid diethylamide (LSD) is an extremely potent synthetic hallucinogen. It is the most widely used of this class of drugs. It is almost always taken orally. It too received a great deal of publicity in the sixties when its use was advocated by Timothy Leary. It is believed to act by altering synapses using the neurotransmitter serotonin in such a way that sensitivity to sensory input is augmented. Psychologically its effects are similar to those of mescaline; however, unlike mescaline, it produces those effects in almost infinitesimal doses. The hallucinations and alterations of consciousness produced by LSD are particularly intense and vivid. It can produce bad trips, flashbacks, and psychological dependence.

CONCLUSION

Problem drugging and addiction are strikingly similar to problem drinking and alcoholism. It's the old story of a friend turning into an enemy, with the victim being taken by surprise. Denial, knowing yet not wanting to know that drugs have become a problem, is the problem. Once denial is overcome, the "cure" is relatively easy.

This chapter has discussed the sources, the mechanism of action, and a bit of the chemistry and pharmacology of the principal drugs of abuse. All of these drugs can be toxic, but none is as toxic, poisonous to the body, as alcohol. The next chapter will illustrate how alcohol can damage virtually every organ in the human body if consumed in a high-enough dosage for a long-enough time.

Chapter 3

Somatic Illnesses Associated With Alcohol Abuse

Alcohol abuse can damage any part of the body. The damage may be direct, the consequence of alcohol's effect on a particular cell, tissue, organ, or system, or it may be indirect, the consequence of alcohol's profound alteration of the body's internal chemical environment. The most common sites of damage are the nervous system, liver, and blood. The gastrointestinal system, heart, muscles, and reproductive organs also may be damaged.

Although the mechanisms by which alcohol destroys cells and damages organs are multiple, complex, and only partly understood, it is believed that alcohol's ability to penetrate membranes and disrupt membrane phenomena leads to cell death and is one of the most important pathways to somatic damage secondary to alcohol abuse.

THE NERVOUS SYSTEM

The structure of the nervous system is extremely complex. For our purpose a simple description will suffice. The nervous system consists of two main divisions: the *central nervous system* and the *peripheral nervous system*. The central nervous system consists of the brain (Figure 3.1) and the spinal cord. The peripheral nervous system consists of the nerves connecting the brain and spinal cord to the muscles, glands, and sense organs. It has two parts: the nerves supplying the "voluntary" muscles and those supplying the "involuntary" muscles known as the *somatic* peripheral nervous system, and the glands of the internal organs, the *autonomic* nervous system.

The brain and spinal cord are hollow structures filled with fluid, called *cerebral-spinal fluid*. The brain is organized in a hierarchical manner. The higher centers, known as the *cerebral cortex*, are responsible for voluntary muscle control, interpretation of sensory input, memory, language, abstract thought, and rational planning. It is divided into two *hemispheres* that are somewhat specialized in function. Each hemisphere is divided into four lobes: *frontal*, *parietal*, *temporal*, and *occipital*. Folded beneath

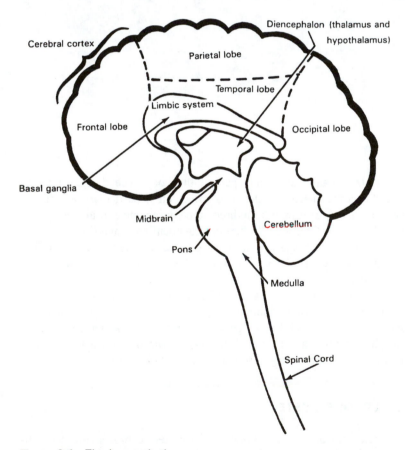

Figure 3.1 The human brain.

the cortex is the *limbic system*, an interconnected group of structures involved in the experience of emotion, among other things. Beneath the limbic system are the *basal ganglia*, clusters of nerve bodies that relay motor and sensory information to the cortex.

The next lower part of the brain is the *diencephalon*. It consists of two main structures: the *thalamus* and *hypothalamus*. The thalamus is primarily a sensory relay; the hypothalamus has many important regulatory functions and is involved in the expression of emotion. The *midbrain*, which is beneath the diencephalon, receives and processes auditory and visual sensory input. The *medulla*, or brain stem, lies between the midbrain and the spinal cord. It controls involuntary (vegetative) activities, such as respiration and heart rate. The *cerebellum*, or little brain, is behind the medulla. It coordinates fine motor activity. The *pons*, which is involved in sleep regulation, is in front of the medulla. The spinal cord begins where the central nervous system leaves the skull. All of these structures have more functions than have been noted here.

Alcohol affects *every* part of the nervous system. Alcohol abuse can damage any or all of them. Alcohol first depresses the cerebral cortex, resulting in disinhibition. This depression is indirect. The state of arousal—the level of activity—of the cortex is controlled by structures in the brain stem. It is believed that alcohol depresses the arousal system, which in turn depresses the cortex. As dosage increases, alcohol directly depresses cortical activity. In higher doses it depresses the cerebellum, resulting in slurred speech and staggering gait. In very high doses alcohol can depress the respiratory centers of the medulla, resulting in death.

Functionally, the nervous system can be viewed as a mechanism for the reception, transmission, and interpretation of information from the external and internal environments. It then originates and transmits responses to that information. Alcohol abuse can derange all of these functions.

As discussed in chapter 1, alcohol's primary pharmacological action is the depression of synaptic transmission in the central nervous system. This is what makes a person "high." Although asymptomatic social drinking may have some enduring effects on the nervous system, they are usually assumed to be of little practical significance. (Some recent research has questioned this.) This is not necessarily the case when drinking turns into problem drinking or alcoholism. The possible deleterious neurological effects of prolonged heavy drinking are manifold. Some of them are the result of the addictive properties of alcohol, including the development of tolerance, requiring progressively larger amounts to "get the same high"; development of psychological dependence; development of physiological dependence; and withdrawal symptoms of varying degrees of severity. Other possible neurological sequelae—consequences—of chronic alcoholism include diffuse damage to the brain, degeneration of specific structures in the brain, damage associated with the nutritional deficiencies often concomitant with alcoholism, and damage to the peripheral nervous system. Additionally, alcohol abuse impairs both cognitive functioning and normal sleep patterns. These impairments may occur in the absence of gross neurological changes. The neurological sequelae of alcoholism are sometimes transient and reversible; unfortunately, they are also sometimes permanent and irreversible. Let us examine each of the possible neurological complications of alcoholism, beginning with the phenomenon of tolerance.

Tolerance, Dependence, and Withdrawal

The nervous system accommodates, or becomes less sensitive to, the effects of alcohol. The mechanism of this accommodation is unknown. Its practical consequences may include an increase in alcohol consumption by the drinker as he or she seeks to reexperience his or her old high. Since alcohol induces (increases the production of) the MEOS enzymes, prolonged heavy drinking also results in the liver metabolizing alcohol more rapidly. These nervous system and metabolic effects are additive. They set up an addictive cycle in which the drinker must drink more to get the same effect, while the increased alcohol consumption builds further neuronal tolerance and induces more MEOS enzymes. The alcoholic drinker finds him or herself in a situation analogous to that of the laboratory rat who must run ever faster on the treadmill to receive the same reward. The chronic heavy drinker may require three or four times the amount of alcohol initially needed to get equally high. (This is a modest multiplier compared to heroin and cocaine tolerance. Those addicted to those drugs may need 100 times the initial dose to get the same high.) There are limits, however, to this cyclical process. In advanced alcoholism, a point is reached when the integrity of the nervous system is compromised and tolerance to alcohol decreases. At that point, liver damage may also intervene, lowering the rate of metabolism of alcohol. Advanced chronic drinkers frequently report such a loss of tolerance. This loss of tolerance is pathognomonic (characteristic) of advanced alcoholism.

Long before becoming *physiologically dependent* on alcohol a drinker may come to rely on it to relax, assuage anxiety, self-medicate depression, speak in public, have sex, or function comfortably in a social situation. When a drinker cannot do something without alcohol, he or she has become *psychologically dependent* on it. To that extent, the drinker is "hooked." I have heard several patients say, without irony, "I'm so nervous I just can't drive my car without having a drink." Psychological dependence may or may not progress into physiological dependence; the reverse, however, is not true. Physiological dependence by definition entails psychological dependence, because the physiologically dependent drinker cannot function at all without alcohol. Psychological dependence on alcohol may be limited and of little practical significance, as in the case of the nervous public speaker who must get a "little high" before a semiannual speaking engagement; or it may be all encompassing, as in the case of the alcoholic who cannot love, work, or play without alcohol. Highly specific psychological dependencies on alcohol do not necessarily progress, but like any chemical dependency they are indicative of a failure to deal with a conflict in a more adaptive way.

Physiological dependence is defined rather simply. If withdrawal symptoms accompany the cessation of drinking, the drinker is physiologically dependent. Alcohol is a central nervous system depressant. Chronic heavy alcohol use chronically depresses the central nervous system; it gets used to functioning in a depressed state. When the depressant is removed, there is a *rebound effect*, and the central nervous system becomes hyperactive. It is as if a coiled spring were suddenly released. Withdrawal symptoms range from anxiety and tremulousness to hallucinations and convulsions. Withdrawal from alcohol can be fatal. The physiologically dependent drinker must continue to drink to prevent the occurrence of withdrawal symptoms. The drinker's position is the reverse of that of the man who banged his head against the wall because it felt so good when he stopped; the physiologically dependent drinker drinks because it feels so awful when he stops.

Withdrawal reactions are difficult to predict. Generally speaking, the longer the duration of the binge and the greater the quantity of absolute alcohol consumed, the greater the risk of a serious withdrawal reaction. General health, nutritional status, age, and a history of previous difficulties during alcohol withdrawal are also of prognostic significance. Although mild withdrawal symptoms may occur even after a few days of steady drinking, serious withdrawal symptoms are not common until the drinker has consumed at least a pint of whiskey (10 drinks) or its equivalent per day for at least 10 days (Butz, 1982). It is good to bear in mind, however, that atypical reactions do occur.

Withdrawal symptoms begin several hours to several days after the last drink. They tend to peak between the second and fourth days, the third day being most commonly reported as the worst, and they generally abate, at least in their acute manifestations, within a week. Three stages of withdrawal are generally recognized by physicians. They are of progressively greater severity. Withdrawal syndromes do not, of course, come in neatly labeled packages, and a continuum of symptom severity is probably closer to reality than the conventional trichotomy.

The first stage, the mildest, is characterized by tremulousness, restlessness, appetite loss, insomnia, anxiety, and intense feelings of apprehension. Patients describe themselves as "ready to jump out of their skins." Pulse and heartbeat are rapid. Most withdrawals do not progress beyond this stage, which is very uncomfortable but not in itself dangerous. The main danger is that the patient will drink to relieve the pain.

The second stage is marked by intensification of symptoms: the tremors become more severe; the patient feels that he or she is "shaking inside"; pulse, heart rate, respiration, and blood pressure continue to elevate; and anxiety and dread become more intense. During this stage the patient may suffer *alcoholic hallucinosis.* As one of my patients put it, "Doc, I had the audio-visuals." These hallucinations do not have any prognostic significance; they are not indicative of schizophrenia or other psychoses and should not be diagnosed as such. I have seen hospital records of patients who experienced a single episode of alcoholic hallucinosis many years ago but who still carried a diagnosis of schizophrenia. Patients experiencing alcoholic hallucinosis are usually oriented as to time, place, and person and are in fairly good contact with reality. That is, they realize that their hallucinations have no basis in external reality, even though they are powerless to stop them. They are, inevitably, extremely frightened. They require, and usually respond well to, reassurance.

The presence of hallucinations is a consequence of the hyperactivity of the nervous system; it is a physiological phenomenon. The content of the hallucinations is, at least in part, expressive of emotional and intrapsychic conflicts; it is a psychological phenomenon. Alcoholic hallucinations, like all hallucinations, can be analyzed in much the same manner as dreams. Although this is rarely possible, or therapeutically desirable, during detoxification, the clinician should attend to and try to and understand what the hallucinations mean to the patient. Convulsive seizures of the grand mal (epileptic) type may also occur during alcohol withdrawal. They too are a rebound phenomenon and should not be misdiagnosed as epilepsy. They are dangerous mostly because of the risk of self-injury during a seizure. In rare instances, *status epilepticus,* a life-threatening condition of continuous seizures, develops. Seizures, when they occur, usually develop 48 hours after the last drink. Unfortunately, brain damage from prolonged excessive drinking *can* lead to epilepsy, but withdrawal seizures in and of themselves do not indicate the kind of structural changes in brain tissue that would render a person epileptic.

The third and most dangerous stage of withdrawal is know as *delirium tremens* (DTs). Most withdrawals do not progress to this stage. During DTs, the withdrawal symptoms become even worse. The alcoholic enters a state of abject terror. Hallucinations, often of small crawling animals or insects, become persecutory and are now tactile as well as visual and auditory. Psychomotor agitation becomes intense. Pulse becomes even more rapid, blood pressure continues to rise, and fever develops. Orientation and contact with reality are lost, and confusion and paranoia set in. Nausea, vomiting, explosive diarrhea, and drenching perspiration are also common. Sometimes the patient must be restrained to prevent self-injury or injury to others. Even with the best care, there is significant mortality during DTs.

I recall a patient who finally achieved stable sobriety after an excess of 20 attempts. He told me how de-humanized he felt when he was first restrained during DTs. But he went on to say, "You know it was funny, Doctor, after a while I looked forward to being put into a straitjacket on the 'flight deck' (AA slang for closed psychiatric ward). When the cops brought me in they all knew me. An aide would say, 'Shit, Jack, you back again? You better get in the jacket before you get too bad like you always do,' and I would feel kind of warm and safe and secure when they laced me in."

Some researchers consider an ordinary hangover to be a mild, self-limiting withdrawal syndrome. Others consider it to be a direct consequence of the toxicity of alcohol. It is both. The proportion of toxicity and withdrawal vary with the hangover.

The medical treatment of withdrawal from alcohol is called *detoxification*. It is accomplished in a variety of ways, but all involve the use of sedative drugs, which are *titrated* downward (systematically reduced) to zero over several days to a week. Currently, the most popular drug used for this purpose is the tranquilizer Librium. Other sedative-hypnotic drugs are also used. These drugs can themselves be addicting, and their use must be time-limited. Treatment of vitamin, mineral, and other nutritional deficiencies is vital. Anticonvulsive medication also may be used. Close supervision, nursing care, and emotional support are important during detoxification. Many medical complications can occur. The technical aspects of detoxification from alcohol, such as choice and dosage of withdrawal drug, are medical issues and will not be discussed here.

Withdrawal from alcohol can be dangerous. Assessment of how and where detoxification should be carried out is a medical decision. It should be made by a physician experienced in and knowledgeable about alcoholism and the management of withdrawal. It should *never* be made by a nonmedical therapist or counselor. Referral for medical evaluation is always appropriate for the alcoholic patient, who has been using a highly toxic substance indiscriminately. In many cases detoxification can be carried out in an outpatient setting, with or without medication. If the patient has an intact social support system, the risk associated with outpatient detoxification is lessened. However, if the alcoholic is debilitated, if the intoxication has been prolonged, or if there is a history of seizures or DTs, detoxification should be accomplished in an inpatient setting. Hospitalization offers the additional advantage of providing external controls and an opportunity for educational interventions, if the patient is capable of hearing them. Detoxification is a medical procedure, not a treatment for alcoholism. Therefore, it is vital that counseling and alcohol education, which *are* treatments for alcoholism, be provided by the detoxification facility.

Wernicke's Syndrome and Korsakoff's Psychosis

As noted, alcohol's interaction with the human nervous system is complex. The slowing of synaptic transmission, first in inhibitory and then in excitatory synapses, is responsible for both the subjective inner experience, the high, and the objective behavioral effects of drinking. Furthermore, the neurons become acclimated to the presence of ethanol, possibly resulting in physiological dependence, and withdrawal symptoms when the chronic user attempts to stop drinking. The nervous system can become damaged by alcohol abuse in at least three additional ways: (1) from the toxic effects of the alcohol itself, (2) from the poisoning of brain cells by toxins circulating in the blood as a result of the failure of a diseased liver to metabolize them, and (3) as a consequene of the nutritional deficits concomitant with alcoholism. Wernicke's syndrome and Korsakoff's psychosis result from such a nutritional deficiency— explicitly, from a lack of *thiamine*. Thiamine is also denoted vitamin B_1.

Wernicke's syndrome is an acute condition initially characterized by confusion, delirium, and hyperactivity. The patient frequently is also suffering from *peripheral neuropathy*, a condition resulting from damage to the peripheral nerves by alcohol and/or nutritional deficits. (Peripheral neuropathy will be discussed more fully in the next section.) As Wernicke's syndrome develops, double vision (*diplopia*) ensues, and, if treatment is not instituted, the patient becomes quiet and sinks into a terminal stupor. There is strong evidence that Wernicke's syndrome is a nutritional deficiency disease. If caught in time, it is rapidly and dramatically reversible by the intravenous (IV) administration of thiamine. Complete recovery is possible but not usual. Although Wernicke's syndrome will occur whenever there is severe thiamine deficiency from any cause, its occurrence is overwhelmingly associated with advanced alcoholism.

Thiamine serves several vital metabolic functions. It is required for the process by which neurons "burn" glucose in order to obtain energy, and it is needed to build *myelin*, a fatty substance that serves as an "insulator" for some axons. Although all cells require thiamine to help meet their energy requirements, brain cells require a great deal of energy to perform their functions and are therefore highly sensitive to oxygen deprivation or thiamine deficiency. The primary lesions in Wernicke's syndrome occur in the midbrain. However, other brain structures are damaged too.

Korsakoff's psychosis is a chronic condition believed to be a residual of Wernicke's syndrome. It may also result from an insidious subclinical process—that is, a process without manifest symptoms. In either case, Korsakoff's psychosis is the long-term result of brain damage caused by a thiamine deficiency not caught in time. Korsakoff patients have severe short-term memory deficits, which they attempt to conceal by filling in the gaps. This is called *confabulation* and is primarily an unconscious process, a defense against catastrophic anxiety. Korsakoff patients lack insight and suffer from impaired judgment. There may also be general intellectual deterioration. Various sensory and motor impairments resulting from damage to the peripheral nerves also commonly accompany Korsakoff's psychosis. Some patients fully recover with thiamine therapy and abstinence from alcohol; partial recovery, however, is much more common, and some patients do not improve at all. Although thiamine deficiency is definitely etiological in Korsakoff's psychosis, some authorities believe that alcohol abuse per se is also involved in the etiology of this syndrome. In street parlance, Korsakoff's psychosis is called "wet brain." (The term wet brain may also refer to alcoholic dementia.)

Thiamine must be processed by the liver before the body can use it. Therefore, liver disease complicates the treatment of Wernicke-Korsakoff syndrome. The mineral magnesium is required for the liver to convert thiamine into usable form. Unfortunately, *hypomagnesemia* (magnesium deficiency) is also common in advanced alcoholism, and it too must be treated. Other nutritional deficiencies, particularly of niacin, are common as well. Extreme niacin deficiency causes *pellagra*, which is characterized by skin lesions ("wine sores"), psychiatric symptoms, and brain damage. Vitamin, mineral, and other nutritional deficits are so common in alcoholism that the nutritional status of all alcoholic patients, including functional middle-class ones, should be evaluated and appropriate remediation instituted.

Peripheral Neuropathy

Just as demyelinization of nerve tracts in the central nervous system (the brain and spinal cord) can occur as a result of nutritional deficiencies associated with advanced alcoholism, demyelinization can also occur in the peripheral nerves, which transmit sensory and motor information to and from the muscles and central nervous system. The loss of myelin is believed to be primarily the effect of thiamine deficiency, as thiamine is a coenzyme required for the synthesis of myelin. However, the process is probably more complicated, involving deficiencies of all B vitamins. Some authorities believe that the direct toxic effects of alcohol itself also play a role in the etiology of *peripheral neuropathy*. Loss of myelin slows the transmission of information through the nerves (peripheral nerves are axons or bundles of axons). This slowing results first in various sensory abnormalities, usually in the lower extremities, including burning, tingling, and prickling sensations; pain; and eventually numbness. If the drinking continues and the thiamine deficiency is not corrected, the degenerative process continues and the axon itself, rather than just its sheath, degenerates. At this point motor symptoms occur, ranging from gait disturbances to foot drop to paralysis. Since the distance from the feet to the spinal cord is greater than the distance from the hands to the spinal cord, symptoms in the feet and legs usually occur first. Later the hands and arms become involved. The final stage of degeneration involves the destruction of the nerve cell body. Muscle wasting may also occur. Advanced cases may involve the autonomic as well as the somatic peripheral systems.

If damage is restricted to demyelinization, abstinence and nutritional repair lead to rapid recovery. If the axons have been damaged, recovery will be slow, taking months or even years. If the *neuron somata*, the cell bodies located in the anterior horns—horn-shaped gray matter on the belly side—of the spinal cord, have been destroyed, the damage will be permanent, and normal function will not be restored. Since alcoholic peripheral neuropathy is not uncommon, alcoholism counselors and therapists will encounter clients suffering from this disorder. *Alcoholic polyneuropathy*, as this condition is also known, is treated by abstinence from alcohol and massive dosages of B vitamins, initially intramuscularly. If drinking continues, further nerve degeneration is the rule. The clinician should remember that peripheral neuropathy can have many causes and that it is a rare side effect of the drug Antabuse.

Degenerative Diseases of the Brain

In addition to brain damage caused by avitaminosis (disease resulting from vitamin deficiency) associated with alcoholism, alcohol itself can damage nervous tissue, including brain tissue. How does alcohol damage the nervous system? Researchers are not quite sure, but several factors seem to be operative.

First, alcohol may induce a form of *autoimmune* response in the brain. There is evidence that it does so by releasing *sequestered* (chemically bound) *antigens*. Antigens are proteins whose normal function is to stimulate the production of antibodies, which attack invaders such as viruses. They are part of the body's defense (immune) system. Unfortunately, the cells' defense signals can get mixed up, and the defensive halfback, so to speak, tackles the defensive guards instead of the offensive ball carrier, causing an autoimmune response. It is thought that alcohol mixes up the defense signals, releasing antigens when there is no need for them. The antigens and/or the antibodies produced by them react with brain proteins. Such an autoimmune response destroys neurons.

Second, alcohol causes red blood cells to *agglutinate*—clump or sludge—and these agglutinated cells have trouble getting through the tiny blood vessels, the capillaries of the brain. The agglutinated cells block and sometimes break the capillaries of the brain. The result is a series of microstrokes. Cumulatively, they may result in considerable *necrosis* (death of brain tissue).

Third, alcohol, by its deleterious effects on neuronal membranes, disrupts protein synthesis in the brain, which if severe enough also results in the death of neurons. Since central nervous system neurons do not regenerate, they are lost forever. Some necrosis is an inevitable accompaniment of normal aging. In people with good health this does not result in significant functional loss. Alcohol abuse can greatly accelerate the process, and the result is premature senility.

When these processes result in diffuse damage to the cerebral cortex, *alcoholic chronic brain syndrome* develops. This is a form of dementia and is known as *alcoholic dementia* or sometimes *alcoholic deterioration.* The syndrome is marked by confusion, memory loss, and general intellectual deterioration. Personality changes, including the development of emotional lability (instability) and paranoia, are common. The patient is moody and suspicious. The syndrome may progress to motor involvement, stupor, and death. As the disease progresses, the hollow spaces of the brain, the *ventricles,* enlarge and the cortex shrinks. There is considerable evidence that subclinical cortical shrinkage is common in alcoholics. Thus, the neurological requisites of recovery from alcoholism, the capacities to learn and to control impulses, may be compromised by alcoholism itself. If the alcoholic continues to drink, deterioration usually continues. If the alcoholic's dementia is mild, abstinence and rehabilitation may result in a social recovery. Many of these cases, however, require institutional care.

Other parts of the brain may also degenerate. When the damage is to the pons, the result is *central pontine myelinolysis.* This relatively rare condition is found in chronic alcoholics who are also severely malnourished. It is marked by rapid deterioration and death. When the damage is primarily to the *corpus callosum,* the nerve fibers connecting the right and left cerebral hemispheres, the result is *Marchiafava-Bignami disease.* This condition is usually fatal. When the damage is to the cerebellum, the result is *cerebellar degeneration.* Symptoms include progressive unsteadiness of gait and slurred speech. If drinking continues, the condition worsens. With abstinence, however, improvement is usually possible. Nutritional factors may play a role in this condition. The optic nerve and other parts of the visual system also may be affected. When this happends the result is known as *alcoholic amblyopia,* a condition characterized by blurred vision and blind spots. Again, treatment consists of abstinence from alcohol and remediation of nutritional deficits. Some cases improve; others do not.

Alcohol's Effect on Learning

As noted, alcohol interferes with the synthesis of proteins in the neuron. It is believed that *messenger RNA* (ribonucleic acid) a cytoplasmic protein, plays a role in encoding new information. It is precisely the normal biochemical processes by which RNA is built and modified that are deranged by alcohol. The synthesis and processing of other cytoproteins are also negatively influenced by alcohol. When alcohol abuse is mild, the derangement is of function only, and no cell destruction takes place. Nevertheless, there are cognitive deficits; learning is impaired. There is evidence that mice and other experimental animals require more trials to learn a maze following alcohol ingestion than they did before. This effect persists for some time after the mouse's last drink. Psychological testing has demonstrated that similar effects can, and frequently do, occur in humans. DeLuca and Wallace (1981) found that cognitive deficits in alcoholics are more common, more severe, and more enduring than previously believed. Although there is some evidence and considerable theoretical speculation that minimal brain dysfunction may be etiological in the development of some forms of alcoholism, the kinds of cognitive dysfunction researchers have recently found in alcoholics are almost certainly consequences, not antecedents, or causes, of alcoholism. This means that restitution of cognitive capacities will require a prolonged period of abstinence and will be less than complete for many alcoholics who do achieve stable sobriety. As they say in AA, "It takes five years to get your marbles back and the rest of your life to learn how to use them." Verbal abilities return more quickly and completely than do perceptual ones, and most recovering alcoholics with sobriety of any duration compensate so well for whatever residual damage they have that no functional impairment is noticed.

Nonetheless, these alcohol-related learning decrements and cognitive impairments have obvious and important practical significance in counseling active or recently sober alcoholics. It is prudent for the alcoholism counselor to assume that the active alcoholic, however socially intact, is suffering from some degree of cognitive deficit. The counselor must take into account the fact that his or her client, no matter how well dressed and well educated, is not playing with a full deck. Neurological impairment and psychodynamic denial combine to interfere with the alcoholic patient's capacity to hear the counselor. Interventions, therefore, should be short, simple, clear, and redundant.

There is an interesting phenomenon called *state-dependent learning*. When experimental animals learn a task under the influence of a drug (such as ethanol), they will therefore perform the task better under the influence of the drug than without it. It is as if the total organismic state is part of the "learning set." This is also true of people, so an alcoholic who has "learned" to make love, write a poem, give a speech, or ride a bike under the influence of alcohol will find it difficult to do these things without it. He or she must learn them all over again when sober. When the recently sober person comes to counseling upset that he or she cannot function in some way, it is wise to inquire whether or not the particular skill in question had ever been exercised while the person was sober. If not, the counselor can explain that one can do anything sober that one can do while drinking but that it may take some time to be able to do so, since new learning is involved. There are exceptions. I knew a man who had been a highly skilled "second story man" while drunk, but who complained that he had never regained his abilities as a "cat burglar" in sobriety.

It is interesting to note that if a subject has learned a task under the influence of one sedative-hypnotic drug, such as alcohol, he or she will "remember" it just as well under the influence of another sedative-hypnotic drug, such as phenobarbital. The same is true of other classes of drugs.

Sleep Disturbances

Sleep disturbances are extremely common in both active alcoholism and recovery from alcoholism. Alcoholics, both active and recovering, frequently complain of an inability to fall asleep; or restless or tormented sleep; of disturbing or anxiety-ridden dreams; and, less frequently, of early morning awakening. Although psychological factors undoubtedly have a role in these disturbances, it is known that the pharmacological effect of alcohol itself is a powerful determinant of these abnormalities.

Sleep is neither a uniform state nor a passive happening. On the contrary, the sleep cycle is characterized by a regular, rather complex, sequence of discrete sleep states, and falling asleep is an active process mediated by the neurotransmitter *serotonin*. The sleep cycle has been studied by monitoring the electrical activity of the brain using an *electroencephalograph* (EEG). The EEG records composite pictures of the electrochemical activity of the cortex; these composite pictures are brain waves. A calm, resting normal young adult shows a brain wave pattern of 8 to 12 cycles per second while awake with his or her eyes closed. This is the *alpha rhythm*. As one becomes drowsy, the alpha rhythm is replaced by lower-voltage waves of 4 to 6 cycles per second. These are the *theta waves* of *stage 1 sleep*. After a few minutes the EEG waves slow in frequency and increase in amplitude. This is *stage 2 sleep*. It is marked by "sleep spindles" of 12 to 15 cycles per second and occasional bursts of high-voltage patterns. After several more minutes, slower (1 to 4 cycles) higher-voltage waves called *delta waves* begin to appear. This is *stage 3 sleep*. When the slow waves predominate, *stage 4 sleep* is reached. This slow-wave sleep appears to be a biological necessity, although it is not known why. The sleeper remains in stage 4 for about half an hour and then enters a stage of *rapid eye movement (REM) sleep*. REM sleep is associated with dreaming, which is also a biological necessity. The cycle then repeats itself. Slow-wave and REM sleep make up about 40% of a night's sleep.

Alcohol disturbs and disrupts the sleep cycle. It reduces the amount of slow-wave and REM sleep, and it distorts the normal brain wave patterns of stage 2 sleep. When a person is deprived of slow-wave and/or REM sleep, there is a "rebound effect" on subsequent nights, and the sleeper tries to make good the lost slow-wave and REM sleep. This happens when alcohol abuse ceases. At first REM rebound predominates, and the newly sober alcoholic complains of restless, tormented sleep. Complaints of insomnia and frequent awakening during the night are common. There is evidence that the neurotransmitter serotonin is used by a part of the brain stem called the *raphe nuclei* to induce and maintain sleep. Alcohol is known to profoundly alter the metabolism of serotonin. Additionally, the metabolism of other neurotransmitters in the *biogenic amine* family, which are believed to mediate REM sleep, are also affected by alcohol. The metabolism of one of these, the neurotransmitter norepinephrine and of the enzyme *monoamine oxidase* (MAO), both of which play a vital role in sleep phenomena, are profoundly altered by alcohol.

The practical meaning of all of this is that there is a physiological basis for the wide-ranging sleep disturbances of alcoholism. Of equal importance is the fact that these abnormalities continue long into sobriety. AA takes a hard line on early-recovery sleeplessness, telling its members, "Nobody ever died of lack of sleep." The counselor can assure the sleepless early recovery patient that his or her sleep disturbance is a symptom of withdrawal and of neurological recovery and that it will correct itself in time, as long as the recovery process is not disrupted by drinking.

Subacute Alcohol Withdrawal Syndrome

Subacute alcohol withdrawal syndrome, also known as the *attenuated or prolonged withdrawal syndrome*, consists of the cognitive deficits, sleep disturbances, and concomitant emotional dysphoria that are characteristic of at least the first year of sobriety. The syndrome does not include any unmistakable pathology (structural neurological damage) that may have resulted from alcoholism. One might view it as a shakedown period during which the nervous system is reestablishing its health. The emotional dysphoria that sometimes accompanies this healing process can serve as a "drink signal." If the drink signal is acted on, the recovery is aborted and active alcoholism resumes. The duration and severity of the subacute alcohol withdrawal syndrome vary widely. Usually, the heavier and more prolonged the drinking has been, the greater and more intense the attenuated withdrawal syndrome will be. Recent evidence suggests that prolonged withdrawal symptoms are far more common, more disabling, and longer lasting than previously suspected. Psychotherapeutic interventions during the first year of sobriety must take into account this syndrome and its possible effects on the recovering alcoholic's feelings and behavior. The counselor should tell the client that he or she is likely to have mood swings and otherwise inexplicable emotional discomfort during the first year of sobriety and that we will try to find an emotional or interpersonal reason for (or determinant of) that discomfort, but that often we will not find a reason because what you will be experiencing is neurochemical, not psychological, part of the recovery process during which your nervous system is readjusting itself.

Hepatic Encephalopathy

Liver disease is a common complication of alcoholism. If damage to the liver is severe, it may not be able to do its metabolic work. This can result in the presence of toxins in the bloodstream, which carries them to the brain. Although other toxins are probably involved, ammonia seems to be the main culprit. Therefore, *hepatic* or *portasystemic encephalopathy* (brain disease) is also known as *ammonia intoxication*. Its effects include confusion, drowsiness, and, in severe cases, unresponsiveness. The patient may develop a characteristic flapping tremor. Treatment includes addressing the underlying liver pathology and restriction of protein intake. Except in severe cases, ammonia intoxication is intermittent, often occurring when the patient eats too much protein. From a counseling viewpoint, it is important to be aware that ambulatory alcoholics with liver disease may be subject to period confusion from ammonia intoxication. They may appear to have been drinking, although they have not.

Alcoholic Hypoglycemia

As noted, the metabolism of alcohol profoundly alters the biochemical environment of the hepatocyte. Specifically, the supply of NAD is depleted as it is converted to NADH. NAD is necessary for the liver to convert stored carbohydrate (*glycogen*) into sugar (*glucose*). If an alcoholic has not been taking in sufficient sugar during a prolonged drinking bout, his or her liver may not be able to maintain an adequate level of blood glucose. Since the brain requires a constant supply of both oxygen and glucose to meet its energy needs, coma may ensue. If intravenous glucose is not administered in time, brain damage and even death may occur. Although brain damage from alcoholic *hypoglycemia* is not common, it is seen in clinical practice. Its clinical manifestations depend on the site and extent of the damage.

Trauma

Alcoholics are far more subject to head injury from automobile and other accidents, falls while drunk, and fights than the average person. Therefore, alcoholics presenting themselves for treatment of alcoholism may be suffering from slow intracranial bleeding resulting from a head injury. Such a *subdural hematoma* may cause brain damage and can be fatal. The confusion and other symptoms of such an injury are often mistaken for withdrawal symptoms or the effects of intoxication. The possibility of such an injury must always be considered in a detoxification setting.

Blackouts

Blackouts, or *alcoholic amnesias*, are memory losses during drinking episodes. In effect, the drinker has a temporary loss of the capacity for recent memory. Such loss can be partial ("grayouts") or total. Presumably, memory losses during drinking episodes are caused by alcohol's power to disrupt protein synthesis in the neuron. The encoding and storage of information—the memory process itself—are theorized to require just such intraneuronal synthetic processes. Blackouts are also called *alcoholic palimpsests*. Palimpsest means *sand writing* in Greek. In a blackout, whatever is written in the memory bank is wiped out like writing in the sand because it cannot be converted into a more permanent *engram* (that is, it cannot be permanently stored in neural tissue).

Blackouts are a rather common symptom of problem drinking. Social drinkers also have been known to experience them occasionally. They are often casually dismissed by the drinker; many authorities, however (such as Jellinek, 1960) consider them to be *prodromal* (precursory) signs of alcoholism. This casual dismissal may or may not conceal profound apprehension on the part of the drinker. Psychologically, blackouts can be understood as failures of the synthetic powers of the ego; experientially, they are disruptions in the experience of the self. They are often a source of great anxiety and guilt for the drinker, who does not know what he or she may have done during the blank period. Unfortunately, such guilt and remorse may have a basis in reality, since auto accidents and serious crimes have been known to occur during blackouts. Additionally, the disruption in the sense of continuity of self and the experience of fragmentation are uncanny, causing great anxiety apart from concern over unknown acts. Frequent blackouts are pathognomonic of alcoholism.

THE LIVER

Alcoholic liver disease is a complex phenomenon. It was once believed to be a consequence of the poor nutrition so frequently associated with severe alcoholism. It is now know that this is not the case. Alcohol abuse itself can cause both functional and structural derangement of the liver, because the metabolism of alcohol greatly alters the biochemical milieu of the hepatocyte, the liver cell. This is not to say that poor nutrition does not exacerbate this pathogenic (disease-causing) process, or that nutritional therapy is not a vital part of the treatment of alcoholic liver disease.

Heavy drinking alters the inner environment of the hepatocyte in two fundamental ways: (1) it reduces the availability of NAD, replacing it with NADH, and (2) it induces enzymes in the MEOS, resulting in a thickening of the *endoplasmic reticulum*, which contains these enzymes. The first change can be conceptualized as a decrease in the concentration of available hydrogen ion acceptors or, in electrochemical terms, as a decrease in the "oxidizing" capacity of the cell. The second change, which can be observed under the microscope, alters the way the liver metabolizes many substances, including drugs, since these substances are also acted on by the enzymes of the MEOS. This is the basis of the alcoholic's cross-tolerance for barbiturates and other drugs.

The decreased availability of acceptors results in an increase in the concentration of hydrogen ions in the liver cells which in turn increases the production of fat, while the lack of NAD inhibits the metabolism of that fat. The liver, in effect, now begins to use hydrogen as its fuel instead of fat, its normal fuel. This leads to a buildup of fat in the hepatocyte. There is also an accumulation of extracellular fat. This overall increase in hepatic fat results in the *first stage* of alcoholic liver disease—*alcoholic fatty liver*. The energy-producing organells of the hepatocyte, the mitochondria, are also damaged by this alteration in the normal oxidation of fatty acids. These intracellular changes may persist for months after the cessation of drinking. Accumulation of fat in the liver per se is initially asymptomatic, although laboratory tests may show abnormalities in the levels of liver enzymes. Later there is abdominal pain or discomfort. As the liver swells, it may grow large enough to press against the ribs and to be felt by the drinker. An enlarged liver can easily be palpated (that is, felt) during a medical examination.

Secondary consequences of the increased production and reduced oxidation of lipids (fat) by the liver are also possible. The mitochondria may try to burn off some of the excess lipids by utilizing abnormal biochemical pathways, which causes a class of organic chemicals known as *ketones* to be released into the bloodstream. This condition, which also occurs in untreated diabetes, is called *ketoacidosis* and can be dangerous. The level of fat in the bloodstream may also increase, mostly in the form of an excess of *triglycerides*. This condition is known as *hypertriglyceridemia* and increases the risk of cardiovascular disease.

As discussed earlier, excess hydrogen also interferes with the synthesis of sugar from the liver's stores of glycogen, making the alcoholic subject to hypoglycemia, especially if he or she has not been eating.

Finally, the excess of hydrogen ions leads to a buildup of *lactic acid* in the blood, which decreases the excretion of *uric acid*. The resulting high blood level of uric acid is called *hyperuricemia*. High levels of lactic acid are associated with anxiety; high levels of uric acid are associated with *gout*.

Prolonged drinking thus alters the cofactor balance in the liver, which increases the concentration of hydrogen ions, leading to accumulation of fat. These changes greatly alter the overall chemistry of the liver and indeed the entire body. Fatty liver in itself is not a serious condition. If drinking ceases, the liver will repair itself and return to functional and structural normality.

Unfortunately, the disease process does not necessarily stop here. An active inflammatory process may ensue. This is the *second stage* of alcoholic liver disease and is called *alcoholic hepatitis*. Alcoholic hepatitis should be distinguished from hepatitis in general, which simply means liver inflammation. Liver inflammation can have many causes, the most common being viral infection. When alcoholic liver disease progresses to the stage of alcoholic hepatitis, cell destruction occurs, and the liver is, to some extent, permanently damaged. It is not understood why fatty liver is universal in chronic alcoholics while only a minority develop alcoholic hepatitis. Duration and severity of drinking, genetically determined susceptibility, and associated malnutrition may play a role. At this stage the alcoholic experiences liver swelling, jaundice, hepatic pain, and fever. This is the active phase of alcoholic liver disease, the phase in which the damage is actually done. The disease process may be slow and insidious or rapid and dramatic. Alcoholic hepatitis is extremely serious. If its progress is not reversed, it can be fatal. Treatment consists of total abstinence from alcohol and vigorous supportive medical care.

The active inflammatory process of alcoholic hepatitis kills off a varying number of liver cells. These cells do not regenerate; instead they are replaced by fiber and scar tissue. This infiltration of the liver by scar tissue is called *alcoholic cirrhosis* or *Laeannec's cirrhosis*. In this *third stage* of alcoholic liver disease, the ability of the liver to perform its wide-ranging metabolic functions is impaired, and irreversible structural changes compromise the architecture of the liver. The liver now has a hard time doing its job. The chemistry of the body may be deranged in a variety of ways. Additionally, the fibrous nature of the cirrhotic liver interferes with the flow of blood and other fluids through it. Thus, chemical change and mechanical blockage occur. As the liver's capacity to perform its metabolic tasks becomes marginal, the level of toxins, especially ammonia, in the blood increases, causing hepatic encephalopathy (ammonia intoxication). This condition often comes and goes, depending on the condition of the liver and the patient's diet. When hepatic encephalopathy is mild, the alcoholic may act as if he or she has been drinking, when in reality the liver is diseased. Mechanical blockage may result in fluid accumulation in the abdomen (*ascites*) or in backflow of the hepatoportal circulatory system, causing pressure on the veins of the esophagus (*esophageal varices*). This may result in *esophageal hemorrhage*, which is a medical emergency. If the hemorrhage is not stopped, the patient will die. *Edema*, which is fluid accumulation in other parts of the body, is another possible complication of cirrhosis.

Treatment of alcoholic cirrhosis consists of total abstinence from alcohol; a carefully controlled diet; and a variety of medical and possibly surgical interventions to reduce the ascites, alleviate pressure on the esophageal varices, and minimize or eliminate ammonia intoxication. If drinking continues, further episodes of alcoholic hepatitis usually occur, worsening the cirrhosis. Unabated, this process is fatal. If the alcoholic stops drinking, the outcome is variable. Some cases of cirrhosis can be managed medically. Others cannot, and death results either from liver failure or esophageal hemorrhage.

Alcoholics are also at increased risk for liver cancer. Unfortunately, this is the case even for recovered alcoholics.

Liver disease also has secondary consequences. Among its many functions, the liver regulates the supply of many substances essential for the body's metabolic economy. This can be called this *homeostatic* function of the liver. The liver accomplishes this regulation by storing nutrients, that have been derived from food and absorbed by the small intestine, that pass through it by way of the hepatoportal circulatory system, the liver's direct link with the intestinal tract. As discussed earlier, the liver helps maintain a relatively constant level of blood glucose by converting excess glucose into glycogen, storing the glycogen, and reconverting it into glucose as needed. The liver performs a similar regulatory function for many vitamins and minerals. It may also modify these substances so the body can use them. This is the case with thiamine. The liver also has an important role in regulating the supply and use of *magnesium, zinc,* and *folic acid*, all of which perform vital metabolic functions. Magnesium is involved in muscle function, including that of the heart muscle; zinc is a component of many enzymes; and folic acid is required for the formation of red blood cells. Cirrhotic liver disease compromises all of these liver functions. Additionally, the liver produces the hormone *erythropoietin*, which activates the production of red blood cells. This process, too, is interfered with by liver disease.

THE DIGESTIVE SYSTEM

The digestive system is essentially a hollow tube in which food is digested and from which it is absorbed. The tube has various sections called the mouth, pharynx, esophagus, stomach, small intestine, and large intestine. Two outlying organs, the pancreas and liver, also have digestive functions.

Alcohol is an irritant, and constant irritation can damage tissue, including the lips, tongue, mouth, and pharynx, through which or over which alcohol passes. The chronic alcoholic is at increased risk of cancer of all these organs. The heavy smoking so frequently concomitant with alcoholism undoubtedly also plays a role in the etiology of these cancers. In general, the effects of heavy smoking and nutritional deficits confound the role of alcohol in the pathogenesis of many conditions. However, as already shown, whatever the role of these other factors, alcohol alone can do more than enough damage.

The zinc deficiency sometimes associated with chronic alcoholism may lessen the taste acuity of the tongue, further diminishing appetite and worsening an existing malnutrition. The esophageal varices that may have resulted from backwards pressure created by the blocked hepatoportal circulation that is secondary to cirrhosis may hemorrhage, or even be ruptured by violent vomiting. Vomiting may also cause blockage of the air passages and/or aspiration pneumonia—that is, pneumonia caused by foreign particles in the lungs. More than one intoxicated drinker has died in this way. Alcoholism is also associated with increased risk of esophageal cancer.

The stomach produces hydrochloric acid, which plays an essential role in digestion. The stomach has a natural barrier that prevents the acid from digesting the stomach itself. Heavy consumption of alcohol strips away this protection. This can result in *gastritis* (inflammation of the stomach lining). Gastritis causes pain, nausea, and other gastric distress. It is a common complaint among chronic alcoholics. Chronic alcoholism contributes to the formation of peptic ulcers and is associated with a greater risk of stomach cancer.

Chyme, the product of gastric (stomach) digestion, passes into the small intestine. The small intestine is the entry site of ducts carrying digestive juices from the pancreas and liver. The damage that chronic alcohol abuse causes the small intestine is usually functional rather than structural. However, derangement of enzymatic activity and intestinal function can cause severe problems. Prolonged heavy drinking can result in malabsorption of minerals, folic acid, vitamin B_{12}, fat, and other substances. It is believed that alcohol does this by interfering with the active transport of these substances across the intestinal *mucosa*, or mucous membranes. This malabsorption may be the cause of the nutritional deficiencies sometimes found even in alcoholics who continue to eat reasonably well. Alcohol abuse also increases the motility of the intestine, causing severe diarrhea. The enzymes necessary for the digestion of complex sugars are deficient in advanced alcoholics. Inability to digest these sugars also contributes to chronic diarrhea.

Alcohol does not significantly interfere with the production of *bile*, a fluid that the liver contributes to the digestive process to aid in the utilization of fats. Alcoholism can, however, damage the pancreas. The mechanism is obscure, but spasm of the duct that conducts pancreatic juice to the small intestine as well as direct toxicity are believed to be involved in this pathogenic process. Whatever the nature of the process, alcohol abuse may result in *pancreatitis*, or inflammation of the pancreas, which is a common complication of alcoholism. The pancreas has two functions. First, it products pancreatic juice, which contains enzymes necessary for digestion. Pancreatic juice is transported to the small intestine via the pancreatic duct. Second, the pancreas produces the hormone *insulin*, which regulates the utilization of sugar. Insulin is released directly into the bloodstream. Pancreatitis can compromise both of these functions. In acute pancreatitis the patient is nauseous, vomiting, and in great pain. He or she seldom continues drinking. *Acute pancreatitis* sometimes responds to supportive medical measures, although mortality is high. If the patient survives the acute attack, there is still the ominous possibility of underlying damage to the pancreas, that could lead to *chronic pancreatitis*. In this condition functional tissue is replaced with fiber, and the pancreas has difficulty performing either of its tasks. Exacerbation of acute symptoms and chronic pain may complicate this state of affairs. Chronic pancreatitis can be insidious and occur in the absence of acute attacks. If the patient abstains from alcohol, chronic pancreatitis can usually be managed medically. However, if the patient continues to drink, the prognosis is poor.

THE BLOOD

Blood consists of a fluid (plasma) and three main types of blood cells, or *corpuscles*: red blood cells (*erythrocytes*), white blood cells (*leukocytes*), and platelets (*thrombocytes*). Erythrocytes carry oxygen to the cells, leukocytes defend the body against foreign invaders, and thrombocytes are necessary for normal blood clotting. Dissolved in the plasma are a wide variety of biologically necessary substances, including nutrients, hormones, inorganic ions, and antibodies—proteins that are an important part of the body's immunological system. Alcohol abuse can derange the process by which erythrocytes, leukocytes, and thrombocytes mature and enter the bloodstream, resulting in *anemia*, lowered resistance to disease, and increased risk of hemorrhage, respectively. The most common, and hence the most important clinically, of these alcohol-related abnormalities of the blood is anemia. Let us examine how alcohol interferes with the normal production of red blood cells.

All types of blood corpuscles develop from a common ancestor, the *hemocytoblast*, which is a cell in the bone marrow. Through a complex series of cell divisions and modifications, the various types of blood cells are formed. Since any rapidly dividing cell is particularly sensitive to toxins, it is not surprising that alcohol can interfere with this process of blood cell formation. Erythrocytes, for example, have a characteristic life cycle: They develop in and are released by the bone marrow into the bloodstream, where they flourish and live productive lives carrying oxygen to the tissues for approximately 100 days. Then they age and are ultimately destroyed by the spleen, which returns iron and vital amino acids to the body for storage and reuse. *Hemoglobin* is the protein in the red blood cells that combines with oxygen in the lungs and transports it throughout the body. Iron is a vital constituent of hemoglobin. In order for this cyclical process of red cell proliferation, maturation, activity, aging, and destruction to operate normally, thereby maintaining an optimal level of red cells, the bone marrow must be normal, the hormone erythropoietin must be present, and both iron and folic acid must be available in sufficient quantities.

Erythropoietin is produced by the liver and activated by the kidneys. Given the effects of alcohol on the basic chemistry of the liver, it is not surprising that normal production, storage, release, and regulation of erythropoietin can be radically altered by alcohol abuse. Inflammatory processes associated with alcohol-induced diseases of the liver and the pancreas suppress the production of erythropoietin. The result is a failure of normal proliferation of red cells in the marrow.

Folic acid is required for the replication of DNA during cell division. Since the production of red (and other) blood cells involves several stages of cell division, this process is particularly sensitive to deficiencies of folic acid. Alcohol abuse may affect the level of available folic acid in several ways: (1) drinking without eating may result in inadequate folic acid intake, (2) alcohol interferes with the absorption of folic acid from the small intestine, and (3) alcohol blocks the metabolic pathways involved in the storage (again by the liver) and release of folic acid to meet the body's requirements. The result is ineffective red cell development, which if severe leads to the formation of giant abnormal red cells called *macrocytes*. *Macrocytic anemia* is associated with prolonged alcohol abuse and poor nutrition.

Finally, alcohol asserts a toxic effect on the internal metabolism of red cells, leading to iron encrustation of the mitochondria in the erythrocytes. These iron rings can be seen under the microscope, and the resulting condition is called *ring sideroblastic anemia*. It is associated with severe and prolonged alcohol abuse.

In addition to these problems in red cell proliferation and maturation, alcohol-related illnesses may accelerate the destruction of red cells, exacerbating the anemia. The treatment for all of these anemias is total abstinence from alcohol and nutritional repair, particularly supplementation of folic acid. These anemias are stubborn, and recovery is usually quite slow.

The body's immunological system consists primarily of the white blood cells that fight bacterial infection and special serum proteins (antibodies), that defend against viral infection. The leukocytes develop from the common bone marrow ancestor, the hemocytoblast, through a process similar to that of red blood cell maturation. They, too, require normal levels of folic acid, which may not be present in alcoholics. The result is *leukopenia*—poverty of white blood cells, which makes the alcoholic suffering from this condition particularly vulnerable to infection. Given the effects of alcohol on protein synthesis, it is also likely that the antibody system is affected by alcohol abuse. In any case, the chronic alcoholic suffers heightened vulnerability to infections of all sorts and depleted resources to fight infection if one occurs. In an era of AIDS, any depression of the immune system is frightening and the alcoholic with heightened susceptibility to infection may escalate his or her alcohol consumption to dampen the fear of having AIDS when the real problem is the drinking itself.

Similarly, deficiency of available folic acid and possibly direct toxicity may result in *thrombocytopenia*, a deficiency in the number of blood platelets. This shortage slows clotting time and increases the risk of hemorrhage. Again, the treatment is abstinence from alcohol and folic acid supplementation.

THE HEART

The heart is basically a muscle that pumps blood through the body. Alcohol asserts a direct toxic effect on the heart. *Myocardial* (heart muscle) cells leak potassium, phosphate, and enzymes after alcohol ingestion, evidence that alcohol adversely affects the internal metabolism of the heart muscle cell. The result of repeated episodes of such transient toxicity may be *alcoholic cardiomyopathy*. In effect, the heart muscle is replaced with fat and fiber; it enlarges and becomes flabby. The result is a characteristic type of *congestive heart failure*. Alcoholic cardiomyopathy is a slow and insidious disease. By the time it is diagnosed there may be considerable damage. The patient may also develop irregularities in heartbeat (*arrhythmias*). The prognosis depends on the extent of damage. Treatment consists of complete and permanent abstinence from alcohol and standard medical measures for the control of congestive heart failure. It is believed that heavy beer drinkers are most subject to alcoholic cardiomyopathy, possibly because preservatives added to beer can also damage heart muscle.

Alcohol abuse can also adversely affect the heart in various indirect ways. Nutritional deficiencies may damage it. Thiamine deficiency in particular can result in an inflammatory, degenerative condition known as *beriberi*, which affects the nerves and digestive system as well as the heart. Abnormally low levels of serum potassium, a condition known as *hypokalemia*, commonly found in heavy drinkers, adds to the stress on the heart by making contraction of the myocardial cells more difficult. The associated low level of serum magnesium, *hypomagnesemia*, also adversely affects heart muscle cells. The *hyperlipidema* (abnormally high levels of fat in the blood) that is secondary to the altered chemistry of the hepatocytes that is associated with prolonged heavy drinking increases the risk of atherosclerotic cardiovascular disease, commonly known as hardening of the arteries. This damage to the circulatory system significantly increases the risk of heart disease in chronic alcoholics. Additionally, alcohol in sufficient quantities raises blood pressure. Therefore, alcohol abuse contributes to high blood pressure, which in turn increases the risk of heart attack and stroke. It is my experience that alcoholics who suffer from moderately high blood pressure often experience a dramatic return to normal blood pressure when they achieve stable sobriety. However, the heavy cigarette smoking which is so frequently associated with problem drinking, makes matters worse, since smoking also adversely affects heart function and blood pressure. Heavy smoking is a confounding variable in the association of alcoholism and heart disease.

The most extensive longitudinal study of problem drinking to date (Vaillant, 1983) found heart disease to be the most common medical complication of alcoholism. This was unexpected and may be a result of not following the drinkers for a long enough time for liver disease to develop. There is no question, though, that prolonged heavy consumption of alcohol considerably increases the risk of cardiac disease and stroke.

THE SKELETAL MUSCLES

The skeletal muscles can be damaged by chronic alcohol abuse in much the same way as cardiac muscle. Although the exact mechanism by which alcohol damages the muscles is not known, electron microscopic examination of alcohol-damaged muscle cells reveals swelling of the mitochondria and fragmentation of the *myofilaments* (the organelle of the muscle cell that actually contracts), which are also findings in alcoholic cardiomyopathy.

Acute alcoholic myopathy is an acute syndrome of muscle pain, tenderness, and swelling following binge drinking. The muscles of the pelvic and shoulder girdles, as well as the adjacent arm and leg muscles, are most likely to be affected. The chest muscles may also be involved. Abstinence from alcohol usually leads to recovery within a month. However, if the patient resumes drinking, the symptoms are likely to recur.

Chronic alcoholic myopathy is a slow wasting away of these muscles, without pain or tenderness. It is characterized by progressive muscle weakness, and is a prolonged and insidious process. If the patient abstains from alcohol, slow recovery is the rule. Depending on the severity of the damage, recovery may or may not be complete. Both acute and chronic myopathy are often associated with nutritional deficiencies, and these also must be remediated. The primary damage, however, is from the direct toxic effects of alcohol on the muscles, not from malnutrition. Alcoholic myopathy is often complicated by alcoholic polyneuropathy. The two tend to occur together.

ALCOHOL-INDUCED ANXIETY AND DEPRESSION

People often drink to alleviate depression and anxiety. This is true for the occasional relief drinker as well as the problem drinker and the alcoholic. As noted, alcohol is actually a pharmacological depressant that worsens the original depression. The early disinhibitory effects of alcohol are deceptive, since the initial euphoria is followed by a "down." Of course, pharmacological depression of the nervous system asserts an anesthetic effect, which is experienced as a cessation of pain, especially emotional pain. Drinkers do not therefore experience either their preimbibing depression or the pharmacological depression. Additionally, drinking may be an aggressive act that serves to externalize anger that had been turned against the self, thereby at least temporarily alleviating the depression. Unfortunately, this aggression is usually followed by guilt, which deepens the depression. Thus alcohol does not cure depression; it merely masks it. Inevitably, with a hangover the depression, worsened by the depressant effects of the alcohol itself and sometimes by guilt, returns in spades. Ultimately the drinker can no longer find cessation of pain, let alone euphoria, in the glass. Often enough the futile search for the old effect continues indefinitely. If the drinker occasionally reexperiences relief from depression, learning theory teaches that this intermittent reinforcement will be an extremely powerful maintainer of the dysfunctional drinking. In short, alcohol is a terrible antidepressant. It causes what it purports to cure.

Alcohol also enjoys a reputation for tranquilizing, anti-anxiety effects. What is the scientific status of this popular conception? In small quantities (up to three drinks), alcohol's depression of synaptic transmission does assert a tranquilizing effect on the drinker. Subjectively, it dampens anxiety. The initial effect of alcohol in low dosage—inhibition of inhibitory neural circuits—often results in the drinker feeling carefree, exuberant, and free of mental and emotional distress. Alcohol is especially effective in assuaging anxiety caused by the superego—the anxiety caused by guilt over forbidden impulses and desires. In experimental animals, sedative-hypnotic drugs increase the frequency of behaviors previously extinguished by punishment.

Further, the anesthetic effect of alcohol contributes to a general reduction in anxiety. However, the subjective reports of the anxiety-reducing effects of alcohol indicate a much greater reduction than do experimental measures of the objective correlatives of anxiety (for instance, measures of galvanic skin resistance or of heart rate). In fact, some data indicate an increase in the objective signs of anxiety. To make matters worse, the habitual drinker soon becomes acclimated to the anxiety-reducing effects of alcohol and requires progressively greater amounts of alcohol to achieve the same effect. Further, the anesthetizing effects of alcohol soon wear off, leaving the drinker with the same conflicts and, perhaps, with a physical and emotional hangover, with its concomitant guilt.

Alcohol in doses greater than two or three drinks actually causes anxiety. There is nothing subjective or psychological in this process itself; it is a purely biochemical phenomenon. Alcohol causes the release of adrenalin-like substances, the catecholamines, which mediate sympathetic nervous system arousal—the fight or flight reaction. Subjectively, sympathetic arousal (rapid heartbeat, rapid breathing, elevated blood pressure, and general body tension) is experienced as anxiety. Heavy and even moderate drinking causes a massive release of catecholamines (dopamine, norepinephrine, and epinephrine, or adrenalin), which are all neurotransmitters as well as in the case of the latter two, hormones released by the adrenal medulla, which cause sympathetic arousal. Catecholamines can be measured in urine following heavy drinking. Thus, the habitual drinker, who drinks to decrease anxiety, is actually drinking to reduce the anxiety caused by the alcohol already drunk to reduce anxiety. This cycle may be repeated ad infinitum. In this respect heavy drinkers drink because they drink. This is truly a case of a dog chasing its tail, a quintessential exercise in futility. The rebound effect of the alcohol-depressed nervous system makes the next day's anxiety even worse.

Feelings of guilt for damage to self and others, fear of retaliation for aggressions committed during a binge, psychological conflict about drinking itself, and fear of the consequences to one's health, interpersonal relationships, and job performance all exacerbate the pharmacologically induced anxiety.

Alcoholism counseling has traditionally maintained that anxiety in alcoholics is a consequence and not a cause of their alcoholism. Since so many alcoholics maintain that they drink to relax, to reduce their anxiety, and since this so clearly makes no sense pharmacologically, their belief has been seen as self-deception and a rationalization for their drinking. More recent research (National Institute on Alcohol Abuse and Alcoholism, 1983) has shown that such conditions as purely synchronized alpha waves, which improves with alcohol consumption, characterize nonalcoholic male children of alcoholics. Subjectively, poor-quality alpha rhythms in EEGs of brain waves would be experienced as tension and anxiety, and their alcohol-induced synchronization would be experienced as reduction of tension and anxiety. It has been suggested that this would make drinking highly attractive to the male children of alcoholics and that this could lead to alcoholism. These EEG findings, which suggest that the popular belief that heavy drinkers drink to reduce tension and anxiety may have some truth to it, are important in our attempts to understand why some people become alcoholics and some do not. Cumulatively, the evidence suggests that at least one group of alcoholics, those who have a certain kind of genetic susceptibility to alcoholism, may have higher than average levels of anxiety that is tranquilized by alcohol with more than average efficiency. None of this is certain, but it is increasingly seen as probable. However, as suggestive for etiology as these findings may be, they do not change the fact that heavy, let alone alcoholic, drinking causes anxiety. (These and related findings will be discussed in more detail in chapter 5).

In summary, if alcohol is a poor antidepressant, it is a not much better tranquilizer, except in small doses used infrequently. Drunk frequently and heavily, it is the antithesis of a tranquilizer—it is an anxiety-inducing drug.

THE REPRODUCTIVE ORGANS

According to Masters and Johnson (1970), the most common cause of sexual dysfunction in the United States is excessive drinking. Alcohol does help some people overcome sexual repression, and in low doses alcohol undoubtedly increases sexual pleasure for many people. However, objective measures clearly demonstrate that alcohol in more than minimal quantities decreases sexual performance. Measures of penile tumescence show an inverse, nearly linear, relationship between the quantity of alcohol ingested and the firmness of erection. High and hard are antithetical conditions. An experiment in which a measuring device was inserted into the vaginas of volunteer female college students who viewed erotic films while drinking indicated a similar inverse relationship between quantity of alcohol ingested and vaginal pulse pressure (a measure of sexual arousal) (Wilson & Lawson, 1978). Although one cannot help but wonder how representative of the general population this sample was, there is considerable evidence that, although drinking may be sexually disinhibiting for many women as well as men, decreased arousal, lowered sensitivity, difficulty achieving orgasm, and less satisfying orgasm are linearly related to the quantity of alcohol ingested. Subjective reports do not necessarily agree with these findings, which are based on objective measures of female sexual performance. Thus, the evidence is that for both men and women the more alcohol consumed, the more difficult consummation of the sexual act becomes.

Impotence is an extremely common complaint of alcoholics. Alcohol asserts a direct toxic effect on the gonads (ovaries and testes). Liver disease can also contribute to sexual dysfunction. *Testicular atrophy* is not uncommon in chronic alcoholics. The testicles become smaller and softer than normal. Although not common, alcoholic peripheral neuropathy may affect the nerves serving the sexual organs. The result is impotence based on neurological impairment secondary to alcoholism. Additionally, feminization may result from abnormally high levels of blood estrogen found in some male alcoholics. The feminized male alcoholic has enlarged breasts (*gynecomastia*), loss of body hair, and thinned, softened skin. The liver metabolizes estrogen, and alcohol-related liver disease may compromise the ability of the liver to do this work. The result is a rise in the level of blood estrogen. Additionally, testosterone, perhaps already abnormally low as a result of testicular atrophy, may be metabolized too rapidly by the alcohol-induced enzymes in the MEOS. A clinical picture of cirrhosis of the liver, testicular atrophy, and enlargement of the breast is called *Silvestrini-Corda syndrome*. In women, prolonged excessive drinking may damage the ovaries, resulting in infertility.

Alcoholic impotence often remits spontaneously with abstinence; however, this is not always the case. The physical damage may be too great or the emotional inhibition too deep. Sometimes sobriety results in impotence in men who were potent while drinking. Alcohol-induced sexual dysfunction in both sexes is treated by Masters and Johnson–type behavioral techniques and/or insight-oriented psychotherapy to resolve intrapsychic conflict.

THE ENDOCRINES

The *endocrines* are glands that discharge their secretions, called hormones, directly into the bloodstream, where they are distributed throughout the body. Some hormones affect every cell and tissue, while others act primarily on specific receptors. We are already familiar with ethanol's effect on the catecholamines—adrenaline and its relatives, some of which serve as hormones as well as neurotransmitters, on the sex hormones, particularly testosterone, and on the pancreas, which as an endocrine gland produces insulin. Alcohol's effect on some of the other endocrine glands is not as clearly established, but it is known that alcohol can damage the body's mechanism for dealing with stress, the *hypothalamus-pituitary-adrenal (HPA) axis*. The hypothalamus is a part of the brain involved in emotionality and the regulation of such behaviors as eating and drinking. It tells the pituitary, the master gland of the body, what and how much hormone to secrete. The hypothalamus does this by sending hormones to the pituitary. The pituitary, in turn, releases hormones that regulate the other endocrine glands, including the adrenal glands, which have several functions and secrete several hormones. Alcohol disrupts this delicate feedback system, resulting in the release of catecholamines from the adrenal medulla and the steroid *cortisol* from the adrenal cortex. Thus, alcohol produces abnormalities in the two major adrenal functions. By impairing the stress response system, alcohol can cause the very stress that it is consumed to reduce. Although these effects are usually functional rather than structural, abnormalities in the HPA axis can persist long into sobriety, and permanent damage is possible. It is also probable that alcohol affects other endocrine functions and feedback systems as well.

THE KIDNEYS

The damage alcohol does to the kidneys is believed to be secondary to (that is, to follow from) liver disease. However, alcoholics with or without liver disease suffer far more kidney damage than nonalcoholics if they contract urinary tract infections, and alcoholics are at increased risk for infections of all kinds.

DAMAGE TO THE FETUS

Women who drink alcohol during pregnancy risk damaging their unborn children. Ethanol readily cross the placenta and affects the fetus. Children have been born with alcohol on their breath. Since rapidly dividing cells are especially vulnerable to the toxic effects of alcohol, it is not surprising that heavy alcohol consumption by a pregnant woman can damage her fetus. The damage appears to be due to an inhibition of growth, particularly of neural tissues. The result is *fetal alcohol syndrome*. Babies born with fetal alcohol syndrome are small, often have facial abnormalities, and may have varying degrees of brain damage. Sometimes the heart also displays abnormalities. These children have a variety of emotional and learning problems. Even with the best remediation and social rehabilitation, they remain gravely damaged individuals. According to one early study (Jones, Smith, Ulleland, & Streissguth, 1973), approximately one third of the offspring of chronic alcoholic women have this syndrome, and approximately one half will show some degree of retardation. Later estimates of prevalence vary widely. It is not known why some children of alcoholic mothers are born normal and others are not, but it is known that the risk is dose related. The greater the maternal alcohol consumption, the greater the risk of fetal alcohol syndrome. Experiments with animals support these clinical findings; in both rodents and chickens, alcohol consumption adversely affects the fetus, and both risk and severity of damage are dose related (Sandor, 1968).

There are group differences in fetal reactivity to alcohol. Black women are far more likely to produce fetal alcohol syndrome babies than White women who drink the same amount during their pregnancies (National Institute of Alcohol Abuse and Alcoholism, 1994). Social, nutritional, and constitutional factors have all been implicated in this differential, but it is not really understood.

It is also known that beer drinking does far more damage to the fetus than wine or distilled spirits drinking. Again, it is not known why.

Additional evidence of the toxicity of alcohol on the fetus is found in the abnormally high rate of spontaneous abortion among alcoholic women. This is also true for experimental animals. Alcohol-drinking pregnant rats have higher rates of spontaneous abortion.

There is also evidence that in humans and experimental animals that moderate (two drinks per day) alcohol ingestion decreases the average size of the neonate, although no other ill effects of moderate drinking are known. Although there is no reason to believe that an occasional glass of wine will damage a fetus, it is wisest to abstain from alcohol during pregnancy. Certainly heavy drinking exposes the fetus to great risk. Evidence for humans and experimental animals indicates that children born to recovering alcoholics are *not* at increased risk of abnormality.

CONCLUSION

Thus far we have concentrated on the pharmacology of alcohol and to a lesser extent of other drugs, as well as on the profound damage that these drugs can do to the body and to the mind. The alcoholism or substance abuse counselor must be knowledgeable about these matters; that knowledge will play a vital role in his or her function as an educator, as well as inform his or her understanding of what is going on for the client. When the client has difficulty understanding the counselor, the counselor will know that this may be the effect of the prolonged recovery syndrome or even of organic brain damage; the client's statement "I drink because I am so depressed" will be met by the counselor's "You are so depressed because you drink." Counselors do not need to retain detailed knowledge of the mechanism of alcohol's damage to the various organs—they have this text as a reference; but they do need fingertip awareness of the nature of that damage and how it manifests itself behaviorally. Human beings are, however, more than the sum total of their biochemical transactions and pathologies; they are also social beings, and their social surroundings profoundly influence what and how they drink or use drugs. The next chapter will focus on how men and women have used alcohol across time and across cultures and how they have felt about that use.

Chapter 4

How Alcohol Has Been Used

Almost every culture has discovered the use of beverage alcohol. Since any sweet fluid will soon ferment when exposed to the yeast spores omnipresent in the air, spontaneous fermentation must have been a common occurrence. One might say that prehistoric peoples discovered alcohol early and often. Apparently, when they tasted the beers and wines produced by serendipity, they liked them. At any rate what was once produced by accident was soon produced intentionally, and the production of alcoholic beverages became one of humanity's earliest technological achievements.

With the exception of some Pacific island peoples and most Native American tribes, every culture has developed a technology to convert some species of plant or plant product into alcohol. Fermentation served as a means of preserving food, and the products of fermentation were used as medicines. Alcoholic drink provided people with a means of altering their mood and feelings in ways that they liked. The changes in mood and feelings were associated with the supernatural, and alcohol became an integral part of religious rituals. Alcohol probably became a mediator re-lating to the sacred for two reasons: (1) its disinhibiting properties enabled states of emotional ecstasy or frenzy and (2) its power to promote dedifferentiation facilitated feelings of merger with the divine. The first has to do with alcohol's ability to release intense and primitive emotions; the second has to do with alcohol's ability to blur ego boundaries and promote feelings of closeness and integration. The result can be a pharmacologically induced mystical experience. Alcohol was also used as an offering to the gods, a *libation*. Alcohol continues to play a role in many modern religious rituals, including its use in Judaism to sanctify the Sabbath and its use in Christianity to symbolize the blood of Christ.

In most societies, alcohol did not remain a monopoly of the priesthood. On the contrary, secular use of alcohol is extremely widespread. It has been used as a daily beverage, a marker of ceremonial occasions, and in socially sanctioned drinking orgies. Many literate societies, including the ancient Chinese, the biblical Hebrew, the ancient Greek, and the Roman left records of both socially integrative drinking and alcohol abuse. It is known that ancient societies were concerned with the social regulation of alcohol use. Preliterate societies, of course, did not record their drinking practices; however, anthropologists have studied the relationship of alcohol use to culture, both intraculturally and cross-culturally. Let us look at some of their findings.

ANTHROPOLOGICAL STUDIES

Ruth Bunzel: Cultural Dynamics of Drunkenness

The first important anthropological study of drinking behavior was conducted by Ruth Bunzel in 1940. She investigated the use of alcohol by two culturally distinct groups of Mayan Indians: the *Chichicastenango* of Guatemala and the *Chamula* of Mexico. At the time of her study, both groups spoke Mayan and retained many elements of their native culture, although they were surrounded by and interacted with the majority White culture. Heavy drinking was integral to the lives of both Indian groups. The Indians did not think of their drinking as personally or socially damaging, although Bunzel did. The importance of her study lies in her careful and convincing demonstration that the drinking behavior of these Indians could not be totally explained by the pharmacological effects of alcohol or by the individual personalities of the drinkers; on the contrary, their drinking behavior could only be fully understood by taking into account the meaning of drinking for the culture, the social norms and mores surrounding the drinking, the childrearing practices, and the predominant character structure in each Mayan subculture. Pharmacology, personality, and culture were all important determinants of individual Indian drinking behavior. I believe that this is always the case.

The drinking patterns of each of these hard-drinking Mayan sub-cultures were heavily influenced by the traditional emphasis on drinking on ceremonial occasions and as a part of Mayan religious rituals, and by the white man's vested interest in the "drunken Indian," who could be more easily economically exploited. But the emotional meanings of the drinking, which were largely culturally determined, were different for the Chichicastenango than for the Chamula. The Chichicastenango were a highly repressed people with rigid social controls and a puritanical morality for whom drinking provided a socially sanctioned moral holiday during which forbidden sexual and aggressive wishes could find expression. Bunzel related this character structure to Chichicastenango child-rearing practices and to the culture as a whole, which had a fear-ridden ancestor cult and many guilt-inducing beliefs. The Chamula, on the other hand, were much more relaxed, less plagued by guilt, and more tolerant of instinctual expression. In many ways they were the opposite of their fellow Mayans, the Chichicastenango. They indulged their children, long delayed weaning, and did not fear their ancestors. They encouraged close bonds—virtual mergers—between children and their mother or her substitute. With adulthood came the necessity for independent initiative, separation, and competition, which evidently engendered great anxiety. Drinking allowed an intrapsychic reestablishment of the merger with mother.

The Chichicastenango drank primarily to gratify forbidden wishes, and the Chamula drank primarily to dedifferentiate and reexperience union with the mother. The first can be viewed as an instinctual regression and the second as an ego regression. Each had the sanction of the culture, yet the Chichicastenango experienced guilt and hangovers after binge drinking, while the Chamula did not. The importance of Bunzel's study for the alcoholism counselor is that it teaches the importance of understanding the drinker's cultural situation. To be an upper-class, educated, White male alcoholic is both the same and different from being a lower-class, uneducated, Black female alcoholic. Clinically, it is vital not to lose sight of either the commonality or the differences in these alcoholic behaviors.

Dwight Heath: Frequent Drunkenness Without Alcoholism

More recently, Heath (1958, 1991) studied the drinking patterns of the Bolivian Camba, a tribe of mestizo (mixed European and Native American) peasants who drink large quantities of extremely high-proof alcohol at their frequent fiestas. In addition to special occasions, fiestas are held every weekend. Although these drinking parties have a prescribed structure and the drinking is essentially ritualized, all participants become drunk, a state highly valued by the Camba. Although the women drink less, Camba style drinking is engaged in by everyone. During his first study, Heath observed no manifestations of aggression, sexuality, or sentimentality associated with drinking, and problem drinking (drunkenness being seen as positive and not a problem) let alone alcoholism are unknown among the Camba. There is no guilt associated with drinking, and even the heaviest drinkers return to work the next day with no apparent detriment to their performance. Heath hypothesized that Camba drinking served an integrative function in a society of predominantly introverted people who had few other socially sanctioned means of bonding. When he returned thirty years later, he found radical changes in the Camba's economic situation and many political changes, but their character structure and drinking behavior had remained virtually the same. The implications of Heath's studies are intriguing in that they suggest that alcoholism cannot be accounted for by the pharmacology of ethanol, but, on the contrary, that the culturally determined *meaning* of drunkenness and the "proper form of drunken behavior" learned from one's culture are highly determinative of whether or not heavy drinking turns into alcoholism. What is called *expectancy theory* (MacAndrew & Edgerton, 1969) maintains that one's response to alcohol depends on what one expects alcohol to do, and that even drunken behavior is heavily influenced by what one expects a drunk to do. Expectancies are *cognitive structures* (sets) that are acquired from the culture at large or from the immediate social surround of parents, family, and peers. Expectancy theory draws on both cultural data and experimental evidence to support its central hypothesis of the saliency of culturally mediated cognitive structures in the reaction to alcohol.

In his study of drinking in a technologically advanced, industrialized "modern" society (Spain), Rooney (1991) also emphasized the culturally determined meaning of heavy drinking. Although drunkenness is infrequent and not socially sanctioned, drinking is part and parcel of Spanish life. The total amount of alcohol consumed is substantial, yet "alcoholism" is rare. (Rooney acknowledges that Spanish-style drinking may result in health problems and notes that withdrawal symptoms like mild morning "shakes" are not regarded as a problem since everyone knows that taking a drink will "cure" the problem.) Rooney attributes the low rate of alcoholism to the Spanish view that alcoholic beverages are just that, something to drink, and to the association of drinking and sociability. Unlike Camba drinkers, the Spanish do not drink to oblivion, although for the Spanish as for the Camba, drinking serves an integrative function. Once again, culture rather than pharmacology, individual character structure, or psychopathology is understood as the most powerful determinant of whether or not heavy drinking eventuates in alcoholism.

Michael Maccoby: Drinking in a Mexican Village

Michael Maccoby (1972) also studied drinking, including alcoholic drinking, in a mestizo culture—in his case, in a Mexican village. Maccoby was an analysand and student of Erich Fromm, and his study reflects Fromm's theories of *social character* (1964), the unconscious assumptions, values, and character structure one internalizes from one's culture, as well as Fromm's integration of Marxist, existential, and Freudian thought and theory. Maccoby found that alcoholic drinking by the male villagers resulted from the interaction of four types of vulnerability: cultural, psychological, psychosocial, and economic. He saw the *cultural vulnerability* as the consequence of a lack of alternative activities and a loss of patriarchal or matriarchal structure, a condition going back to the destruction of Aztec culture by the Spanish. Although the Mexican villagers, unlike the Camba, the Chamula, and the Chichicastenango, disapproved of heavy drinking, 18% of the adult males were alcoholic and an even higher percentage were heavy (problem) drinkers.

The *psychological vulnerability* consisted of an *oral-receptive* character structure characterized by narcissism, sadism, and mother fixation. In his analysis of psychosocial vulnerability, Maccoby distinguished between those alcoholics most fixated on the mother, who were unmarried and dependent on her, and those who had married and attenuated their mother fixation. The former were oral-receptive, while the latter had an *anal-hoarding* character structure. Only the moderate drinkers and abstainers attained the higher developmental level reflected in a *productive* character structure. Maccoby's two types of alcoholics seem to be a primitive equivalent of Knight's essential and reactive alcoholics (discussed in Chapter 4).

The *psychosocial vulnerability* consisted of a hostile relationship between the sexes, which the more regressed alcoholics compensated for with *machismo*, an exaggerated masculinity that Maccoby sees as a pathetic attempt to defend against wishes to merge with the mother.

Those villagers who were relatively rich had leisure time, and that leisure constituted an *economic vulnerability*. In the course of time, all of the alcoholics fell to the lowest economic rung. Interestingly, the abstainers were those who had most absorbed nontraditional ways, who found "modern" activities to engage in, who had the least mother fixation, and who had found nonmachismo male ideals and values. (For a discussion of other contributions by Fromm to the understanding of alcoholism, see chapter 7.)

Bunzel's study discussed above contrasted two tribes' drinking practices by looking closely at their cultures; it is a *microstudy*, as are Heath's and Maccoby's. The anthropological contributions discussed next are different. They examine the drinking behaviors of many cultures in a less detailed way; they are *macrostudies*. These large-scale cross-cultural studies are ingenious, but they risk generalizing from insufficient evidence. They are inferential and their conclusions are far removed from direct observation. Their conclusions are what philosophers of science call *experience-distant theories*. Although these methodological weaknesses restrict our confidence in their results, these studies are of heuristic value and offer valuable insights into the dynamics of alcoholism.

Donald Horton: Anxiety and Drunkenness

The earliest and best known study is Donald Horton's 1943 research based on data, from 56 cultures, deposited in the Yale University anthropology department's archives. Horton tested several hypotheses relating drinking behavior, especially drunkenness, to psychocultural variables. His basic hypothesis was that alcohol is anxiety-reducing and that cultures with the highest levels of anxiety will display the most drunkenness. He identified several sources of anxiety, including (1) anxiety about lack of supplies, which he called *subsistence anxiety*, and (2) anxiety attributable to cultural disapproval of drunkenness, which he called *counter anxiety*. According to this hypothesis, the amount of drunkenness in a culture is directly proportional to the level of subsistence anxiety and inversely proportional to the level of counter anxiety. What the data showed was that there is a statistically significant direct relationship between the level of subsistence anxiety and drunkenness. There was no relationship between drunkenness and counter anxiety as Horton measured it. Of course, equating poor or unreliable sources of supplies, which is an objective datum, with high levels of anxiety, for which there is no direct evidence, is an inference. It is a reasonable inference, though, and Horton's study established that there is a relationship between high levels of anxiety and heavy drinking in cultures in which alcohol is believed to be anxiety reducing. At any rate there can be no doubt that people sometimes drink, however unwisely, to reduce anxiety.

Peter Field: Social Structure and Drunkenness

Peter Field (1962) reanalyzed Horton's data and came to a different conclusion. He saw a relationship not between subsistence anxiety and drunkenness but between lack of social structure and drunkenness. That is, he saw that the societies with the poorest and least reliable sources of supplies were the ones that had the least highly developed social structures, and he attributed drunkenness not to subsistence anxiety but to a weak or absent social structure and the accompanying lack of social control. Another way of looking at this interpretation would be to say that the societies with the most drunkenness were the ones that suffered the greatest degree of what sociologist Emile Durkheim (1897) called *anomie*, the absence of social norms. We know that societies such as some American Indian tribes whose traditional cultures have been undermined by more technologically advanced societies have extremely high rates of alcoholism. Field's theory would predict this. Further, cultural norms must be learned, so it would be entirely reasonable to predict that societies lacking firm social structures would be deficient in producing the kind of parenting that is internalized as norms and controls and that they would therefore have high rates of drunkenness.

Samuel Klausner: Menstrual Taboo and Drunkenness

Samuel Klausner (1964) looked at the relationship between sacred ritual drinking and secular ceremonial drinking. Sociologists had pointed out that observant Jews who do a great deal of carefully controlled ritual drinking as a part of religious ceremonies have a very low rate of alcoholism. Klausner wondered if this relationship held for other cultures. He looked, therefore, cross-culturally at the relationship between sacred drinking and secular drinking using the data in the Yale Human Relations Area files. He did not find a relationship. He then speculated about the symbolic meaning of alcohol and hypothesized that it most often symbolized blood; certainly it does in many religious rites in which a libation, a symbolic blood offering, is made to the gods. Klausner then suggested that the cultures that held blood to be most sacred would be the ones with the most successful social controls of drunkenness. The abuse of the sacred would be unacceptable to the culture and its members. Klausner further hypothesized that cultures that regarded blood as sacred or as related to the sacred would have the strongest menstrual taboos. The societies with the strongest menstrual taboos therefore should have the lowest rates of drunkenness. The anthropological data supported this ingenious hypothesis, which was suggested by the strong menstrual taboos of Semitic cultures. Of course one could postulate that the strong menstrual taboos and the low rates of drunkenness were both manifestations of powerful systems of social control. Be this as it may, this study has an important clinical implication, namely, that the alcoholism counselor should be alert to the symbolic meaning or meanings of alcohol for the drinker. Although the symbolic meanings are highly variable, the most common associations are to milk, mother, magic fluid, source of power, blood, and semen.

Child, Bacon, and Barry: Dependency Needs
And Drunkenness

The most important cross-cultural anthropological study is that of Child, Bacon, and Barry (1965). They studied 138 preliterate societies and demonstrated that drunkenness was positively correlated with the punishment of open expression of dependency needs and with cultural pressures toward individual achievement. Although drunkenness is not necessarily alcoholism, this anthropological finding supports one psychodynamic theory of the etiology of alcoholism, the *dependency conflict theory* (see chapter 8). Child, Bacon, and Barry's analysis further demonstrated that culturally integrated drinking in highly organized societies was not related to the prevalence of drunkenness. Their conclusion was that societies that demand independence, individual achievement, and self-reliance while frustrating the meeting of dependency needs and that also give social sanction to secular drinking will have high rates of drunkenness. For many of us, ours is such a society.

David McClelland: Male Solidarity and Drunkenness

McClelland, Davis, Kalin, and Wanner (1972) took a different approach to the cross-cultural study of drinking behavior. They studied folktales in preliterate societies to determine (among other things) the societies' psychological attitudes toward drinking. They found that cultures which do not institutionally stress maleness are the ones that drink. McClelland et al. reasoned that unstructured societies with low male solidarity do not provide sufficient social support for men to mediate the conflict between achievement and obedience. This is not too different from Child et al.'s (1965) discovery that societies that drink heavily frustrate dependency needs. However, McClelland and associates have a different view; they argue that men solve their conflicts between achievement and obedience by drinking in order to feel powerful, and that this feeling of power gives the drinker the feeling or illusion that he can achieve whatever he wants without having to fear punishment for disobedience. Drinking allows men to feel powerful in a primitive, non-instrumental, impulsive way—that is, through drunkenness. McClelland et al. used this anthropological study of primitive folktales along with other data to formulate the theory, to which we will return later, that men drink in order to feel powerful.

HISTORY OF ALCOHOL USE

The use of alcohol, pioneered by preliterate peoples, continued in the great cradles of civilization in the valleys of the Tigris-Euphrates, Indus, and

Yellow rivers. From the records these societies left behind, it is known that the classical civilizations of the Near East, India, and China made copious use of alcohol. In all of these places, alcohol consumption was secularized and widespread.

In modest amounts, alcohol allows one to feel less anxious, to express normally inhibited feelings, and to feel closer to others. Alcohol can facilitate feeling more or less hostile toward, either more isolated from, or more in communion with, other people. Dosage and expectancy interact to determine which reaction will occur. The muting of hostility and feelings of communion are socially facilitating and help explain the use of alcohol to mark contractual agreements of all sorts. Mild expressions of hostility while drinking may be socially useful as a means of reducing the ambivalence inherent in all human relationships. This paradoxical power of alcohol, to simultaneously permit some expression of hostility (which later can be discounted as "the booze talking") in primary groups where it would normally be forbidden and to enhance one's feelings of identification and union with others and with the totality of things, understood as the sacred, is socially useful. It also helps explain the social sanction that alcohol consumption had in these diverse and culturally autonomous civilizations. It is these effects of alcohol consumption that sociologists point to when speaking of the socially integrative function of some drinking, which they refer to as *integrative drinking*. However, alcohol consumption, particularly in large amounts, can also be socially disruptive. It often leads to uncontrolled aggression, social withdrawal, or both. Sociologists refer to the use of alcohol to induce particular feelings in the individual drinker without regard to the effect of the drinking on others as *instrumental drinking*. Essentially, this is drinking to get drunk. The ancient civilizations of the Near East, India, and China were aware of both of these possible social consequences of alcohol consumption and their literature both praised and warned against the effects of wine. Various means of social control were attempted, and each society made abortive attempts at prohibition. It was only when abstinence had religious sanction, as it did for devout Buddhists and some castes of Hindus, that members of these cultures were willing to not drink. For the majority, however, drinking remained an important part of life.

The classical civilizations of Greece, Rome, and ancient Israel demonstrated the same widespread use of alcohol and the same awareness of its dangers. The Bible praises wine and recommends it to cheer the sorrowful. In his dialogue *The Symposium,* Plato depicts Socrates as the only sober member of the company after a night of drinking devoted to the discussion of love. Socrates' capacity for drink is presented as evidence of his spiritual superiority. The Israelites succeeded in associating wine drinking with the sacred through their extensive ritualization of its use, and alcohol abuse ceased to be an important social problem for them. For the most part, the New Testament presents wine as socially and personally beneficial. Indeed, one of the miracles of Jesus is turning water into wine. When Western civilization developed out of the Greek, Roman, and Hebrew cultures, it took over the fairly positive attitudes these peoples had toward drink and drinking. Although gluttony and drunkenness were considered sins, it was not until the Reformation, more than a thousand years after the rise of Christianity, that groups within Christendom came to regard drinking per se as sinful.

Distillation was discovered in about the 7th century either in Arabia or India. Perhaps it was an idea whose time had come and was discovered independently in both places. Distillation made possible the manufacture of stronger alcoholic beverages. Use of the new technique quickly spread beyond the countries of its origin. The use of distilled liquors soon became common in Europe. From the evidence of such epic literature as *Beowulf* and the Icelandic sagas, heavy drinking was very popular in pagan Europe. This trend did not disappear with the Christianization of various European tribes, and alcohol was consumed daily by most people in Europe during the dark ages and into medieval times. Given the lack of sanitation and the dangers of drinking much of the available water, this was a rational practice. Chaucer's 12th-century pilgrims certainly enjoyed their daily drinking, although Chaucer also helped make the besotted monk a stereotype.

While all social classes in Europe drank and drinking had social and religious approval, this was not true elsewhere. The Koran, the sacred text of Islam, condemns drinking, and the first, perhaps only, successful prohibition of alcohol was in Moslem countries. Some contemporary Moslem societies continue prohibition, and alcohol abuse is minimal in these cultures.

Early modern times brought increased urbanization and industrialization to Europe. With the growth of an urban proletariat, people increasingly drank to assuage their misery. In 18th-century England, the enclosure laws, which restricted access to land, drove people from their ancestral homes and into the cities, where the availability of cheap gin contributed to a virtual epidemic of drunkenness. The English parliament imposed social control through the taxation of alcohol and the restriction of sales, and the gin epidemic receded. The relationship of alcohol abuse to the availability of cheap spirits in situations where social controls are weak, cultural supports are removed, and alternate satisfactions are not available is well documented. Similar epidemics of alcohol abuse occur when traditional native cultures are undermined or destroyed by contact with technologically more advanced societies. Many sociologists believe that such alienation is etiological in drunkenness and alcohol abuse. The Marxists attribute such social pathology to the dehumanizing effects of the exploitation of workers by owners in capitalist societies.

The colonists brought alcohol to America. In fact, the availability of beer and other spirits on board the ships that brought them was a major concern of these pioneers. The Puritans regarded rum as "God's good creature," and drinking was very much a part of prerevolutionary American life. Although drunkenness was disapproved of and punished, the tavern was a center of social, economic, and political activity. Taverns were very much a part of colonial life, and drinking there was more or less socially integrative. The triangular trade in rum, molasses, and slaves played a vital role in the economy of New England. It was not until the end of the 18th century, when the increased use of distilled spirits made for more socially disruptive drinking, that opposition to drinking arose in America. Benjamin Rush (1785/1944), who was surgeon general of the Revolutionary army, was one of the first to treat alcohol abuse as a medical problem, as a disease. He wrote the first "scientific" treatise on alcoholism in which he blamed the use of hard liquor for socially disruptive drinking and prescribed treatments ranging from a form of psychotherapy to severe whippings. In the 19th century Rush, who was not a prohibitionist, became a hero of the *temperance movement.*

With increased industrialization and urbanization, drinking became less socially integrative and more socially disruptive. More and more, drinkers were solitary and isolated individuals with little attachment to family or community. Public drunkenness became more common. By the early 19th century the temperance movement was gathering momentum. At first the movement wanted to outlaw hard liquor only; it was seeking social control of alcohol use, not prohibition. However, by the middle of the century it was predominantly a prohibitionist movement. Clerical opposition to alcohol increased, and many religious groups made abstinence one of their central tenets. The temperance movement entered into uneasy alliances with other reform groups, at times cooperating with the abolitionists and with the women's suffrage movement. The struggle between the "wets" and "drys" was an important factor in late 19th and early 20th century American politics. American prohibition began in 1919 and lasted until its repeal in 1933. It was partly successful, and the death rate from cirrhosis of the liver, a measure of alcohol abuse, did indeed decline. However, prohibition never had the widespread social support in America that forbidding the use of alcohol has had in some Moslem countries. The American experiment with prohibition gave drinking the allure of the forbidden, it glamorized gangsters and bootleggers, and it made cynics, if not criminals, out of many ordinarily law-abiding citizens.

DEMOGRAPHIC STUDIES OF AMERICAN DRINKING PRACTICES

Since the repeal of prohibition, drinking has become the norm in most American subcultures. Although alcohol consumption is socially acceptable and extremely widespread except with some fundamentalist religious groups, the old ambivalence remains and finds expression in a patchwork of inconsistent and contradictory laws by which states try to regulate the sale and consumption of alcoholic beverages. American drinking practices vary with age, gender, ethnicity, religion, geographic region, educational level, and social class. In fact, sociological variables are better predictors of alcohol use and of problem drinking than psychological variables.

There are two large-scale pioneering demographic studies of American drinking practices: the Cahalan, Cisin, and Crossley survey of 1969 and the Harris survey of 1971. Their findings are remarkably consistent. A more recent study (Clark & Midanik, 1982) showed little alteration in American drinking behavior. These surveys found that Americans are highly ambivalent about drink and drinking. Cahalan et al. found that 68% of adults drank at least once a year (77% of the males and 60% of the females). Harris's figures were somewhat higher, and there is reason to believe that drinking increased in the 1970s. Cahalan et al. found that 12% of respondents were heavy drinkers. Half of their sample drank more often than once a month and half did not. Clark and Midanik found that one third of the adult population abstained, one third were light drinkers, and one third were moderate or heavy drinkers (at least two drinks per day). They also found that *10% of the population drank half of the total alcohol consumed.*

Consumption of alcohol increased until 1982 and has decreased since. The National Institute on Alcohol Abuse and Alcoholism (NIAAA) conducts ongoing surveys of alcohol consumption and alcohol abuse. Its 1988 report indicates that alcohol consumption continued to decline, as it had done for the preceding five years. High school and college students appear to be drinking less than they used to, on average, although the most recent studies show an increase in heavy drinking among people, male and female, in their 20s. The NIAAA also reported that, during the 1980s, drinking increased among women aged 35 to 50, and that Native Americans, followed by Hispanic American men, have the highest rates of alcohol use and abuse. The *New York Times* (Hall, 1989), citing liquor industry data, reported sales of hard liquor had dropped 23% since 1980 and that beer and wine sales dropped 7% and 14%, respectively, during the decade. Apparently, Americans were drinking less.

Those most likely to be drinkers were men under 45 years; men and women of higher social status; professional, business, and other white-collar workers; college graduates; single men; residents of the Mid-Atlantic, New England, upper Midwest, Midwest, and Pacific areas; residents of suburban areas or cities; those whose fathers were born in Ireland or Italy; and Jews or Episcopalians. Those most likely to be heavy drinkers were men aged 45 to 49; those of lower social status; blue-collar workers; men who completed high school but not college; single, divorced, or separated men and women;

residents of the Mid-Atlantic, New England, and Pacific areas; residents of the largest cities; those whose fathers were born in Ireland, Latin America, the Caribbean, or the United Kingdom; and Protestants of no specific denomination, Catholics, and those without religious affiliation.

Put differently, men of all ages are more likely to drink than women; young and early middle aged more than the late middle aged and the old; the urban more than the rural; the secularly oriented more than the religious; the unattached more than the attached; the better educated more than the less educated; and the economically better off more than the poor. Italians and Jews are rarely abstainers. In the older surveys, Blacks had approximately the same proportion of drinkers as Whites, although Black women were more likely to drink than white women. In the most recent study (Williams & DeBakey, 1992), both Black women and Black men were significantly less likely to drink than their White gender counterparts. Of Black males, 43% reported being abstinent as against 30% of White males, while 67% of black females reported being abstinent as against 50% of White females in 1988. Another 1988 survey reported that Hispanics were somewhat less likely to drink than non-Hispanics. Thirty-five percent of Hispanic males as contrasted with 31% of non-Hispanic males were abstainers; the corresponding figures for females were 66% and 52% (Williams & DeBakey, 1992).

The one group that has shown a consistent increase in the percentage of drinkers and of heavy drinkers is young women. Homosexual women (Wilsnack, 1991) report more drinking and more heavy drinking than do heterosexual women. Otherwise, the distribution figures across region, religion, gender, and age for both drinkers and heavy drinkers have remained constant, from the Cahalan and Harris data on the late sixties right up in the present.

Although the poor are less likely to drink, if they do they are more likely to be heavy or problem drinkers. The same is true of those with less education and those who rank lower on other measures of socioeconomic status. Men of all ages and socioeconomic levels are more likely than women of comparable age and status to be heavy or problem drinkers, as are city dwellers more likely than country dwellers. Ethnicity is also correlated with heavy drinking. For example, Jews, who are rarely abstainers, have an extremely low rate of problem drinking, while the Irish, among whom abstinence is not uncommon, have a high rate of problem drinking. Italians and Chinese also have low rates of problem drinking. An important finding of Cahalan's and later survey research is that problem drinking is most prevalent among men in their twenties, although frank alcoholism is more prevalent in men in their forties. Clavis and Midanik reported that the young drink more than others, a finding which turns up on all the surveys. This strongly suggests that many youthful heavy drinkers mature and outgrow problem drinking.

Although the decision to drink, as well as the development of problems associated with drinking, is more highly correlated with sociological
variables than with psychological ones, it is important for the alcoholism
counselor to remember that these are statistical generalizations and that
people of all backgrounds become addicted to alcohol. If one works long
enough in this field, sooner or later an elderly, poorly educated, economically disadvantaged, Orthodox Jewish woman from rural Arkansas will
walk in the door and she will be an alcoholic. Furthermore, as our melt-
ing pot melts, as more and more Americans are assimilated into the common middle-class culture, as regional differences blur, and as sex roles
become less rigid, gender, residence, socioeconomic status, and ethnicity
are likely to become less predictive of both the use of alcohol and of
problem drinking. It may also be that the relatively low rates of problem
drinking in some groups may, in part, be an artifact of those groups'
ability to protect their problem drinkers from some of the social consequences of uncontrolled drinking. Be that as it may, there are certainly
cultural differences in attitudes toward drinking that affect the way members of those cultures drink.

Survey research and its findings are notoriously fallible. For all of the
methodological sophistication of such researchers, their results are still
subject to sampling errors, possible failure to find those most affected by
heavy drinking (who are less likely to respond to questionnaires, or who,
at the extreme, may be homeless), and most seriously by the inherent
fallibility of self reports. These shortcomings are especially applicable in
a population known for minimization and denial. Having said this, there
is no question that survey research, however fallible, does contribute in
important ways to our knowledge of alcohol use and abuse.

There are two main ways that epidemiologists avoid the pitfalls of
self report research: *consumption studies* and *prevalence of cirrhosis reports*. The 1990 NIAAA study (National Institute of Alcohol Abuse and
Alcoholism) showed that liquor sales continued to fall, but that beer and
wine sales had not declined since 1988. Cirrhosis mortality peaked in
1973 at 15.0 deaths for every 100,000 people; by 1986 it had fallen to 9.3
deaths per 100,000. These data indicate that both frequency and quantity
of alcohol consumption dropped during the 1980s and that consumption
now appears to be stable. This trend has been found throughout the industrialized West. The percentage of drinkers who manifest problem drinking
has remained remarkably consistent since the 1969 Cahalan study being
reported at 7% to 10% by all researchers. In 1990, one million Americans
described themselves as alcoholic. An extremely important finding of
Cahalan and his associates is that problems associated with drinking seem
to come and go. That is, individuals reporting problems with alcohol one
year may not report them another year, and if they report problems in
subsequent years, they may be different problems. These data seem at

variance with the notion that alcoholism is a progressive disease. It could be that these findings reflect the fact that problem drinking and alcoholism are different things, or that denial contaminates this type of research. (See the discussion of the disease concept of alcoholism in chapter 5 for more on this issue.)

SOCIOLOGICAL THEORIES OF DRINKING BEHAVIOR

Historically, alcoholism has been understood in three competing but not necessarily mutually exclusive ways—as *immorality*, as *illness*, and as *deviance*. Sociologists regard alcoholism as a form of *social deviance*. This view takes the focus off the individual alcoholic and his or her genetic endowment and psychological conflicts and moves it onto the social forces that make for deviance, with alcoholism seen as but one expression of these forces.

Labeling, Reference Groups, and the Normative Model

Related to the concept of deviance is the sociological notion of *labeling*. Labeling may serve as a self-fulfilling prophecy, as in the case of the label "drunken Indian." The person so labeled may come to believe that he or she will be a drunk, and that belief may be instrumental in its fulfillment. Similarly, persons labeled "hopeless" may continue to relapse because they believe (at least as far as drinking is concerned) that they *are* hopeless. Labeling may be self labeling, but sociologists are more interested in the effects of labeling on "out" groups by the dominant members of the culture. Thus, one possible cause of deviancy is labeling. From the point of view of deviancy theory, there is no such thing as a "disease" of alcoholism; rather, alcoholics are simply those drinkers whose drinking is not normative in a given culture. Abstinence can also be a deviant behavior. Deviancy theory gets incorporated into most definitions of alcoholism, which include drinking more than is considered normative in the drinker's world. Needless to say, the relativism of such definitions offends moralists and troubles "hard nosed" scientists.

In general, sociologists emphasize the role of attitudes and beliefs in both the use of alcohol and the response to alcohol. They have found empirical support in the already mentioned expectancy literature which purports to demonstrate that people learn from their cultures how to be drunk. Since drunken comportment is seen as a learned affair, problems associated with drinking (such as domestic violence) are believed to come not from drinking or the disinhibiting effect of alcohol on aggression but from the drinker's culturally learned belief that drinking will make him aggressive. Critics of expectancy theory have pointed out that as dosage goes up, the role of expectancy goes down. Although this is true, there can be little doubt that the sociologists are onto something here. Cultural attitudes do impact powerfully on drinking behavior.

Sociologists have also highlighted the importance of one's *reference group* in determining how one drinks. If the reference group (for instance, Jews) is thought to drink little, then its members are likely to drink little. A Jewish college student may shift his reference group to one in which heavy drinking is positively regarded, and his drinking may increase. Such examples are endless, but the saliency of the reference group's attitude toward drinking in determining drinking behavior is well established.

Some sociologists have emphasized the function of drinking as a "time out" from adult responsibilities, even as a "moral holiday." This view is related to the *tension reduction model* of drinking motivation first introduced into the social science literature by Horton (1943) in his slightly different version, *anxiety reduction*. Although the degree to which alcohol is actually tension reducing has been challenged (see Chapter 6), sociologists have hypothesized that the greater the tension in a culture, other things being equal, the higher the rates of drunkenness, while the more alternate modes of tension reduction there are available, the lower the rates of drunkenness. This has obvious implications for treatment.

Another theory is the *normative model* of drinking behavior, which holds that the less ambivalence, the more consistency, and the more moderation are the norm in a culture or subculture, the lower will be the amount of alcohol consumed and the lower will be the prevalence of alcoholism. Writing from a social-psychodynamic perspective, Meyerson (1940) had implicated ambivalence toward alcohol as an etiological factor in problem drinking, and his formulation has had a more recent vogue. According to this view, *permissive* norms toward drinking and drunkenness make for high rates of both, but *ambivalent* norms result in even higher rates.

The evidence is still out on this one.

Anomic Depression, Magical Potency, and Single Distribution

Perhaps of more interest is the notion of heavy, socially disruptive drinking as a response to *anomic depression*, that is, depression resulting from the destruction of, or devaluation of, one's culture, with consequent obliteration of its norms. Such explanations have been applied to Native American drinking and to alcoholism in urban ghettos. Such drinking can be seen as simultaneously a self medication of anomic depression and as a passive-aggressive expression of rage. As such it is a kind of protest. Native American drinking has been referred to as the longest running protest movement on record. Drinking that serves such a protest function is called *symbolic interactional* drinking.

Social scientists have also been interested in the degree to which a culture believes that alcohol has "magical" qualities. In particular, the belief that drinking alcohol confers *magical potency* correlates with high rates of drunkenness. There is no lack of Ivy League Ph.D's who, at least unconsciously, subscribe to this view. Advertising, sometimes subtly, sometimes not so subtly, often encourages such a belief.

The epidemiologists have come up with the *single distribution model* of problem drinking, which holds that the more "normal" or "social" drinking there is, the more problem drinkers and alcoholism there will be, and that the way to "treat" alcoholism is to establish social policies (such as high taxes on alcohol and restricted hours of sale) that reduce alcohol consumption. The extreme of this approach would be prohibition. Since the problem is seen to reside in alcohol itself, cultural attitudes, constitutional predisposition, and psychopathology are played down by single distribution theorists. Nevertheless, their "treatment" recommendation is a social-political one.

Jessor and Problem Behavior

Richard Jessor (1987) and his associates (1968) have studied the development of *problem behavior* in the young for nearly a generation. In Jessor's view, problem drinking and alcoholism are most usefully regarded as a manifestation of problem behavior. Jessor developed an extremely complex multivariate model that is entirely psychosocial to predict problem behavior. Using three categories of variables—antecedent-background, social-psychological, and social-behavior—his model is "successful" in so far as it has been able to predict which constellations of values on his antecedent-background and social-psychological variables result in which values on his social-behavior variables. That is, he has been able to identify what social-psychological factors make for problem behaviors, including alcoholism. His "predictions" are statistical, not individual. Jessor's research is additional evidence that biology and genetically determined neurochemistry are not the only significant determinants of alcoholism. Indeed, these factors play no role in his model. Interestingly, Jessor points out that coming to terms with alcohol and drugs is an important developmental task and that in some subcultures, adolescent alcohol and drug abuse is normative and best regarded as a developmental stage rather than as a psychopathology.

Cultural Contrasts

Sociologists have long been interested in demonstrating the role culture plays in drinking behavior by comparing contrasting drinking norms. Two examples of cultural contrast in attitudes toward drinking have especially interested sociologists: the contrast between French and Italian drinking practices and the contrast between Irish and Jewish drinking practices. Both France and Italy are viniculture countries—that is, they cultivate grapes for wine-making purposes—but there the resemblance ends. The French drink with and without meals, drink both wine and spirits, drink with and away from the family, do not strongly disapprove of drunkenness, and consider it an insult to refuse a drink. The Italians, on the other hand, drink mostly with meals, drink mostly wine, do most of the drinking with the family, strongly disapprove of drunkenness, and do not assert social pressure on people to drink. Not surprisingly, France has the highest rate of alcoholism in the world, while Italy has a much lower rate. Clearly, the social control imposed by the strong sanction against drunkenness and children's learning to drink moderate amounts of low-proof alcoholic beverages with food has something to do with the lower rate of Italian alcoholism. However, this merely describes *how* this culture drinks; it does not explain *why* it drinks in this way.

Studies of Irish and Jewish drinking practices show them to be in sharp contrast as well. The Irish have a high proportion of abstainers and problem drinkers; the Jews have a low proportion of both. The Irish drink largely outside the home in pubs; the Jews drink largely with the family and on ceremonial occasions. The Irish tend to excuse drunkenness as "a good man's fault"; the Jews strongly condemn it and make it culturally alien: *Shicker ist ein Goy*, "The drunkard is a gentile." The high rate of Irish problem drinking has been related to the use of alcohol as a *social remission*, a culturally approved release, in an impoverished, puritanical culture, while the low rate of Jewish problem drinking has been related to the ritualization of drinking and its association with family celebrations of all sorts. Irish drinking tends to be relief or escape drinking, while Jewish drinking tends to be ceremonial.

Robert Bales (1959) studied Irish American and Jewish American drinking practices and described four basic attitudes toward drinking: *abstinence*, *ritual*, *convivial*, and *utilitarian*. Abstinence prohibits the use of alcohol. The ritual attitude prescribes the use of alcohol in religious ceremonies in which it usually symbolizes communion with the deity. The convivial attitude is a secular one in which drinking symbolizes social solidarity, which is assumed to preexist the drinking. The utilitarian attitude treats drinking as a means of individual gratification, whether or not the drinking takes place in a group. Bales thought that cultures with a utilitarian attitude toward drinking predispose their members to problem drinking and alcoholism, while cultures with a ritual attitude inoculate their members against both. Bales concluded that Irish American drinking was convivial-utilitarian, but more utilitarian than convivial, and that Jewish American drinking was ritualistic. Bales generalized this conclusion and hypothesized that sacred ritual drinking inhibits secular drunkenness. However, sacred ritual drinking can be to the point of drunkenness, and many rituals prescribe just such drunkenness on the part of participants. Even Judaism prescribes drunkenness on the feast of Purim, and secular convivial drinking can also be and often is to the point of drunkenness. So the two forms of what Jellinek (1962), combining Bales's ritualistic and convivial categories, called *symbolic drinking*, which symbolizes communion with the divine and community among men, respectively, are not necessarily temperate. In his theory, Jellinek contrasts the symbolic with the utility function of drinking. *Utility drinking* tends to be egotistical and devoted to personal ends. Cross-cultural data do not seem to support Bales's hypothesis that sacred drinking inhibits secular drunkenness. Perhaps the real connection between Jewish ritual drinking and low rates of Jewish problem drinking lies in learning to drink in a situation of strong social control, in which moderation is the norm and guilt is not concomitant with drinking. (It has also been suggested, perhaps not altogether seriously, that the use of wine as an anesthetic during ritual circumcision serves as a one trial adversive conditioning in which alcohol is associated with pain and castration anxiety.) It is this socialization into moderation, rather than the fact that the drinking is part of religious ritual, that supposedly accounts for the relatively low rates of alcoholism. This hypothesis is consistent with the findings on Italian drinking patterns and makes more sense to me. The social norm of moderation in well-integrated cultures, which is learned in situations of powerful affectivity, rather than the connection with either sacred or secular rites, is what makes for low rates of problem drinking. The cultural controls are internalized and only break down only in the face of genetic susceptibility or an individual psychopathology that the drinker has learned to self-medicate with alcohol. Unfortunately, this does not tell us what it is about a culture that results in making drinking in moderation one of its mores.

CONCLUSION

This chapter has explored how people have used alcohol in diverse places and times and some of the reasons that they drank. In the process, it has reviewed theories of the social and cultural determinants of drinking and drunkenness and shown how sociologists and anthropologists have theorized about those determinants. It has also looked at their research strategies, and recognized the enormous methodological difficulties they encounter. Closer to home, the chapter has reviewed how Americans and late 20th-century industralized men and women drink. In the process, it has examined what the demographers have concluded about who is most likely to become alcoholic. The next chapter investigates possible ways to define alcoholism so that it can be studied and diagnosed, exploring whether there are a variety of "alcoholisms" or one unitary disorder. As the chapter will show, these apparently simple tasks are incredibly complex and problematic.

Chapter 5

What Is Alcoholism?

One reasonable conclusion that can be drawn from a perusal of the literature on alcoholism is that nobody knows what alcoholism is. An equally reasonable conclusion is that everybody knows what alcoholism is, but that they just happen not to agree. It is as if alcoholism were the elephant and the researchers the blind men in the parable of the blind men and the elephant. Depending on where they make contact with the beast, the researchers define it as trunklike, earlike, or taillike, when it is really a large thick-skinned mammal with a trunk, ears, and tail. People have argued, and still argue, whether alcoholism is a form of moral turpitude, a bad habit, a disease, or a symptom of an underlying emotional or psychological disorder. Depending on their perspective, they see it as a product of the devil, of the culture, of the genes, of the body, or of the mind. All of these positions have their defenders. Believers in the moral turpitude theory are still with us. The story comes to mind of the fundamentalist preacher who was giving a hell-and-brimstone sermon. As his preaching reached a crescendo, he bellowed out, "Tell me if anyone here is in favor of sin?" A little old lady in the back of the church stuck up her hand. "What! you're in favor of sin?" screamed the preacher. "Oh no," said the little old lady, "I thought you said gin." For her, sin and gin belonged to different categories, but this is not so for many of her fellow Americans. Clearly, something more than perspective is involved here; values also enter into these various ways of defining and understanding alcoholism. Definitions are partly decisions; they are prescriptive as well as descriptive.

The view that alcoholism is a disease goes back at least as far as Benjamin Rush (1785/1994), surgeon general of the Revolutionary army, but it was the pioneer alcohologist Emil Jellinek who made the disease concept scientifically respectable. Jellinek's notable predecessors include the early 19th-century British naval physician, Thomas Trotter (Jellinek, 1994), who held that alcoholism was caused by heredity and premature weaning, and William Silkworth, a physician who treated Bill Wilson (who went on to found Alcoholics Anonymous) and taught him that "alcoholism was an allergy of the body and an obsession of the mind." Wilson incorporated Silkworth's conceptualization into the AA literature.

Suppose we accept the viewpoint of most contemporary writers and agree that alcoholism is a disease. Does that solve the problem? No, not at all. As Jellinek (1960) demonstrated, the disease concept of alcoholism is far from clear or unitary. If alcoholism is a disease, is it a physical disease? An emotional disease? A mental disease? All three? At the advanced stage in which the patient may have a history of DTs, cirrhosis, or brain damage, there is no question but that the patient has a disease, indeed diseases, that are physical—diseases of the body. But are these physical diseases the alcoholism? It seems more reasonable to say that they are the physical consequences of the excessive drinking and secondary to it, rather than the alcoholism itself, although they may contribute to further excessive drinking by impairing the biological equipment necessary for the inhibition of impulsive behavior. In what sense then, if at all, is this excessive drinking per se a disease? Is it a genetic or metabolic disorder? An emotional disorder? If there is an emotional disorder, is it a result of the excessive drinking rather than its cause? Or as this question is sometimes put, is there a "prealcoholic" personality?

There is a vast and vexed literature devoted to answering these questions. It is inconclusive. Similarly, there is an extensive literature on the distinction between *problem drinking* and alcoholism. When does the drinker cross what AA calls the invisible line? Again, there is confusion and uncertainty. The issue of definition is seemingly inexorably linked with the question of etiology. Yet there is no reason why this should be so. We define many things the causes of which we do not understand or know with certainty. There is no reason not to do so with alcoholism. Therefore, let us attempt to cut this Gordian knot. For practical purposes, and in a rough and ready way, alcoholism can be defined as *drinking more than is good for one over an extended period of time*. There are three essential elements in this definition: (1) the drinking does serious harm of various sorts to the drinker; (2) the drinking continues despite its harmful consequences (that is, it is compulsive), and (3) the harmful drinking continues over an extended period of time.

For me, the essential characteristic of alcoholic drinking is its compulsiveness. The drinker continues to drink regardless of the consequences to his or her health, relationships, emotional stability, or financial well-being. The problem drinker also harms himself or herself by drinking, but the damage is usually not so severe and the behavior is not so chronic. The distinction is hard to make, but it is vital both clinically and for research purposes. Problem drinkers sometimes become social drinkers; alcoholics do not. Of course, this is tautological: If you can drink without doing serious harm to yourself or your environment, then you are not alcoholic, although you might have had problems connected with your drinking in the past; conversely, if you cannot drink without harming yourself, then you are alcoholic. The key issue is the ability to drink safely (that is, without returning to compulsive drinking). Unfortunately, there is no way of knowing which problem drinkers will become social drinkers and which will become alcoholics, although it is known that problem drinkers with a family history of alcoholism are themselves at risk for developing alcoholism.

The question of definition is of great importance in the epidemiology of alcoholism. Epidemiological researchers' findings as to the prevalence and distribution of alcoholism in the population vary with and are dependent on their definitions of alcoholism. However, this is a research question and not our primary concern here. The question of definition is also of clinical importance, but in a different way. You cannot diagnose what you cannot define. In cutting the Gordian knot of the problem of the proper definition of alcoholism, several *decisions* are necessary. Since definitions are prescriptive as well as descriptive, they are, in their very nature, decisions. First, the question of etiology will be held in abeyance, and our definition will be purely phenomenological. Regardless of the cause or causes, certain behaviors will be defined as alcoholic and others as not. Second, I will assume that any behavior that is as dysfunctional and self-destructive as alcoholism is a disease. For an organism to destroy itself is pathological, regardless of the source of the pathology. In these prescriptive acts I am accepting the stances of the World Health Organization (WHO), the American Medical Association (AMA), and the American Psychiatric Association (APA), all of which define alcoholism as a disease (or behavioral disorder) and all of which remain agnostic as to the etiology of the disease, confining their definitions to the descriptive.

The purpose of a working clinical definition is to diagnose—to spot the critter if it is there. An understanding of etiology is more important in treatment than in diagnosis. Undoubtedly, there is more than one type of alcoholism (in fact, some authors speak of alcoholisms), and each comprises a different mix of biological, cultural, and psychological factors. However, since the primary treatment of any of these alcoholisms is to help the patient stop drinking, the first step must be diagnosis of the problem. To this end, descriptive definitions are most helpful. Therefore, let us look at the WHO and APA definitions.

WORLD HEALTH ORGANIZATION DEFINITION

The WHO adopted Mark Keller's (1958) definition of alcoholism, which states that alcoholism is "a chronic behavioral disorder manifested by repeated drinking of alcoholic beverages in excess of the dietary and social uses of the community and to the extent that it interferes with the drinker's health or his social or economic functioning. . . . Alcoholics are those excessive drinkers whose dependence upon alcohol has attained such a degree that it shows a noticeable mental disturbance or an interference with their bodily and mental health, their interpersonal relations, and their smooth social and economic functioning, or who show the prodromal signs of such developments."[1] This is a clear and useful definition that stresses both cultural deviance and damage to the drinker. It can be used as a rough index for diagnostic purposes.

AMERICAN PSYCHIATRIC ASSOCIATION
DIAGNOSTIC CRITERIA

The APA publishes a series of *Diagnostic and Statistical Manuals of Mental Disorders* (DSM-I, DSM-II, DSM-III, DSM-III-R, and DSM-IV). The DSM-III was published in 1980. It was followed by the DSM-III-R (1987), a revision of the DSM-III, and by the recently published DSM-IV (1994). I continue to find the DSM-III most clinically useful. It contains a category of *substance use disorders*, which are classified according to severity as either substance abuse or substance dependence. The pathological use of alcohol is treated this way in the DSM-III. Since the DSM-III definitions of alcohol abuse and alcohol dependence provide very clear guidelines for the diagnosis of alcoholism, they will be quoted at length here.

> *Diagnostic criteria for Alcohol Abuse.* The essential feature of Alcohol Abuse is a pattern of pathological use of at least a month that causes impairment in social or occupational functioning.
>   A. *Pattern of pathological alcohol use*: need for daily use of alcohol for adequate functioning; inability to cut down or stop drink-

[1]From Keller (1958, p. 2). Reprinted by permission of publisher and author.

ing; repeated efforts to control or reduce excess drinking by "going on the wagon" (periods of temporary abstinence). . . . or restricting drinking to certain times of the day; binges (remaining intoxicated throughout the day for at least two days); occasional consumption of a fifth of spirits (or its equivalent); amnesic periods for events occurring while intoxicated; continuation of drinking despite a serious physical disorder that the individual knows is exacerbated by alcohol use; drinking of nonbeverage alcohol.

    B. *Impairment in social or occupational functioning due to alcohol use*: e.g., violence while intoxicated, absence from work, loss of job, legal difficulties (e.g., arrest for intoxicated behavior, traffic accidents while intoxicated), arguments or difficulties with family or friends because of excessive alcohol use.

    C. *Duration of disturbance* of at least one month. The essential features of *Alcohol Dependence* are either a pattern of pathological alcohol use or impairment in social or occupational functioning due to alcohol, *and* either tolerance or withdrawal. Alcohol Dependence has also been called *Alcoholism*.[2]

These definitions are very useful to alcoholism counselors. They are simple and clear; and they provide behavioral criteria upon which to base a diagnosis. According to the DSM-III definition, alcoholism entails physiological involvement. This is similar to Jellinek's category of gamma alcoholism, discussed later.

    The DSM-III-R has "shopping lists" for both psychoactive substance dependence and psychoactive substance abuse. Alcohol is, of course, a psychoactive substance. Here are the lists. (It should be noted that the DSM-III-R avoids the term alcoholism, speaking only of abuse and dependence, thus sidestepping the "Is alcoholism a disease?" debate, although the inclusion of abuse and dependence in the manual makes them psychiatric disorders. Is a disorder a disease? If so, this is a distinction without a difference.)

DSM-III-R Diagnostic Criteria for Psychoactive Substance Dependence

A At least three of the following:
    (1) substance often taken in larger amounts or over a longer period than the person intended
    (2) persistent desire or one or more unsuccessful efforts to cut down or control substance use

---

[2]Reprinted with permission from the *Diagnostic and Statistical Manual of Mental Disorders* (3rd ed. [pp. 164–165]). Copyright 1980 by the American Psychiatric Association.

(3) a great deal of time spent in activities necessary to get the sub-
     stance, taking the substance, or recovering from its effects
(4) frequent intoxication or withdrawal symptoms when expected to
     fulfill major role obligations at work, school, or home or when
     substance use is physically hazardous (e.g., drives when intoxi-
     cated)
(5) important social, occupational, or recreational activities given up
     or reduced because of substance use
(6) continued substance use despite knowledge of having a persistent
     or recurrent social, psychological, or physical problem that is caused
     or exacerbated by the use of the substance (e.g., having an ulcer
     made worse by drinking)
(7) marked tolerance; need for markedly increased amounts of the
     substance in order to achieve intoxication or desired effect, or
     markedly diminished effect with continued use of the same amount
(8) characteristic withdrawal symptoms
(9) substance often taken to relive or avoid withdrawal symptoms
B   Some symptoms of the disturbance have persisted for at least one month,
     or have occurred repeatedly over a longer period of time.

Diagnostic Criteria for Psychoactive Substance Abuse

A   A maladaptive pattern of psychoactive substance use indicated by at
     least one of the following:
(1) continued use despite knowledge of having a persistent or recur
     rent social, occupational, psychological, or physical problem that
     is caused or exacerbated by use of the psychoactive substance
(2) recurrent use in situations in which use is physically hazardous
     (e.g., driving while intoxicated)
B   Some symptoms of the disturbance have persisted for at least one month,
     or have occurred repeatedly over a longer period of time
C   Never met the criteria for Psychoactive Substance Dependence for this
     substance.[3]

The DSM-IV

The long-awaited DSM-IV was published in June 1994. Although her-
alded as a major revision, it does not in fact substantially differ from the
DSM-III-R in most regards; however, the secton on substance-related

[3]From the *Diagnostic and Statistical Manual of Mental Disorders (Third Edition,
Revised* [pp. 167–169]), by the American Psychiatric Association, 1987, Washington,
DC.

disorders does depart from the DSM-III and III-R in some importnat ways. Although adhering to the substance-dependence/substance-abuse distinction of previous editions, the new criteria for substance dependence no longer require physiological dependency. Rather, tolerance and withdrawal are two of seven symptoms, three of which must be present for the diagnosis to be made. Physiological dependence or lack of it is now specified as a qualification of the diagnosis, as is the degree and conditions of remission, if the disorder is indeed in remission. As in previous editions, substance abuse is defined as a less severe condition than substance dependency. Substance abuse is diagnosed if the patient meets at least one of four criteria and has never met the substance dependence criteria. Alcohol abuse and dependence are defined as a subset of the substance abuse and dependence criteria and do not differ from it. As the editions have progressed, the shopping lists for diagnoses have grown more complex, and in that growing complexity, they have become in some ways less useful, although the specification of physiological dependence is a gain in diagnostic clarity. For this reason and because the DSM-IV is a widely available standard reference, it will not be quoted in detail here. However, in most treatment settings the clinician will be expected to use the DSM-IV criteria to diagnose and, accordingly, should consult it.

The DSM-IV has a new and useful category of *substance-induced disorders* including substance intoxication, substance withdrawal, and "substance-induced delirium, persisting dementia, persisting amnestic disorder, psychotic disorder, mood disorder, anxiety disorder, sexual dysfunction, and sleep disorder" (p. 191). This recognition that mental disorders may be caused by substance abuse and persist long into abstinence is important, although the differential between what is consequent and what is antecedent to substance abuse is often hard to establish.

In addition to tolerance and withdrawal, criteria for dependence include increasing use, failure to cut down or control, substantial time devoted to gaining supplies or recovering from use, neglect of other activities, and continued use despite knowledge that use is seriously hurting the user. Criteria for substance abuse emphasize recurrence. What must recur are impairment in a major life area such as work, dangerous risk taking, legal problems, and social or interpersonal problems. Although less severe than dependence, abuse is a serious disorder.

The WHO and APA definitions of alcoholism are useful clinically, but sometimes the counselor needs a more global evaluation instrument. A highly structured intake form called the *Comprehensive Drinker Profile* (CDP) is available from Psychological Assessment Resources, in Odessa, Florida. I prefer a more informal approach that gathers the same information without inducing as much defensive reaction, but many beginning counselors feel more secure with a structure to follow.

Some philosophers of science maintain that the meaning of a concept is uniquely determined by how it is measured. Once the *operations* (steps) necessary to measure it have been specified, all that can be meaningfully said about it has been said. According to this school of thought, a concept whose meaning cannot be *operationalized* is meaningless and cannot be a subject of scientific discourse. So a definition is simply a statement of the measurements that specify the concept. Implicit in the *operationalists'* understanding of the nature of scientific definition is the notion of *quantification*—some sort of number derived from the measurement must be assignable to particular measurements of the concept. By this standard, the above definitions of alcoholism are semi-operationalized.

Several appendixes at the end of this chapter contain a number of "instruments" that have been devised to measure (and thereby operationalize) alcoholism. Each is a self-report device that defines alcoholism by a score and is intended to facilitate self-diagnosis. The first two, the *Johns Hopkins University Drinking Scale* and the *Michigan Alcoholism Screening Test* (MAST), are "scientific" instruments developed by researchers; the third is a more "folksy" instrument developed by AA, which is no less an operationalization of the concept of alcoholism. Since the three instruments differ, they provide three different operational definitions; however, a person who "scores" alcoholic on one will in all probability score alcoholic on the others. These instruments have great clinical utility.

The above definitions assume that alcoholism is a unitary phenomenon. There are, however, many ways of classifying alcoholic behavior and alcoholics. They delineate alcoholisms and types of alcoholics. Some authorities believe that there is more than one type of alcoholism. They draw dividing lines around clusters of personality traits, presumed dynamics, heritability, or drinking behaviors. Some students of alcoholism regard these classificatory schemes as misguided and diversionary, as distinctions without a difference. In a sense they are right. Alcohol is alcohol, and if you drink enough of it, you will get hooked, regardless of your age, gender, psychiatric diagnosis or lack of one, personality, or cultural background. However, this hard-nosed traditional alcoholism counseling orientation is unpleasantly "know-nothing" and hardly scientific. For all of their limitations, the various attempts at classification have been important historically, and they do shed light on our all too obscure topic. In addition to the vexed but important distinction between problem drinking and alcoholism, illuminating typologies have been constructed by Jellinek (1960); Knight (1937); Blane (1968); Winokur, Rimmer, and Reich (1971); and Cloninger (1983, 1987b). Jellinek distinguishes among drinking patterns, Knight among personality types, Blane among dynamics, Winokur, Rimmer, and Reich among psychiatric diagnoses or their absence, and Cloninger among patterns of heritability.

JELLINEK AND THE DISEASE CONCEPT
OF ALCOHOLISM

Jellinek's *The Disease Concept of Alcoholism* (1960) was a groundbreaking book. In it Jellinek made the disease concept of alcoholism scientifically respectable. He did this by taking a very careful and painstaking look at each of the possible ways of understanding alcoholism as a disease. In doing so, he evaluated available empirical evidence and the conceptual strength of each approach. Two major findings emerged. One was the concept of alcoholism as a *progressive* disease culminating in *loss of control* (that is, the inability to stop drinking after having begun). Jellinek derived this view largely from responses to a questionnaire on drinking histories that he submitted to a sample of AA members. Few pieces of survey research have had such influence. Every alcohol rehabilitation program has a chart of Jellinek's stages of progression, which it uses to teach the disease concept of alcoholism to patients. According to this scheme (Jellinek, 1952), alcoholism progresses from "occasional relief drinking" to "obsessive drinking continuing in vicious cycles," having passed through such stages as "onset of blackouts," "grandiose and aggressive behavior," "family and friends avoided," and "indefinable fears." The order of progression is seen as invariant. This concept of alcoholism as a progressive, fatal disease is canonical in AA. Later research (Park, 1973; Vaillant, 1983) has shown that neither progression per se nor Jellinek's order of progression is inevitable or invariant. However, Jellinek's basic finding holds. For most problem drinkers, things do not get better; if they continue to drink, they get worse, and their problems get worse in pretty much the way the respondents to Jellinek's questionnaire said they do.

It is this progression that is the essence of Jellinek's and later versions of the disease concept. Alcoholism thus seen has a "course" just like other medical illnesses.

CRITICISMS OF THE DISEASE CONCEPT

Although Jellinek's conceptualization of at least one form of alcoholism as a disease is based on a nuanced, subtle analysis that recognizes that not all problem drinking is best understood as a disease (see below), his ideas have come under increasing attack from a host of critics. Their arguments point to the fact that the progression is not inevitable nor invariant, and to experiments that show that alcoholics do not always drink themselves to oblivion when they have the opportunity. The critics maintain that the medicalization of addiction, including alcohol addiction, is essentially a political decision, which has had the at least partly intended effect of increasing compassion for alcoholics and rendering the treatment of alcoholism reimbursable by insurance companies and government, and has, in general, made it easier to obtain financial support for alcoholism rehabilitation. This may be true, but it does not in itself constitute an argument against the disease concept. Even if its advocates' motivation is bleeding heartism or a desire to line their pockets, the disease concept must be evaluated on its own merits as scientific explanation.

To demonstrate that Jellinek's notion of progression is untenable, Herbert Fingarette (1988), one of the most thoughtful (and passionate) of the critics, cites both survey research by the Social Research Group at the University of California (Clark & Cahalan, 1976) and the Rand Corporation (Polich, Armor, and Brailler, 1981) that purport to show that symptoms of problem drinking come and go but do not progress, and Vaillant's (1983) longitudinal study showing that youthful problem drinking is a poor predictor of middle age alcoholism and that the rate of "spontaneous recovery" from alcoholism is substantial. He attacks the notion of loss of control by citing Mello and Mendelson's (1972) study that showed that hospitalized alcoholics who had open access to alcohol did not drink themselves into oblivion and that they drank less when they had to "work" for their drinks. He also cites evidence from more naturalistic settings of alcoholics being able to "control" their drinking. Fingarette also attacks the disease concept from a clinical standard point, maintaining that teaching alcoholics that they have an uncontrollable disease becomes a self-fulfilling prophecy. Marlett and Gordon (1985) speak of the *abstinence violation effect* (AVE) in which an alcoholic who believes that if he or she takes one drink, he or she will be unable to stop, will in fact not be able to stop, not because of a "disease" but because of a cognitive expectancy. In fact, the expectancy literature showing that the effects of ethanol, behavioral and subjective, on the drinker are mediated by "mental set," or learned anticipations, is cited by Fingarette to bolster his argument.

Other critics of the disease concept offer essentially the same critique: the course of problem drinking is variable and unpredictable, loss of control is refuted by the scientific evidence, responsibility is denied and undermined by those holding the disease concept (which is morally reprehensible), and, clinically, the disease concept is anti-therapeutic. Sometimes the dubious wisdom of telling teenage problem drinkers (and drug users) that they have an incurable lifelong disease is stressed. Critics like Wendy Kaminer (1993) emphasize their judgment that the medicalization of human problems, including chemical dependency, has unintended, catastrophic moral and political effects and results in a culture of victimization and political apathy. Kaminer's is more a critique of the codependency movement and other spinoffs of AA than a direct attack on the disease concept of alcoholism, yet her argument echoes Fingarette's.

What can be said in reply to Jellinek's critics? Jellinek was well aware that not all problem drinking is progressive and he distinguishes that which is not (behavioral disorders) from that which is (the disease). Researchers seem to have difficulty validating progression; clinicians do not. Their experience tells them that for a certain type of drinker, things do indeed get worse if drinking continues. Vaillant in analyzing his own and other data concludes that progression does occur, but that the time span needed to demonstrate it is long (15 to 20 years), and that neither the evidence of spontaneous remission nor the variable patterns of alcohol abuse undermine either the scientific credibility or utility of the disease concept. I find his argument convincing.

As for the loss-of-control issue, Jellinek's original formulation of it is clearly untenable. What loss of control does mean is that the "alcoholic" cannot predict what will happen when he or she picks up a drink. The social drinker may decide to get drunk, say as a way of dealing with frustration. That may be foolish or immature from somebody's standpoint, but that is not evidence of loss of control. The alcoholic, on the other hand, decides to have one beer and does, but if he or she continues to experiment, he or she finds that sooner or later the desire to have one drink does not prevent him or her from winding up completely smashed. The key issue here is *unpredictability*. Critics of the unpredictability notion of loss of control maintain that the alcoholic has simply decided to get drunk. This contradicts alcoholics' subjective experience, "I found myself drinking in spite of not wanting to," and just about everybody's clinical experience. If the critics mean to say that the "decision" to get drunk is unconscious, that seems indistinguishable from saying that the drinking is compulsive and, if indeed compulsive, reasonably regarded as a disease.

The argument that the disease concept has undesirable social and political implications in its undermining of the experience of personal efficacy and responsibility is simply saying that critics would make a different decision about what constitutes a disease. Having argued above that definitions are prescriptive as well as descriptive, I agree that deciding that alcoholism is a disease is, in part, a political decision—but it is also a clinical and scientific one. Although there is some validity in a position like Kaminer's, hers is a value judgment to be weighed against the positive value of the disease concept.

As for the clinical critique, I have not found that alcoholics who subscribe to the disease concept continue to drink; on the contrary. The disease concept makes sense of a bewildering experience, reduces anxiety and guilt, and facilitates taking responsibility for one's recovery. Although there are occasional alcoholics who say, in effect, "What do you want from me? I have a disease, so of course I drink," I know of no clinicians who report this response other than rarely.

The critics are on more solid ground in suggesting that teaching the disease concept is basically antitherapeutic with young people. Besides,

there is no way of knowing which adolescent rebellion drinkers will become alcoholic, although we have good reason to believe that a family
history of alcoholism is a potent risk factor. As for the AVE, the way to
deal with that is to tell alcoholic patients not that if they have a drink they
will be unable to stop, but rather that if they drink, they cannot predict
what the result will be, and that continuing to drink will almost certainly
lead to serious problems.

Conceptually, to say that alcoholism is a disease can have several
meanings: to the strict determinist it is a tautology, simply meaning that
alcoholism like everything else has a cause or causes; to the geneticist it
means that there is an innate predisposing factor that makes the development of alcoholism probable; to the personality theorist it means that there
is a certain constellation of personality traits, acquired or innate, that predisposes to alcoholism; to the physician alcoholism means that it has a
predictable cause; and to the neurochemist it means that drinking itself
changes the brain chemistry in such a way that the reaction to alcohol is
altered so that control becomes difficult or impossible. A reasonable conclusion seems to be that for some alcoholics there are predisposing factors
of various sorts (the evidence for this appears in chapter 6), which make
for various degrees of inevitability; that for some a predictable course will
follow; and that it is possible that there are consequent factors resulting
from the drinking itself that make drinking safely impossible for some.

Although the disease concept may be based on a decision and be a
metaphor, I regard it as helpful and useful. Therefore, although the reader
is cautioned that this conceptualization has its critics and that their arguments have merit, I will continue to refer to the disease and the disease
process in this text. Vaillant (1983,) after exhaustively reviewing the evidence, concluded that alcoholism is best compared to a chronic metabolic
disease like diabetes, which can be significantly controlled by proper self
care. I agree.

TAXONOMIC SYSTEMS

Jellinek's Types of Alcoholics

Jellinek's second major contribution is his taxonomic (classification) system. It too has its limitations, and drinkers sometimes move from one
category to another. One might say that it has cross-sectional validity but
that its longitudinal validity is questionable. That is, at any given time all
alcoholics will fall into one of the categories, but any given alcoholic may
move across categories with the passage of time. Jellinek's categories are
as follows: alpha, beta, gamma, delta, and epsilon.

Alpha alcoholism is characterized by the presence of such symptoms as hangovers or blackouts and by psychological, not physical, dependence. The alpha alcoholic is the person who needs alcohol on a regular basis and who becomes anxious if it is not available. However, he or she will not experience withdrawal symptoms upon cessation of drinking. The person who "requires" alcohol in order to do a particular thing, such as make love, can also be considered an alpha since this is a psychological dependency on alcohol. Alpha alcoholism is not necessarily progressive. In fact, in Jellinek's formulation it is not, and indeed some drinkers remain psychologically dependent on alcohol for life without deteriorating physically or mentally; nor do they become physically dependent. It is known, however, that some alpha alcoholics do deteriorate and end up in other categories, usually gamma. Jellinek did not consider alpha alcoholism to be a true disease.

Beta alcoholism is characterized by physical symptoms such as ulcers or liver disease but not by physical dependence. The typical beta alcoholic is a heavy drinker, usually of beer, who continues to function socially and economically in a fairly adequate way as he or she continues to inflict somatic injury on him or herself. The beta alcoholic's drinking pattern remains stable in terms of quantity consumed and the relative absence of psychological and social symptomatology. Although beta alcoholism is not a progressive disease, it too is a form of pathological drinking. There is something manifestly crazy about continuing to inflict bodily damage on oneself in this way. Again, Jellinek did not consider beta alcoholism to be a true disease, and he thought that betas remained betas. However, it is known that some betas move into other forms of alcoholism, chiefly gamma. Beta alcoholism is strongly associated with male, blue collar, culturally syntonic (that is, socially approved) heavy drinking.

According to Jellinek, *gamma alcoholism* is the most prevalent form of alcoholism in the United States. Almost all members of AA are thought to be gamma alcoholics. Gamma alcoholics are both symptomatic and physically dependent (at least in the late stages). That is, they suffer emotional and psychological impairment, their social and economic functioning is compromised, and they develop a tolerance to alcohol and experience withdrawal symptoms if they stop drinking. Clearly, they are sick people, and Jellinek did consider gamma alcoholism to be a true disease. Gamma alcoholics include but are not limited to the chronic alcoholics seen in alcoholism clinics and detoxification facilities. It was from his study on the drinking history of members of AA that Jellinek developed and described the category of gamma alcoholism as a chronic progressive disease. He thought that gamma alcoholism was characterized by *loss of control*. That is, once the gamma alcoholic takes a drink, there is no way of knowing when or how the drinking will stop. Loss of control means unpredictability; it does not necessarily mean that the gamma alcoholic will always get in trouble if he or she takes a drink. Nevertheless, this unpredictability means that the gamma alcoholic cannot drink safely. This is important clinically. The alcoholism counselor must often point out to the client that he or she does not know what will happen if he or she drinks again and the fact that nothing bad happened last time does not change this. As AA puts it, "It's the first drink that gets you drunk." This is true for the gamma alcoholic, as is the AA slogan, "One drink is too many, but a thousand isn't enough." The issue of loss of control and the disease concept are scientifically controversial (see earlier discussion). In my experience, however, for all practical purposes both are true enough for those who are deeply into "booze."They are true alcohol addicts. Therefore, it is my position that abstinence, not controlled drinking, is the preferred, indeed the only rational, treatment for gamma alcoholism. The trick is to distinguish the gammas from the problem drinkers who may settle down into less dysfunctional drinking patterns. In general, the more symptomatic and the worse the history, the more likely it is that the patient is a gamma. A history of repeated withdrawal crises confirms the diagnosis. In terms of the APA's DSM-III, the gamma alcoholic is suffering from alcohol dependence; in terms of the DSM-III-R, from psychoactive substance dependence; and in terms of the DSM-IV, from substance dependence with or without physiological dependence, as the case may be.

Delta alcoholism is characterized by physical dependence but few or no symptoms. Jellinek believes that alcoholism in heavy wine drinking countries such as France is largely delta alcoholism. The delta drinker does not lose control; he or she does not get drunk, violent, or pass out, but he or she cannot stop drinking without experiencing withdrawal symptoms. High rates of liver disease are associated with delta alcoholism.

Jellinek's final category is *epsilon alcoholism*. Epsilon alcoholism is binge drinking, which the old psychiatric literature called *dipsomania*. The epsilon drinker goes on binges, often for no apparent reason, of undetermined length that usually lasting until he or she collapses. The epsilon drinker then does not drink at all until the next binge. The interval between binges may be weeks, months, or years. It may remain constant, vary widely, or systematically decrease. In the latter case the epsilon drinker eventually becomes a gamma. The epsilon alcoholic is also known as a *periodic*.

There is an interesting empirical study that attempts to find cultural confirmation of Jellinek's taxonomy. Babor and his associates (1992) reasoned that if Jellinek was right, then diagnosed American alcoholics (presumed gammas) would show greater severity of psychiatric symptoms and give more psychological reasons for drinking than diagnosed French alcoholics (presumed deltas), with diagnosed French Canadian alcoholics being in between. Their data supported their hypothesis for male but not for female alcoholics, a not surprising finding considering that Jellinek's original analysis was based on male drinking patterns.

Jellinek's categories are useful. However, many alpha, beta, and epsilon drinkers become gamma alcoholics. Of course, not all do. In each case, alpha, beta, gamma, delta, or epsilon, the alcohol is doing serious harm to the mind and body. Therefore, at least temporary abstinence must be the treatment goal. For the gamma alcoholic, permanent abstinence is the treatment goal.

Knight's Essential Versus Reactive Alcoholism

Jellinek was a biostatistician and epidemiologist who became an alcohologist. It was not surprising that he devised a typology based on drinking behavior. Robert Knight was a psychoanalyst who spent much of his career as a hospital psychiatrist, first at the Menninger Clinic and later at the Austin Riggs Center in Stockbridge, Massachusetts. His interest was clinical rather than epidemiological. Knight's research interests were in the areas of borderline personality structure, which he was one of the first to describe, and alcoholism. Not surprisingly, his classificatory system, although somewhat dependent on drinking behavior, is essentially developmental. That is, he classifies alcoholism according to the developmental level of the alcoholic. Knight's schema is dichotomous. It is based on his work with institutionalized alcoholics at the Menninger Clinic. By definition, the cases he saw were severe. Within this severity, Knight distinguished between essential alcoholics and reactive alcoholics.

The *essential alcoholics* were the patients who never really established themselves in life. They had trouble from adolescence onward. They were often financially and emotionally dependent on their families; they had spotty educational and work histories with very little evidence of accomplishment or achievement. Their *object relations*, the psychoanalytic term for interpersonal relations, were at the need-gratifying level. They failed to complete the normal developmental task of separation-individuation, and they were fixated at that developmental stage. Using traditional psychoanalytic language, Knight described these patients as oral characters who had not reached the "mastery of the object" characteristic of the anal stage of psychosexual development. Oral character disorder is characterized by angry dependency, impulsivity, and lack of frustration tolerance. These essential alcoholics were in trouble with alcohol from the beginning. They had never drunk normally. The essential alcoholics were those who had a borderline character structure. Fixation at and intense conflict around separation-individuation is characteristic of *borderline personalities*—called so because their level of psychopathology is between neurosis and psychosis. They are severely ill but not overtly psychotic. Borderline personality disorder overlaps with oral character disorder and is characterized by intense rage; wildly fluctuating levels of self esteem; stormy, unstable interpersonal relations; and difficulties at school and work. Knight thought that such borderline, essential drinkers could never drink safely. Therefore, the treatment goal with them was permanent abstinence from alcohol. It is now known that many borderline patients are or become alcoholic, although the vast majority of alcoholics are not borderline.

The *reactive alcoholics*, on the contrary, were those who had managed some life successes. They had achieved economic independence and vocational attainments. They had generally succeeded in marrying and establishing families. The quality of their object relations had once been fairly adequate, even if now they were gravely impaired by their drinking. Most had had a period of social drinking before crossing the "invisible line" into alcoholism. Knight saw their addiction as a reaction to life stresses or losses. From his description of his reactives, they seem to be a mix of "normals" with drinking problems and *narcissistic personality disorders* (N.P.D.). Narcissistic personality disorder is characterized by low self esteem, feelings of entitlement, manipulative interpersonal relations, and psychological deficits in such areas as the ability to modulate anxiety. (This disorder is further discussed in chapter 10.) Knight thought that some of these people could return to normal or controlled drinking once their psychological conflicts had been resolved or ameliorated. This is doubtful.

Knight pioneered the psychoanalytic treatment of alcoholism. It is important to note that he did so within a controlled environment in which patients could not drink. Knight's distinction, however, is a useful one. Essential alcoholics suffer from such massive developmental arrests that they are extremely difficult to treat. They make up the population of many chronic alcoholic wards. The reactive alcoholics are much more functional, although they too may suffer from grave psychopathology, albeit of a different type, much of which is caused by their drinking. Their prognosis is far more hopeful.

Blane's Dependency Types

Howard Blane is another clinician who developed a system of classifying alcoholics based on clinical experience. His system uses a different differential than Knight's. He is a subscriber to the *dependency conflict theory* of the dynamics of male alcoholism (discussed below) and he divides the male alcoholic population according to the ways in which males handle their dependency needs. In Blane's view, no alcoholic meets his dependency needs in a healthy way. In his book *The Personality of the Alcoholic: Guises of Dependency* (1968), Blane divides alcoholics into dependent, counterdependent, and dependent-counterdependent types.

The *dependent alcoholics* are openly dependent on others for financial and other forms of support. Theirs is not a healthy adult interdependence. Blane's dependent alcoholics are very similar to Knight's essential alcoholics. Blane believed that their prognosis is poor.

The *counterdependents* handle their dependency needs by denial and *reaction formation*, the psychoanalytic term for turning things into their opposite for defensive reasons as in turning hate into love and becoming hoveringly overprotective of the "loved" one. They are the "two-fisted drinkers" who "don't need anybody." They are the people prone to break up the bar and give similar evidence of their "independence." Some are overtly sociopathic. Blane believed that their prognosis also was poor. With respect to the more sociopathic of this group, I would agree. However, some counterdependents can be successfully treated psychotherapeutically by a tactful and empathetic understanding of the fear underlying their defiant defense. The trick is to find a face-saving way of keeping them in treatment.

The third group, the *dependent-counterdependent*, are those alcoholics for whom the conflict around dependency is active and intense. They are in the most pain and therefore are the most amenable to treatment. Although the dependency conflict theory of the etiology of alcoholism is out of fashion, there is no question that dependency conflicts get played out in alcoholic behavior, and Blane's typography is of considerable clinical utility. The alcoholism counselor sees dependent, counterdependent, and dependent-counterdependent alcoholics, and it is sometimes useful to think of them in these terms.

Winokur, Rimmer, and Reich's Primary Versus Secondary Alcoholism

Winokur, Rimmer, and Reich (1971) drew a distinction between primary alcoholism and secondary alcoholism. Actually, Winokur et al.'s typology is trichotomous: primary alcoholism, depressive alcoholism, and sociopathic alcoholism. However, both depressive alcoholism and sociopathic alcoholism are secondary to something else, namely, depression and sociopathy, respectively. Therefore, Winokur et al.'s scheme can be viewed as dichotomous, distinguishing between primary and secondary alcoholisms.

Primary alcoholics are those whose alcoholism is not preceded by a major psychiatric illness. *Secondary alcoholics* are those whose alcoholism follows a major psychiatric illness. By major psychiatric illness, Winokur primarily meant a major affective disorder. Most often this is a unipolar depression, that is, one that does not alternate with mania. Clinically, Winokur's distinction is of great importance. Both primary and secondary alcoholics may be seriously depressed. However, the depression associated with primary alcoholism will remit with treatment consisting of abstinence and appropriate psychotherapeutic intervention, while that associated with secondary alcoholism will not. Participation in AA also helps alleviate depression associated with primary alcoholism. This is not the case with patients suffering from secondary alcoholism. Their affective disorders are not a consequence of their alcoholism, which is an attempt at self-medication of that depression, and treatment of the alcoholism will not cure it. On the contrary, the major affective disorder must be treated psychopharmacologically (with therapeutic drugs) as well as psychotherapeutically. Secondary alcoholism is more common in women. Winokur also drew attention to another important differential—that between primary alcoholism and alcoholism that is secondary to sociopathy. Primary alcoholics, while they are active drinkers, may display some sociopathic behavior, but they are not sociopaths; sociopaths, however, are often heavy drinkers without necessarily being alcoholic. Winokur's alcoholism as secondary to sociopathy overlaps with Blane's counterdependent alcoholism. Both are generally found in men and both are extremely difficult to treat. Today Winokur's secondary alcoholics would be called *dual diagnosis* patients.

The terms primary alcoholism and secondary alcoholism are confusing because their usage has not been consistent. They have been used in Winokur's sense, where primary means just that, that the alcoholism is primary and other conditions such as personality disorder or depression are secondary to or independent of the alcoholism, and secondary alcoholism means that the alcoholism is secondary to something else such as a personality disorder or depression. However, other researchers use primary to mean early-onset severe alcoholism, the kind that is generally believed to be largely heritable, and secondary to mean the kind of alcoholism that develops over 20 to 30 years and is more subtle at least in its early manifestations. In this book primary alcoholism means Winokurian primary.

Cloninger's Male-Limited and Milieu-Limited Alcoholisms

C. Robert Cloninger investigated the heritability of alcoholism. The alcoholics in his 1983 study who manifested early-onset severe alcoholism, characterized by inability to abstain, fighting, arrests, and little or no guilt about their drinking, had a type of alcoholism that is heavily influenced by heredity and limited to men. He called this *male-limited* or *type 2* alcoholism. The other group of alcoholics in his study showed late onset, progression, psychological dependence, and guilt about that dependence. This type of alcoholism occurs in men and women, and, although Cloninger believes that genetic factors are involved here too, they do not manifest themselves without environmental provocation. He called this *milieu-limited* or *type 1* alcoholism.

In Cloninger's view male-limited alcoholism will develop independent of the environment, while milieu-limited alcoholism will develop in those who are genetically susceptible and who live in heavy drinking sub-cultures. Cloninger's male-limited alcoholics are much like Blane's counterdependents and Winokur's sociopathic secondaries. His milieu-limited alcoholics do not quite overlap with any of the other categories, but they do seem to have something in common with Jellinek's gammas. Cloninger's differential has had a strong influence on the theoretical understanding of alcoholism during the past 10 years. It is further discussed in the next chapter.

CONCLUSION

Alcoholism in itself is not a personality disorder nor is it a manifestation of another psychiatric condition. Rather, it is a primary disorder that consists of drinking to the point where the drinker and his or her environment are seriously damaged. It is a disease insofar as it is compulsive and not under the control of the drinker. There are many ways of classifying alcoholism and the ones reviewed earlier have great clinical utility; however, alcohol abuse characterizes each and all of these categories. Personality disorders are certainly associated with alcoholism, but they are not the alcoholism, however much the alcoholism may be a futile attempt to treat the personality disturbance, and the alcoholism, the drinking itself, must be addressed before the patient can improve.

APPENDIX 5A
Johns Hopkins University Drinking Scale

Ask yourself the following questions and answer them as honestly as you can:

1 Do you lose time from work due to drinking?   Yes___
                                                                      No ___

2 Is drinking making your home life unhappy?   Yes___
                                                                      No ___

3 Do you drink because you are shy with other people?   Yes___
                                                                      No ___

4 Is drinking affecting your reputation?   Yes___
                                                                      No ___

5 Have you ever felt remorse after drinking?   Yes___
                                                                      No ___

6 Have you gotten into financial difficulties as a result of drinking?
                                                                      Yes___
                                                                      No ___

7 Do you turn to lower companions and an inferior environment
   when drinking?   Yes___
                                                                      No ___

8 Does your drinking make you careless of your family's welfare?   Yes___
                                                                      No ___

9 Has your ambition decreased since drinking?   Yes___
                                                                      No ___

10 Do you crave a drink at a definite time daily?   Yes___
                                                                      No ___

11 Do you want a drink the next morning?   Yes___
                                                                      No ___

12 Does your drinking cause you to have difficulties in sleeping?   Yes___
                                                                      No ___

13 Has your efficiency decreased since drinking?   Yes___
                                                                      No ___

14 Is your drinking jeopardizing your job or business?   Yes___
                                                                      No ___

15 Do you drink to escape from worries or troubles?   Yes___
                                                                      No ___

16 Do you drink alone?   Yes___
                                                                      No ___

17 Have you ever had a complete loss of memory?   Yes___
                                                                      No ___

18 Has your physician ever treated you for drinking?   Yes___
                                                                      No ___

19 Do you drink to build your self-confidence?   Yes___
                                                                      No ___

20 Have you ever been in a hospital or institution on account
    of drinking?   Yes___
                                                                      No ___

Three YES answers indicates a probable problem drinker. From 4–7 indicates definite early alcoholism. From 7–10 indicates an intermediate phase of alcoholism. Above 10 indicates advanced alcoholism.

APPENDIX 5B
Michigan Alcoholism Screening Test (MAST)

Points

0 Do you enjoy a drink now and then?

Yes___
No ___

(2) **1** Do you feel you are a normal drinker?

Yes___
No ___

(By normal we mean you drink less than or more as much as most people)

Yes___
No ___

(2) **2** Have you ever awakened the morning after some drinking the night before and found that you could not remember a part of the evening?

Yes___
No ___

(1) **3** Does your wife, husband, a parent or other relative ever worry or complain about your drinking?

Yes___
No ___

(2) **4** Can you stop drinking without a struggle after one or two drinks?*

Yes___
No ___

(1) **5** Do you feel guilty about your drinking?

Yes___
No ___

(2) **6** Do friends or relatives think you are a normal drinker?

Yes___
No ___

(2) **7** Are you able to stop drinking when you want to?

Yes___
No ___

(5) **8** Have you ever attended a meeting of Alcoholics Anonymous (AA)?

Yes___
No ___

(1) **9** Have you gotten into physical fights when drinking?

Yes___
No ___

(2) **10** Has drinking ever created problems between you and your wife, husband, a parent, or other relative?

Yes___
No ___

(2) **11** Has your wife, husband (or other family members) ever gone to anyone for help about your drinking?

Yes___
No ___

(2) **12** Have you ever lost friends because of your drinking?

Yes___
No ___

(2) **13** Have you ever gotten into trouble at work because of drinking?

Yes___
No___

(2) **14**   Have you ever lost a job because of drinking?   Yes____

No ____

(2) **15**   Have you ever neglected your obligations, your family,
or your work for two or more days in a row because you
were drinking?   Yes____

No ____

(1) **16**   Do you drink before noon fairly often?   Yes____

No ____

(2) **17**   Have you ever been told you have liver trouble? Cirrhosis?   Yes____

No ____

(2) **18**   After heavy drinking, have you ever had Delirium Tremens
(DTs) or severe shaking, or heard voices, or seen things that
really weren't there?**   Yes____

No ____

(5) **19**   Have you ever gone to anyone for help about your drinking?   Yes____

No ____

(5) **20**   Have you ever been in a hospital because of drinking?   Yes____

No ____

(2) **21**   Have you ever been a patient in a psychiatric hospital or
a psychiatric ward of a general hospital where drinking was
part of the problem that resulted in hospitalization?   Yes____

No ____

(2) **22**   Have you ever been seen at a psychiatric or mental health
clinic or gone to any doctor, social worker, or clergyman
for help with any emotional problem, where drinking was
part of the problem?   Yes____

No ____

(2) **23**   Have you ever been arrested for drunk driving, driving
while intoxicated, or driving under the influence of
alcoholic beverage?   Yes____

No ____

(2) **24**   Have you ever been arrested, or taken into custody, even
for a few hours because of other drunk behavior?***   Yes____

No ____

If YES, how many times?   _____

SCORING
* Alcoholic response is negative
** 5 points for the DTs
*** 2 points for EACH arrest

5 points or more: Alcoholism
4 points: Suggestive of Alcoholism
3 points or less: Subject is not Alcoholic

APPENDIX 5C
Twelve Questions of Alcoholics Anonymous

1 Have you ever decided to stop drinking for a week or so, but only lasted for a couple of days?   Yes___ No ___

2 Do you wish people would mind their own business about your drinking—stop telling you what to do?   Yes___ No ___

3 Have you ever switched from one kind of drink to another in the hope that this would keep you from getting drunk?   Yes___ No ___

4 Have you ever had an eye-opener upon awakening during the past year?   Yes___ No ___

5 Do you envy people who can drink without getting into trouble?   Yes___ No ___

6 Have you had problems connected with your drinking during the past year?   Yes___ No ___

7 Has your drinking caused trouble at home?   Yes___ No ___

8 Do you ever try to get "extra" drinks at a party because you do not get enough?   Yes___ No ___

9 Do you tell yourself you can stop drinking any time you want to, even though you keep getting drunk when you don't mean to?   Yes___ No ___

10 Have you missed days of work or school because of drinking?   Yes___ No ___

11 Do you have "blackouts"?   Yes___ No ___

12 Have you ever felt that your life would be better if you did not drink?   Yes___ No ___

If you answered YES to four or more questions, you are probably in trouble with alcohol.

The Twelve Questions from "Is A.A. for You? "are reprinted with permission of Alcoholics Anonymous World Services, Inc.

Chapter 6

What Do We Know About Alcoholism?

In terms of solid, empirically verified, replicated knowledge, surprisingly little is known about alcoholism. Aside from the physiological evidence and some imprecise demographic findings, there are few hard facts about alcoholism. Some studies strongly suggest that there is a genetic component or predisposition to some forms of alcoholism; there are a handful of replicated empirical psychological findings; there are fewer than half a dozen longitudinal studies; and there is a limited body of known fact about special populations suffering from alcoholism. This chapter takes a look at what is known in each of these areas.

EVIDENCE FOR A GENETIC FACTOR

Conceptually there are two basic questions that researchers ask about the heritability of alcoholism. The first is simply whether alcoholism, some forms of alcoholism, a predisposition to alcoholism, or a predisposition to some forms of alcoholism are inherited. The second is, if alcoholism or a predisposition to it is at least partially inherited, what is it that is inherited? An appetite for alcohol? Enjoyment of alcohol? Relief of some dysfunction or dysphoria by alcohol? Or, in terms of learning theory, more than normal reinforcement by alcohol? A capacity for alcohol (a "hollow leg")? A deviant reaction to alcohol by the nervous system or the liver? Some combination of the above? In other words, is it consumption, preference, metabolism, sensitivity and acute reaction to, tolerance (acute and chronic), physical dependency and withdrawal, absence of some protective factor, or some unknown aspect of the alcoholic's relationship to alcohol that is implicated in a predisposition to alcoholism?

It is well known that people have different responses to alcohol. We all know people who love it and people who cannot stand it. Some people really get a lift from a drink, and some people say, "Oh, I just get sleepy," or "I get a headache," from even a few drinks. Is the difference constitutional or is it a result of experience? Is it genetic or acquired? It is not surprising that there are differences in people's responses to alcohol. After all, people react idiosyncratically to all sorts of drugs, and some cats get high on catnip and some do not. For example, there is the phenomenon of the *alcohol flush*, characterized by reddening and other symptoms, including rapid pulse and difficulty breathing, occurring after low doses of alcohol. This phenomenon occurs in very few Caucasians but in a considerable number of Asians. This racial difference in response to alcohol suggests that a genetic factor is involved.

Scientists study the possible heritability of alcoholism in a variety of ways. One is animal studies, particularly those that attempt to breed an appetite for ethanol. Yet another is the study of the prevalence of alcoholism in families, twins, and the relatives of alcoholics, particularly adoptees who are children of alcoholics. Another is studying the reaction to alcohol of nonalcoholic children of alcoholics. Much current research is focused on the search for *biological markers*, usually but not necessarily biochemical abnormalities that accompany or are antecedent to alcoholism. A biological marker can be anything assumed to be carried by the same chromosome as the trait or condition under investigation. For example, color blindness was once thought to be a biological marker for alcoholism. That does not mean that color blindness causes alcoholism, only that the two go together or, as statisticians say, are correlated because they are presumed to be transmitted by the same chromosome. A biological marker *can* have a causal relation to the condition it marks, but this is not necessarily the case.

Animal Studies

Since people are among the very few animals that naturally drink ethanol in more than minimal quantities, finding animal models for alcoholism is difficult. Elephants are apparently an exception, getting smashed on fermented palms and going on rampages, but it is not clear that it is the alcohol rather than the palms that attract them, nor are we certain whether alcoholic elephants see pink elephants. Alcohol does not appear to be strongly reinforcing for most animals. Psychologists define a *reinforcer* as something that increases the frequency of a behavior; that is, if alcohol is reinforcing, drinking it should increase the frequency of drinking it. Animals generally do not want more alcohol to drink after drinking some; that is, they don't find it reinforcing. This is strikingly different from the animal response to cocaine. If a rodent is given a choice of pushing a lever that delivers cocaine and one that delivers food, he or she will choose the cocaine, continuing to do so until he or she collapses. Nevertheless, nonhuman subjects have been used to study drinking behavior and alcoholism. *Appetite for alcohol* and *preference for alcohol* are traits that occur in some but not all rodent individuals and strains. Strains of mice and rats have been bred to drink alcohol, and some in fact prefer it to water. There are even rodents that will voluntarily drink enough alcohol to have withdrawal symptoms when they stop. This is not a normal mouse predilection. The mouse souse is not found in nature; neither is the heavy-hitting rat. The way these anomalies are created is by breeding with each other those animals that show some appetite for alcohol and in turn selecting those of their offspring with the greatest appetite for alcohol to mate with those of the offsprings' generation that are similarly inclined. This process of selective breeding is continued over the generations until a strain of rodents with a distinct appetite for alcohol emerges. Surprisingly, Martini Mickey can be bred in as little as 10 generations. With some such strains, continued selective breeding results in animals that prefer alcohol and even in animals that show a physical dependence. These results argue strongly for the existence of a genetically transmitted appetite for alcohol in rodents. Although extrapolating from animal models to humans is inferential and it is not certain that similar propensities are inherited by humans, the heritability of an appetite for alcohol in rodents is a striking finding that strongly suggests that similar mechanisms exist in humans. Additionally, the heritability of a tolerance for alcohol, as measured by the *righting response* (the ability to remain on or regain one's paws after a heavy dose of ethanol), has been demonstrated in rodents.

One ingenious, if highly speculative, hypothesis to account for the relatively low rate of alcoholism among Jews is as follows. Jews once had rates of drunkenness, problem drinking, and alcoholism as high as any other group. However, living as a persecuted minority in constant danger, the Jews who liked to drink heavily were more vulnerable and more likely to be killed before reproducing than Jews who did not. Over the centuries the genes that mediate a high appetite for alcohol diminished and became infrequent in Jews. For other peoples who did not share the special vulnerability of the Jews, drinking alcohol was safer than drinking the often contaminated water and had survival value, so these heavy drinkers reproduced, while the Jews who were heavy drinkers were less likely to reproduce. An ingenious hypothesis indeed, but the time scale—a mere few hundred years—seems too short. Be this as it may, there are rodents that like to drink and rodents that do not, and the ones that do are the descendants of many generations of rodents with similar inclinations.

Biological Markers

Research on biological markers is "hot." There are several reasons why researchers are intrigued by the search for metabolic, neurophysiological, and other biological correlatives of alcoholism. One reason involves attempts to establish the heritability of alcoholism. If alcoholism, or a subtype of it, is associated with a biological trait known to be heritable, then that association can be interpreted as evidence for the heritability of alcoholism. The establishment of biological markers for alcoholism raises the possibility of developing diagnostic procedures to identify alcoholics or those susceptible to alcoholism early in the disease process and of taking preventive or remedial actions to prevent or limit clinical manifestations of the underlying susceptibility. For example, if an elevation of enzyme X is found to be a biological marker for alcoholism, adolescents who test high on enzyme X could be warned that they are at high risk for alcoholism. Finally, the study of biological markers offers intriguing possibilities for understanding and illuminating the underlying metabolic and neurophysiological concomitants of alcoholism. As in all research on alcoholism, it is often difficult to tell what is the chicken and what is the egg, what is causative of and what is resultant from alcoholism. For example, if high levels of enzyme X are found in alcoholics, is the high level caused by the drinking itself, that is, is it a consequence of the alcoholism? Or is it etiological, that is, did it antedate and contribute to the development of the alcoholism? Or is the elevation of enzyme X a genetically transmitted trait that shares a chromosome with a gene that transmits a trait that increases the susceptibility to alcoholism? That is, is the level of enzyme X a marker neither consequent to nor causative of alcoholism? These are difficult questions to answer. Determining what is cause and what is effect has long been a problem in purely psychological research on alcoholism, and the case is even worse in biological marker research. There are several ways researchers try to tease out cause from effect. The best method would be to use *longitudinal* research designs that follow subjects from childhood into adult onset of alcoholism and gather data on the status of biological markers antecedent to the development of the disease. The next best design is to study children of alcoholics, who are presumed to be at high risk for alcoholism, and see if they are distinguished from controls who are presumed normal on either baseline measures of various biological markers or in their reactions to challenge doses of ethanol. The least rigorous but easiest method is to simply look for correlations between traits and alcoholism.

Color Blindness   The first biological marker discovered for alcoholism was thought to be color blindness (Cruz-Coke & Varela, 1966). However, Varela, Rivera, Mardones, and Cruz-Coke (1969) later demonstrated that the color blindness in the Cruz-Coke and Varela study was the *result* of severe alcohol abuse. Interestingly, Varela et al. also showed that female relatives of alcoholics differed significantly from controls in the occurrence of blue-yellow color blindness, so it is possible that there is a connection between a recessive gene for blue-yellow color blindness and alcoholism. If there is such a connection, it would consist of the sharing of a common chromosome that carries both the gene for color blindness and a gene for some trait that predisposes to alcoholism.

Platelet Enzymes   Researchers study the levels of various enzymes in blood platelets because they are easily assessable and because platelet levels are assumed to reflect brain levels of the same enzymes. Additionally, the base levels of these enzymes are known to be under genetic control.

The two platelet enzymes that have received the most attention are *monoamine oxidase* (MAO), which breaks down norepinephrine and other excitatory neurotransmitters, and *dopamine-betahydroxylase* (DBH), which converts dopamine to norepinephrine. The base levels of both are under genetic control, and both affect the level of the neurotransmitter norepinephrine, high levels of which are associated with anxiety. Tabakoff et al. (1988) found significant differences between alcoholics and nonalcoholics in the degree of MAO depression following drinking. In other words, drinking increases the level of a neurotransmitter, high levels of which are associated with anxiety, more in alcoholics than in nonalcoholics through a differential lowering of the level of the enzyme MAO, which biodegrades norepinephrine and other monoamines. Alexopoulos, Lieberman, and Frances (1983) found depressed levels of platelet MAO in alcoholics and their relatives. This finding has been consistently replicated. Depressed platelet MAO is also associated with a variety of psychiatric illnesses.

Schuckit and Gold (1988) studied the difference between high-risk college students (those who had a family history of alcoholism) and those who had an average risk (they were free of a family history of alcoholism) on a number of biological markers including platelet MAO levels.

Schuckit and Gold found no significant difference at baseline (that is, before drinking).[1]

Challenge doses equivalent to three to five drinks of ethanol (ETOH) increased the difference between the *family history positive* (FHP) and *family history negative* (FHN) groups on levels of platelet MAO, but they did not reach significance. The research on platelet MAO in abstinent alcoholics is inconsistent, but depressed levels persist for a long time. Some studies show no change in this trait with sobriety. It is likely that low platelet MAO is a biological marker for alcoholism. If so, this is important because high levels of norepinephrine are associated with sensation-seeking behavior, which is characteristic of Cloninger type 2 (male limited) alcoholics. Type 2 alcoholics have been found to have significantly lower platelet MAO than type 1 alcoholics (von Knorring, Bohman, von Knorring, & Oreland, 1985).

Studies on platelet DBH are conflicting, and no clear correlation between platelet DBH levels and alcoholism has been established. There is, however, considerable albeit not consistent evidence that plasma, spinal fluid, and platelet levels of DBH are significantly depressed in alcoholics. However, this could be caused by the subjects' alcoholism. If this finding proves to be generally true of alcoholics, it would mean that they have higher levels of dopamine and less dopamine converted to norepinephrine than nonalcoholics. Since high levels of dopamine are associated with serious mental illness, depressed levels of DBH may contribute to the relatively poor reality testing characteristic of active alcoholism and the early stages of recovery from it. Paradoxically, there are studies (Schuckit & Gold, 1988) that show significantly higher DBH levels in high-risk (FHP) than in low-risk (FHN) groups of young men. High levels of DBH are believed to be associated with less subjective feelings of intoxication after alcohol consumption. This could contribute to heavy drinking by the high-risk group. None of this is certain, and it is far from clear what the findings on DBH levels in alcoholics and high-risk groups mean. However, there does appear to be an association between DBH levels and alcoholism.

Tabakoff et al. (1988) also found abnormalities in the stimulation of the enzyme called platelet *adenylate cyclase* by various metabolites in alcohol-

---

[1]Statisticians speak of significant and nonsignificant differences. A *significant difference* is one that is sufficiently unlikely (usually meaning the odds are less than 1 in 20) to be a chance or accidental finding, about which one can be confident that the difference is due to the properties of what is being compared—in this case alcoholism and its absence. *Statistical significance* is a statement about how certain one is of a conclusion, not of how important it is. The degree of certainty does not indicate how large the difference or correlation between groups is; this is expressed differently, usually by a correlation coefficient. Statisticians speak of significance levels, such as the .05 level, which means there is a 5-in-100 or 1-in-20 chance that the finding is random.

ics and thought this might be a biological marker of alcoholism. The abnormality consisted of less stimulation. This is interesting because stimulation of adenylate cyclase enhances the synthesis of cyclic adenosine monophosphate (cAMP), one of the second messengers with which, it is hypothesized, ethanol interferes. The depression of platelet MAO, DBH, and adenylate cyclase activity persists into abstinence in recovering alcoholics and is postulated to contribute to the prolonged withdrawal syndrome (discussed in chapter 2) and to neurological complications of alcoholism.

Blood Levels of Acetaldehyde　Schuckit and Gold (1988) also found significantly higher levels of acetaldehyde, the first breakdown product (metabolite) of alcohol in FHP students after drinking. This finding is intriguing since high levels of acetaldehyde are aversive and presumably would discourage drinking, yet apparently such is not the case in high-risk subjects. Additionally, acetaldehyde is postulated to interact with neurotransmitters to produce the morphine-like *tetrahydrosioquinolines* (TIQs), a mechanism that some investigators believe is involved in the development of alcohol addiction; it is possible, therefore, that high levels of acetaldehyde could be implicated in addiction to alcohol. However, there has been difficulty in replicating this finding either in college-age FHPs or younger ones. It is known that those who are frankly alcoholic tend to produce high levels of acetaldehyde when they drink. But the evidence is not clear-cut. There is, however, no question that people vary in the ways they metabolize alcohol and that the resultant levels of acetaldehyde have something to do with drinking behavior. Presumably acetaldehyde levels interact with a host of other biochemical, cultural, and psychological variables to determine one's risk for alcoholism. High blood levels of acetaldehyde could result from more rapid conversion of ETOH (ethyl alcohol) into acetaldehyde or from the less rapid conversion of acetaldehyde into acetate. The biological substrate (underlying mechanism) of high acetaldehyde levels may be the presence of atypical or *isoenzyme* alcohol dehydrogenase (ADH) or atypical or isoenzyme aldehyde dehydrogenase (ALDH), both of which are genetically controlled. An isoenzyme has the same atomic constituents as the enzyme, but they are somewhat differently configured. The reader will recall the relationship between propyl and isopropyl alcohol illustrated in Figures 1.11 and 1.12, which is a simple isomeric relationship, not different in principle from the isoenzyme relationship in which the molecules are far larger and more complex. The heritability of these liver enzymes and their variants is well established. High levels of acetaldehyde are associated with the alcohol flushing syndrome, and, not surprisingly, Schuckit and Gold's high-risk FHP subjects had significantly higher occurrence rates of flushing after drinking. Again, this is a non-replicated finding.

Static Ataxia   Also known as upper-body sway, *static ataxia* is a measure of unsteadiness that presumably is related to underlying neuro-logical status. To what degree such unsteadiness is genetically controlled or environmentally determined is unknown. Ataxia is the medical term for staggering; static ataxia is staggering while standing still. Some degree of body sway is found in everyone and each of us has a baseline measure of it. Schuckit and Gold (1988) found no difference in baseline measurements of body sway between FHPs and FHNs. They did find a significant difference in the effect of alcohol on body sway in FHPs and FHNs. The high-risk subjects showed significantly less increase in static ataxia after a challenge dose of ETOH. Other research (National Institute on Alcohol Abuse and Alcoholism, 1988) has demonstrated significantly higher baseline body sway in children of alcoholics, and it has been suggested that static ataxia could serve as a biological marker for alcoholism.

Serum Hormone Levels   Schuckit and Gold (1988) also found significantly lower blood plasma levels of the hormones *prolactin* and *cortisol* after challenge doses of ETOH in FHP subjects. The significance of these possible biological markers for alcoholism is not clear; however, persistently low levels of serum prolactin and serum cortisol are found in abstinent alcoholics and may play a part in the protracted withdrawal syn-drome discussed in Chapter 3.

Subjective Experience and Objective Measures of Effects of Drinking
There is a whole set of research findings that suggesting that those who are at high risk for alcoholism have a "hollow leg" (that is, they experience fewer adverse effects than do other drinkers from the same dose of ETOH). They also feel less drunk. Here science supports the folk wisdom of AA, most of whose members report that they could really "sock it away" early in their drinking careers. It makes sense that someone who can easily drink a lot of an addictive drug will be more likely to become addicted to it. Schuckit and Gold's (1988) research supports this. It is one of their findings about the differential response of FHPs and FHNs to challenge doses of ETOH. In fact, the FHPs reported feeling not only less impaired but also better. That is to say that alcohol is highly reinforcing for these subjects. Surprisingly, Schuckit and Gold found objective correlates for these subjective reports. The FHPs either suffered less impairment or im-proved on a variety of objective tests of cognitive functioning and motor performance. This may be because alcohol is highly anxiety reducing for high-risk subjects. If so, this is at variance with the research of Mello and Mendelson (1970) showing that alcoholics are more, not less, anxious on objective measures of anxiety after drinking, although the alcoholics them-selves report the opposite. Apparently, alcoholics react differently to alcohol

after they develop their disease than they did before, at least with regard to anxiety. This may explain one mechanism of addiction. If those who "benefit" most from drinking drink more to obtain those benefits but lose them in the process, they may nevertheless continue to search for the old rewarding experience by continuing to drink long after such reinforcement is obtainable. This is congruent with AA folk wisdom that points to the already mentioned high capacity for drink—the hollow leg—and the futile search for the old magic as antecedents of alcoholism. Both conditions would set one up for alcohol addiction.

Electroencephalograph Studies   The electroencephalograph (EEG) records brain waves, usually by using scalp electrodes to detect the electrical activity of the brain. What is recorded are averages of the electrical activity of millions of neurons. Sometimes the averaging is done by the brain itself, so what is present at the electrodes is the averaged potential. Sometimes the raw input to the EEG is further processed by computer averaging, so that the output is interpretable. There are two main EEG findings about alcoholics: the first concerns *alpha waves* and the second *event-related* or *evoke potentials*.

It has been shown (Pollock et al., 1983; Propping, Kruger, & Mark, 1981) that Cloninger's type 1 milieu-limited alcoholics have low rates of slow alpha waves, high rates of fast alpha waves, and poor synchrony of those waves when they are abstinent. This may be true of other alcoholics as well. Alpha waves are characteristic brain wave patterns found in everyone. Subjectively, minimal poorly synchronized slow alpha activity and excessive poorly synchronized fast alpha activity are experienced as dysphoric. Such a pattern is a neuroelectrical correlative of tension. Type 1 alcoholics show a marked increase in slow alpha activity, which also becomes better synchronized, and a marked decrease in fast alpha activity when they drink ETOH. Again, there is evidence that this may be true of other alcoholics as well. Subjectively, these changes are experienced as calm alertness and relief of tension. In other words, their anxiety levels drop when they drink. Cloninger (1987b) calls this type of anxiety *cognitive anxiety*. Cognitive anxiety is characterized by anticipatory worry and guilt. This suggests that for some alcoholics excessively high levels of anxiety are antecedent to their alcoholism and that alcohol was a particularly effective antianxiety drug for them, at least before their disease progressed. Nonalcoholic FHP subjects have a greater increase in slow alpha tracings and a greater decrease in fast alpha tracings when they drink than do controls (that is, alcohol is more reinforcing for them). Women FHPs were found to have minimal slow alpha activity, suggesting that they would be more subject to type 1 alcoholism, which is exactly what epidemiological research shows.

Evoke (or *event-related*) *potentials* are spikes in the EEG that reflect brain activity in response to a visual or auditory stimulus that is either unpredictable or task relevant but not usual. Porjesz and Begleiter (1983) found that both sons and daughters of alcoholic fathers have significantly higher amplitudes of event-related potentials. They are *stimulus augmenters*— they who experience stimuli with particular intensity. This is a neuroelectrical measure of stimulus augmentation, but alcoholics have also been found to be stimulus augmenters on other measures of this trait. Cloninger type 2 (male limited) alcoholics are stimulus augmenters in terms of the amplitude of their evoke potentials when abstinent. Alcohol either decreases their augmentation or changes it to *stimulus attenuation*, a decrease in *stimulus reactance* that is assumed to be pleasurable and reinforcing. Cloninger (1987b) speaks of his type 2 alcoholics as suffering from *somatic anxiety* (bodily tension) in contrast to the cognitive anxiety of type 1 alcoholics. In both cases, alcohol consumption reduces anxiety: in the first by reducing stimulus augmentation (amplitude of the evoke potential) and in the second by reducing fast alpha brain activity and synchronizing it. Anxiety reduction is reinforcing, and such mechanisms could predispose to alcoholism. Female relatives of type 2 alcoholics have significantly higher rates of somatic anxiety but not of alcoholism than do controls.

An evoke potential known as the *P3* (or *P300*) *wave* has received special attention. There have been several important findings, including the nonreversible flattening in the amplitude of P3 in alcoholics and decreased P3 in the sons of alcoholics (Begleiter, Porjesz, Bihari, and Kissen, 1984). Since P3 is an orienting response, this may correlate with findings (Tarter, 1981) of *attention-deficit disorder* (ADD) in alcoholics shown to have been hyperactive in childhood. Hyperactivity is believed to be antecedent to alcoholism in a considerable number of male alcoholics who are probably Cloninger type 2s for the most part. Tarter thinks their hyperactivity may be etiological or at least predisposing to alcoholism.

The National Institute on Alcohol Abuse and Alcoholism (NIAAA) (1988) found cognitive deficits of various sorts (for instance, impaired problem-solving ability) in nonalcoholic sons of alcoholics. It is hypothesized that these deficits may be manifestations of the same underlying factor that manifests itself in hyperactivity and abnormal P3 waves. Since the NIAAA (1988) also reports studies that it found no significant difference between the cognitive abilities of children of alcoholics and those of children whose parents are not alcoholics, these studies are difficult to interpret. It is not known if the deficits found are the result of environmental or genetic factors or an interaction of the two.

Most of the biological marker research demonstrates something about high-risk males. Research currently is beginning to show similar differences in response to ETOH in daughters of alcoholics.

Family Studies

Family studies (Bleuler, 1955; Amark, 1951; Pitts & Winokur, 1966) consistently show an increased incidence of alcoholism in relatives (parents and siblings) of alcoholics compared with various control groups or the general population. Such studies show a greater risk for male relatives (fathers and brothers) than for female relatives (mothers and sisters), and a higher risk for both male and female relatives than for control groups. These findings do not shed light on how alcoholism is transmitted, whether by culture, learning, or genetic factors. They do establish beyond doubt that children of alcoholics are at risk for alcoholism.

Studies of Twins   Studies of twins have contributed evidence for a genetic factor in alcoholism. Such studies are conducted by calculating the concordance between identical (*monozygotic*) and fraternal (*dizygotic*) twins for alcoholism; the *concordance rate* is the percentage of twins sharing a given trait or condition. In this case, the percentage of alcoholic twins with an alcoholic twin is calculated for populations of identical and fraternal twins. The concordance rates are then compared. Since identical twins are the product of the same fertilized egg, or *zygote*, and fraternal twins are the product of different fertilized eggs, a higher concordance between identical than fraternal twins is taken as evidence of a genetic factor in the transmission of the trait or condition. The results consistently show that identical twins of alcoholics have a statistically significantly higher incidence of alcoholism than do fraternal twins of alcoholics. In a typical study, Kaij (1960), using male twins, found a concordance of 53.5% in identical twins and a concordance of 28.3% in fraternal twins. However, too much should not be made of this evidence for a genetic factor. Environmental factors, including the fact that identical twins are more likely to be treated alike, confound such studies.

Studies of Adoptees   A promising research design is to study the children of alcoholics who were adopted very early in life by nonalcoholic adoptive parents, following them into adulthood and determining their rates of alcoholism and comparing those rates to their generational peers. The first and one of the most important of these adoption studies was conducted by Goodwin, Schulsinger, Hermansen, Guze, and Winokur (1973) in Denmark. Goodwin et al. followed children of alcoholics who were adopted at or shortly after birth and raised by nonalcoholic parents. An early study (Roe, 1945) found almost no alcoholism in children of alcoholics who were raised by nonalcoholic adoptive parents. This result may be confounded by the disproportionate number of girls in the study. Goodwin et al.'s results were the opposite. In their study, chronic alcoholism was four times more common in 55 adopted-out sons of alcoholic fathers than among 78 adopted-out sons of nonalcoholics. The sons of alcoholics had a 25% rate of alcoholism—higher than the 17% rate Goodwin et al. found for male children of alcoholics raised by those alcoholics. This, of course, means that 75% of the sons of alcoholics raised by nonalcoholic adoptive parents did not become alcoholic; therefore, simple Mendelian inheritance of alcoholism (that is, that alcoholism is caused by a gene) is not the case. Moreover, alcoholism was not found to be significantly more prevalent in adopted-out daughters of alcoholics raised by nonalcoholics. It is of considerable interest that Goodwin et al.'s adopted-out male children of alcoholics had significantly higher rates of hyperactivity, shyness, sensitivity, and aggression than adopted-out male children of nonalcoholics. Adoptees whose biological parents were not alcoholics but who were raised by alcoholic parents did not have significantly higher rates of alcoholism. In contrast to their findings on alcoholism, Goodwin et al. found no correlation between problem drinking (alcohol abuse that did not qualify as alcoholism as they defined it) and alcohol abuse in biological parents.

A Swedish study conducted by M. Bohman (1978) and reported by Cloninger (1983) extended and confirmed Goodwin et al.'s findings. It was based on a much larger sample (862 men and 913 women) of known paternity born to single women between 1930 and 1949. As previously noted, Cloninger found a high correlation between what he called male-limited susceptibility (or type 2 alcoholism) in biological fathers and type 2 alcoholism in adopted-out sons of these fathers who were raised by nonalcoholic adoptive parents. It is early-onset severe alcoholism associated with antisocial and even overtly criminal behavior. Type 2 alcoholism was found only in males; the sons of type 2 fathers raised in nonalcoholic families had *nine times* the rate of alcoholism of the sons of all other fathers in the study. Approximately half of the adopted-out sons of type 2 alcoholics became alcoholic, but half did not, so once again the evidence does not support direct Mendelian inheritability but, rather, indicates that in one form of alocholism *biological vulnerability* to alcoholism is inherited. Goodwin (1988) speculates that what makes for the vulnerability may be low levels of the neurotransmitter serotonin, citing evidence that alcoholic rats have low levels of serotonin in certain parts of their brains and that serotonin reuptake blockers like Prozac decrease appetite for alcohol in these rodents. Since alcohol increases serotonergic activity initially, it might be highly appealing to a person with a serotonergic activity deficit, while its biphasic impact on serotonin levels results in its ultimately decreasing serotonergic activity, setting up a vicious cycle resulting in addiction. Goodwin acknowledges the highly speculative nature of this theory of what is inherited. None of the environmental variables measured by the researchers significantly influenced the appearance of this type of alcoholism, increasing the likelihood that it is highly heritable. The Swedish data also indicated that type 2 alcoholism is extremely treatment resistant. An American longitudinal study (Vaillant, 1983) did not find any worse outcome for what it defined as sociopathic alcoholics, at least with regard to recovery from alcoholism, than for its nonsociopathic alcoholics. This is puzzling, since Cloninger's type 2s are presumably similar to Vaillant's sociopaths.

Adopted-out sons and daughters of type 1, late-onset alcoholic parents, who tended to be approval seeking as well as to worry and be guilt prone, were also significantly more likely to develop alcoholism. The type of alcoholism they developed was the same as that of their biological parents. However, this occurred *only* if they were reared in adoptive homes where heavy drinking was the norm. The actual environmental variable measured was working-class, lower socioeconomic status which the researchers argued went with a heavy drinking lifestyle or at least with approval of intoxication as recreation and relaxation. This type of alcoholism was called *milieu-limited susceptibility* and was far less heritable. A reanalysis of the Swedish data (Cloninger, Bohman, & Sigvardsson, 1981) indicated a correspondence between type 1 alcoholism in the mothers and type 1 alcoholism in the adopted-out daughters.

Like Goodwin et al., the Swedish investigators found that children whose biological parents were not alcoholic but whose adoptive parents were did not develop alcoholism at rates significantly higher than children of nonalcoholics raised by nonalcoholics. They concluded that alcoholism in children of alcoholics is not transmitted by learning, modeling, or unconscious identification, let alone by the maladaptive use of alcohol to ameliorate the pain of being raised in an alcoholic home, although environmental provocation is necessary for milieu-limited alcoholism to occur. However, there may be a confounding variable here. It is known that many children of alcoholics become teetotalers, and it may be that the environmental, emotional, and interpersonal, as opposed to the genetic, influences of parental alcoholism may be to increase the likelihood of *either* alcoholism or total abstinence, while decreasing the likelihood of becoming a social drinker. This hypothesis was not tested in either the Danish or the Swedish studies. A more recent American study (Cadoret, O'Gorman, Troughton, & Heywood, 1984) using the same design found that adopted-out sons of alcoholics were three times as likely to develop alcoholism as adopted sons of nonalcoholics. An important additional finding was that these Iowa children of alcoholics had a significantly higher rate of *conduct disorder* than their peers, a finding congruent with the high rates of hyperactivity in the Danish study and with retrospective evidence (Tartar, 1981) of childhood hyperactivity in clinical alcoholic populations.

Goodwin's isn't the only theory of biological vulnerability, and alcohologists have argued about what, if anything, is inherited in alcoholism. A variety of suggestions have been made. The alcoholics in the Danish study were Winokurian primary alcoholics, and Winokur (1974) has argued that there is a genetically transmitted *depressive spectrum illness* in which women are at risk for unipolar depression and men are at risk for alcoholism or sociopathy. He seems to argue that a common mechanism predisposes them to these diseases, but he does not specifiy what that mechanism might be. Others have pointed to the association of childhood hyperactivity and adult alcoholism found in the Danish study and elsewhere as a clue to what might be transmitted. However, hyperactivity has not been consistently found in the childhoods of alcoholics.

What conclusion can be drawn from this? The best evidence we have, which is fragmentary and based on small samples, shows that a predisposition to some forms of alcoholism is inherited. Alcoholisms can probably be arranged in a continuum ranging from those in which constitutional factors play little or no role to those in which constitutional factors play a vital role. One third of alcoholics report no family history of alcoholism. From a clinical standpoint, the most important finding of these studies is that children of alcoholics are at extremely high risk for alcoholism, even if this predisposition is not necessarily exclusively genetic. Treatment is not importantly affected by the presence or absence of constitutional factors in the etiology of a particular person's alcoholism, although familial alcoholism, particularly if it is early onset, increases the odds that the patient can never drink "safely."

EMPIRICAL PSYCHOLOGICAL FINDINGS

There are few consistent empirical psychological findings in alcoholic populations. However, the few facts that have been determined do hold up across studies and populations. Unfortunately, almost all of the studies are about male alcoholism. Recent and current research seeks to remediate this but has thus far produced limited data. Furthermore, for the most part the existing studies are about the characteristics of men *after* they have become alcoholic; that is, insofar as the studies are descriptive of an "alcoholic personality," they describe the clinical alcoholic personality, not the prealcoholic personality). Given these limitations, it is nevertheless known that alcoholics have elevated psychopathic deviance scores on the Minnesota Multiphasic Personality Inventory (discussed below). They are also field dependent (a concept discussed later in this chapter) on a variety of measures, have low self-esteem and impoverished self-concepts, manifest various symptoms of ego weakness, frequently have a confused or weak sense of identity, including sexual identity, and are stimulus augmenters (discussed both in this and in the previous chapter).

Minnesota Multiphasic Personality Inventory

The *Minnesota Multiphasic Personality Inventory* (MMPI) is a 550-item self-report widely used in both personality assessment and research. Subjects respond to each item by indicting if it is true of them. Like all self-reports, it is limited by the subjects' self-knowledge and by their conscious and unconscious desires to "fake good" or "fake bad." Subjects' responses to the items are reported as scores on 11 scales, including psychopathic deviancy, depression, hypomania (a mild mania), masculinity-femininity, hypochondriasis, paranoia, and psychasthenia (neurosis). The most consistent and frequently replicated MMPI finding with alcoholic populations is significant elevation of the *psychopathic deviate* (Pd) *scale* score. This finding goes back to Hewitt's 1943 study of an early AA group in Minneapolis. Subsequent MMPI studies of a wide variety of alcoholic populations have also reported elevated Pd. What does this mean? An examination of the Pd items reveals that a number of them refer to excessive drinking and others to situations likely to be associated with heavy drinking. Are the elevated Pd findings trivial? Not necessarily. Later investigators (MacAndrew & Geertsma, 1963; MacAndrew, 1965) modified the Pd scale to eliminate these items, and the findings of elevated Pd held. The most reasonable interpretation of the elevated Pd scores is that alcoholics tend to have a "devil may care" attitude, or at least they say that they do. This could be seen as a tendency toward mildly sociopathic behavior. Interestingly, Pd scores fall, but not to the average range, with sobriety. It is the abnormal personality measure most resistant to change with continuing sobriety, psychotherapeutic treatment, and participation in AA. Within limits this can be a strength in our society. Furthermore, it is known that at least some prealcoholics also show elevated Pd scores on the MMPI. The University of Minnesota once required entering freshmen to take the MMPI, and Loper, Kammeier, and Hoffman (1973) back-checked the MMPIs of the University of Minnesota graduates admitted to the university hospital for treatment of alcoholism. These alcoholics showed significantly elevated Pd scores 13 years earlier when they were college freshmen. Their average Pd scores were significantly higher than the usual high scores of young males. Thus, there is something extremely persistent and characteristic of (male) alcoholics that is measured by this scale. It is antecedent to their alcoholism, accompanies it in its active phase, and persists with recovery. It is not known whether the presence of type 2 alcoholism accounts for the elevation of Pd scores. The Pd scores of female alcoholics are also elevated relative to nonalcoholic females, but neither their absolute scores nor the differential is as high as that of male alcoholics. (The Pd scale is reproduced in Appendix 6A.)

The other consistent MMPI finding is elevation in the depression (D) scale in alcoholics. The elevation of depression is generally not as high as the elevation of Pd, but it is still at abnormal levels. Unlike elevated Pd, elevated depression does remit with enduring sobriety. The prealcoholic University of Minnesota students scored high on the hypomanic (Ma) but not the depression scale as freshmen; however, they had elevated scores on the depression scale when they were admitted to the hospital for treatment. This suggests that an acting-out hypomanic lifestyle may serve as a *manic defense* against an underlying depression. This hypothesis is controversial and much debated in the field—it is generally held by clinicians and rejected by researchers.

Clinical alcoholics also manifest elevated scores on scale 7, *Psychasthenia* (Pt), of the MMPI. The Pt scale is a measure of neuroticism indicative of high levels of anxiety, irrational fears, ruminative self-doubt, and self-devaluation. Obsessive worry, tension, indecisiveness, and concentration difficulties also correlate with high Pt scores. This finding is corroborated by the consistently high scores of alcoholics on the neuroticism scale of the *Eysenck Personality Inventory* (Cox, 1985). Alcoholics also score high on Zuckerman's (1979) *Sensation Seeking Scale*, a finding that corroborates the widely reported elevation on Pd.

MacAndrew (1965) empirically derived a scale that distinguishes alcoholics from nonalcoholics by determining which MMPI items were responded to differently by alcoholic and nonalcoholic psychiatric inpatients. In that way he identified 49 items (exclusive of two that refer specifically to drinking), which became the *MacAndrew Alcoholism Scale* (MAC). Subsequent research has shown the MAC to be a highly sensitive measure of alcoholism, accurately identifying 85% of male alcoholics. MacAndrew called those who score high on the MAC *primary alcoholics*, using the term slightly differently than Winokur (see page 103). The MAC primaries are reward-seeking, bold, aggressive, impulsive, and hedonistic, sharing traits with high Pd scorers who are characterized by anger, resentment, complaints against family, rebellion against convention, and moodiness. (MacAndrew's items are given in Appendix 6B.)

MacAndrew also developed a scale of 18 MMPI items that identifies the 15% of male alcoholics not identified by the MAC scale. He called them *secondary alcoholics*. They are tense, fearful, depressed punishment avoiders. MacAndrew concluded that there are two types of male alcoholics: high rolling, devil take the hindmost, hell raisers; and depressed neurotics. You, the reader, may then say with Hamlet, "Who shall 'scape whipping?"; between the high rollers and the sad sacks, who is left. The answer is, among active alcoholics, very few; among pre-alcoholics, we are not sure, and even if mild antisocial behavior and depression predispose to alcoholism, that still leaves multitudes who are neither acting out extroverts nor depressed introverts.

Field Dependence

The second important and consistent empirical psychological finding is that alcoholics tend to be *field dependent*. Field dependence refers to the way a person organizes his or her perceptive field. The concept of field dependence–field independence as a relatively enduring individual difference was developed by Witkin, Karp, and Goodenough (1959). Field dependence–field independence is a *cognitive style*, a way of structuring the experiential world. Cognitive styles manifest themselves in the characteristic ways in which a person establishes his or her spatial orientation and in the acuity of his or her figure and ground discrimination. The field-dependent person relies on the environment and on external cues, rather than on introceptive, internal cues, in orienting himself or herself in space. The field-independent person does the opposite. Witkin and Oltman (1967) argued that field dependence was one manifestation of a *global* cognitive style, while field independence was one manifestation of an *articulated* (that is, finely discriminated) style. The field-dependent person experiences events globally and diffusely, with the surrounding field determining the way those events are organized. The field-dependent person is less differentiated from the environment than the field-dependent person, at least in terms of perceptual organization. Although field dependence–field independence is a dichotomous distinction, it is actually a continuous variable, with field dependence at one extreme and field independence at the other. Most individuals fall somewhere in between.

Field dependence–field independence is measured in several ways: by the *Rod and Frame Test* (RFT), the *Body Adjustment Test* (BAT), and the *Embedded Figure Test* (EFT). In the RFT, the subject sits in a darkened room and is asked to adjust a lighted rod to a true vertical position. The rod is surrounded by a lighted square that can be tilted to any angle. The field-dependent person will position the rod parallel to the square. Each subject has a limit (degree of tilt) beyond which they will not align the rod with the square. The field-independent person will position the rod vertically regardless of the tilt of the square. The degree of tilt to which the subject will rotate the rod is a measure of the person's field dependence–field independence. In the BAT, the subject, who is placed in a tiltable chair, must adjust his or her body to an upright position. The chair is positioned in a small room that can also be tilted. The degree from true vertical that the subject will say is upright is taken as a measure of field dependence. Clearly the BAT is similar to the RFT, with the body being the rod and the room the frame. In the EFT, the subject is asked to look for a simple geometric figure within a more complex figure in which it has been embedded. The score is the time taken to find the embedded figure. All three tests measure the ability to differentiate a figure from an organized field, although the degree to which the RFT and BAT measure the same cognitive orientation as the EFT has been questioned.

Ever since Witkin et al.'s 1959 study, alcoholic populations have consistently been found (Goldstein, 1976) to score on the field-dependent side of the field dependent–field independent continuum. In most studies they have been found to be highly field dependent. Further, field dependence persists into recovery. Stably sober alcoholics also have been found to be field dependent, although the degree of dependency tends to decrease with continuing sobriety. It is important to note that these findings are statistical averages. They do not measure the field independence-dependence of any particular alcoholic, who may be field independent.

Sheldon Pisani (personal communication, April, 1994) has recently compared four groups of alcoholism counseling students at the New School for Social Research using the EFT. Her groups were recovering males, recovering females, nonrecovering males, and nonrecovering females. Contrary to expectations, recovering females scored most field independent, while both male and female recovering students scored higher than their nonrecovering counterparts. The presence of presumably codependent women living with active alcoholics in the nonrecovering part of the sample may bias these findings. Although the differences in this small sample just missed reaching statistical significance, they suggest that field dependence has psychosocial as well as organic determinants.

Unfortunately, there are no longitudinal studies in which field dependence–field independence was measured prior to the onset of alcoholism; it is not known, therefore, whether field dependence is a factor in the etiology of alcoholism, a consequence of it, or both. It is known that field dependent subjects have less-articulated and less-differentiated body concepts, as measured by the Draw-a-Person Test in which the subject is asked to draw a human figure, than do field-independent subjects and that this is consistent with other data on the personalities of alcoholics. Further, field dependence is correlated with susceptibility to social influence. The field dependent person looks to the social environment to determine what he or she is feeling. It is probably part of what AA is talking about when it speaks of alcoholics being "people pleasers." Witkin and Oltman (1967) believe that field dependence is correlated with interpersonal dependency. Other researchers disagree. Some researchers think that field dependence in alcoholics is the result of brain damage from drinking, since organically brain-damaged people are field dependent. However, there is no proof that brain damage is the primary cause of field dependence in alcoholics. It is of some interest that hyperactive children, who are postulated to be minimally brain damaged, are field dependent, and the few longitudinal studies that are available suggest that alcoholics tend to have been hyperactive children. Researchers have argued from this and other evidence that field dependence is characteristic of the pre-alcoholic personality. People grow more field independent as they mature and then become less so as they age; it is as if life were a process of progressive differentiation that eventually reverses itself as dedifferentia-tion ensues. However, the field dependence of alcoholics is independent of age. What can be concluded is that alcoholics, whether as a cause or as a consequence, whether through a failure to differentiate or through dedi-fferentiation, are relatively undifferentiated from their physical and social environments and that this trait persists into sobriety.

Impoverished Self-Concept

Elevated MMPI Pd scores and field dependence are the most consistently replicated findings in alcoholic populations. There are also several other findings that surface with considerable regularity in the research literature. One is impoverishment of the *self-concept*. The self-concept is a person's conscious image of himself or herself. It is related but not identical to self-representation, which is an endopsychic (that is, mental) structure that may be unconscious, preconscious, or conscious. Because it lacks an unconscious dimension, the self-concept is an empirical psychological, rather than psychoanalytic, construct. It is usually measured by some form of self-report.

One of the most illuminating self-concept studies is that of Conner (1962). His form of self-report was an adjective checklist. Active alco-holics who were studied early in treatment checked very few adjectives as descriptive of themselves. Thus, the self-concepts of these barely sober alcoholics could be characterized as either not extensive or as impover-ished. The adjectives they did check were either primary traits, those that are functional in primary groups such as adolescent peer groups, or neu-rotic traits such as "anxious" or "depressed." They did not check second-ary characteristics, those necessary to function successfully in the imper-sonal organizations of the modern marketplace. The primary traits are global and diffuse, such as "nice guy" or "soft hearted" The secondary traits are specific and delimited, such as "active," "wide interest," and "logical." In other words, alcoholics thought of themselves as having traits that would enable them to enter into relationships characterized by lack of differentiation but not as having traits that would enable them to enter into the segmental differentiated relationships characteristic of the workplace. Thus, their self-concepts were impoverished, depressed, and diffuse. It could be argued that the primary relationship they sought was that of infant to mother. However, when Conner tested a group of recov-ering alcoholics who had been sober for three years and in AA, he found that their self-concepts were radically different from those of the active alcoholics with whom they were matched on demographic variables. The recovering alcoholics checked many adjectives; that is, their self-concepts were far more extensive than those of the active alcoholics. The neurotic traits found in the actives' checklists were not present. Secondary traits were included, but the primary traits characteristic of the active alcoholics' self-concepts also appeared in the self-concepts of the recovering alcoholics. In my own research (Levin, 1981) I found a similar persistence of diffuseness, into sobriety, operationalized in several ways, in a sample of well-educated, middle-class alcoholics.

Impoverishment of self-concept is a finding that appears with great regularity in the literature on the alcoholic personality. There is no doubt that it is characteristic of the clinical alcoholic personality, but whether it is true of the prealcoholic personality is not known. Constriction of self-concept in alcoholics may be the result of either a regression in personality development or a *premorbid deficit*, that is, a lack that existed prior to the manifestation of alcoholism. Although impoverishment of self has been replicated in many studies, no good evidence exists that it is a premorbid trait of alcoholics; it may be a consequence of the alcoholism and the alcoholic lifestyle. Most likely it is both causal and consequential.

Closely related to impoverishment of self-concept is *low self-esteem*. This is also a consistent finding in a wide range of alcoholic populations. Low self-esteem in alcoholics has been found regardless of how self-esteem is measured.

Ego Weakness

Many personality studies have found evidence of ego weakness in alcoholics. This is true of research using objective measures and of research using projective instruments such as the Rorschach test. Ego weakness is manifested by *impulsivity*, the *inability to delay gratification, low-affect tolerance*, a propensity toward *panic-level anxiety and prolonged depression*, an unclear, *confused sense of identity* and *lack of clear boundaries. Reality testing*, an important ego function, is impaired in ego weakness.

The *Rorschach test* is an instrument used by psychologists to evaluate personality. It consists of a set of ten cards with ink blots on them. A subject is invited to say what he or she sees when shown the cards. Seven of the ten cards have color. The subject is assumed to project some aspect of self onto the cards in his or her responses; therefore, the Rorschach test is considered a *projective test*. The subject's responses are evaluated in terms of both their formal characteristics and their subject matter. Alcoholics show impaired reality testing on this test; that is, the things they see on the cards are not necessarily reasonable interpretations of what is there. Reality testing is measured as a percentage of *Good Form* (%F+) in the Rorschach protocol. Seventy to 80% F+ is considered optimal, higher percentages are seen as manifestations of rigidity and inability to regress in the service of the ego, (that is, to be playful and creative). According to this measure, alcoholics' reality testing is not as low as that of psychotics, but it is not as high as that of nonalcoholics. This has important clinical implications. It confirms and complements the findings of cognitive deficit discussed in chapter 2, and it is additional evidence that poor information processing on both a neurological and a dynamic basis contributes to denial and resistance in clinical alcoholics.

Color on the Rorschach test elicits affective responses that are scored as %FC if integrated with form (for instance, "that is a pink rose") with form predominating; as %CF if integrated with form with color predominating (for example, "that's sand—it's kind of sand-colored there"); and as %C if unintegrated with form (for instance, "blood, it's red"). Alcoholics have difficulty putting form and color together in their responses. Their %FC is generally zero, they have few CFs, and if they respond to color at all, it is in C responses. So alcoholics' Rorschach protocols either have no color responses indicative of emotional blocking and repression, *or* they have one or more pure color responses indicative of an inability to contain feelings and/or being overwhelmed by them. *Lack of affect tolerance* means not being able to stay with feelings; instead, they are repressed, acted-out, or anesthetized (say, by alcohol). This is exactly the picture we get on clinical alcoholics' Rorschach protocols with their absence of all color responses or their presence of pure color (C) and absence of form color (FC) responses, a picture that is congruent with the lack of affect tolerance noted by clinicians and measured by objective tests of various sorts. Since color is an affective stimulus and form a cognitive one, these results are interpreted as an inability to integrate feeling and thought. Both of the Rorschach findings of poor reality testing and lack of affect tolerance are indicative of ego weakness.

The Cattell *Sixteen Personality Factor Questionnaire* (16PF) is a psychometric instrument in widespread use in personality research. (*Psychometric* tests measure psychological traits.) Barnes (1979, 1983) reports that multiple studies consistently find that clinical alcoholics differ on up to 14 of the 16 scales on the 16PF. Of particular interest is the consistently low average scores of alcoholics on the C scale of the 16PF which measures ego strength and emotional maturity. Alcoholics also consistently score high on second order (derivative) measures of anxiety on the 16PF.

Another dimension of personality first elucidated and measured by Rotter (1966) is *locus of control*. Psychologists use a self-report to determine if a subject sees himself or herself as controlling or being controlled by a situation. Those who see themselves as in control of themselves and their actions are said to have an *internal locus of control*; those who see themselves as controlled are said to have an *external locus of control*. Externality is considered a sign of ego weakness. Almost all studies of alcoholics (Rohsenow, 1983) show them to have an external locus of control. Paradoxically, most studies of alcoholics early in sobriety who are patients in rehabilitation units show them to be moving toward greater externality as they progress through rehabilitation. This is probably a result, however, of their relinquishing grandiosity, denial, and projective defenses. They are now more realistic in that they are aware that they are not in control of their drinking. Stable recovery results in a move toward internality.

The evidence is overwhelming that ego weakness is characteristic of clinical alcoholic populations; however, it is not known if it is characteristic of prealcoholic populations.

Antecedent Neurological Deficit

Tarter and Alterman (1989) have accumulated evidence from retrospective studies and studies of alcoholics' childhoods that learning difficulties and poor school performance are overrepresented in at least male alcoholic populations. They argue for a cluster of problems: hyperactivity, attention deficit disorder, and childhood conduct disorder being antecedent to some forms of alcoholism, and they hypothesized that both the childhood problems and the alcoholism are consequent upon an inherited neurological deficit. This would seem to be particularly the case with Cloninger's type 2 alcoholics. Other studies fail to confirm their findings on children of alcoholics and their theory has not found general acceptance. Most likely, they have identified the antecedents of one type of alcoholism; their dismissal of possible environmental causality, however, particularly given the fact that most of these children grow up in alcoholic homes, is unconvincing. The most robust of their findings is the high prevalence of childhood *hyperactivity* in clinical alcoholic populations (established by retrospective study). Goodwin et al.'s (1973) Danish adoption study also found a correlation of hyperactivity and alcoholism, while Vaillant (see below) hedges on whether or not hyperactivity was a significant antecedent of alcoholism in his populations.

A possibly related and intriguing finding is the statistically significantly higher occurrence of *left-handedness* (London, 1990) in alcoholic populations. Left-handedness in alcoholics was highly correlated with alcoholism in the father and with Cloninger'stype 2 male limited alcoholics. London believes that left-handedness is indicative of underlying difficulties with cerebral laterality (that is, differentiation of function between left and right hemispheres), possibly originating in abnormal intrauterine levels of hormones, especially testosterone. He hypothesizes that these factors may be operative in alcoholism, particularly type 2 alcoholism.

Confused Identity

There is considerable evidence of tendencies toward confused identity, including sexual identity, in alcoholics. Irgens-Jensen (1971) gave draftees into the Norwegian Navy the Draw-a-Person test. He found that those judged to be problem drinkers by a psychological interviewer or who became problem drinkers during their tours of duty drew figures with many pathological features. These features can be interpreted as evidence of poorly differentiated, confused body images and insecure gender identity. Many studies, including those reviewed in this chapter, of clinical alcoholics using interviews, objective tests, and projective techniques support Irgen-Jensen's conclusions. Alcoholism counseling students, using the first edition of this text, who work as art therapists with alcoholics, have told me that the figure drawings that they see are strikingly similar to Irgen-Jenson's. Further, there is considerable clinical evidence that alcoholics suffer a great deal of sexual role conflict. Here the problem is not lack of gender identity but rather conflict over masculine strivings in female alcoholics and conflict over feminine characteristics in male alcoholics. These conflicts are, of course, endemic in our society during this period of changing role expectations. However, it is possible that those who suffer the most severe sex role conflicts turn to alcohol to attenuate the tension.

Stimulus Augmentation

The last important consistent finding in alcoholic populations is stimulus augmentation. The concept of *stimulus augmentation–stimulus attenuation*, discussed earlier in this chapter, was developed by Asenath Petrie (1978). She studied the way that subjects responded to the pressure of a wooden block pressed against their hands but out of their sight. It was found that the perception of the size of the block and the intensity of the pressure was an individual difference that ranged along a continuum from those who perceived the block as greatly magnified and the pressure as highly intense (stimulus augmenters) to those who perceived the block as smaller and the pressure as less than it was (stimulus attenuators). Alcoholics are stimulus augmenters. Petrie's findings have been confirmed by EEG studies of evoke potentials. Since stimulus augmentation–stimulus attenuation is a relatively stable personal characteristic, there may be something either constitutional or acquired in alcoholics that leads them to experience stimuli in a particularly intense way. This would help explain their apparent lack of affect tolerance; the affects they experience may well be more intense. Although constitutional factors may play a role, from a psycho-analytic developmental standpoint stimulus augmentation can be seen as the consequence of failure to internalize the functions of the mother as a "stimulus barrier."

Cox (1987), reviewing the empirical psychological findings just presented and the longitudinal studies discussed below organizes these findings differently and concludes that there is compelling evidence of a pre-alcoholic (male) personality characterized by nonconformity, impulsivity, and reward-seeking characteristics, which would make for high scores on the MacAndrew primary alcoholism scale. There is even more compelling evidence that clinical alcoholics are characterized by negative affect (depression and anxiety) and low self-esteem, as well as by a cognitive perceptual style that includes field dependence, external locus of control, and stimulus augmentation. The negative affect and low self-esteem are characteristic of MacAndrew's secondary alcoholics for whom they are antecedent. Cox points out that the proportion of male and female alcoholics in each group is quite different, with many more females being secondary alcoholics. He argues that negative affect and low self-esteem are consequences in primary alcoholics although they may be antecedents in secondary alcoholics. Citing Tarter and Alterman's (1989) studies, he speculates that the alcoholic perceptual style may be largely antecedent and be a manifestation of a specific inherited neural dysfunction. Other investigators see the alcoholic perceptual style as either a consequence or as importantly environmentally determined. In this chapter, my category of ego weakness cuts across Cox's organization of the data, but we are in agreement on the factual content of the empirical psychological research.

LONGITUDINAL STUDIES

Most of the findings so far discussed, except the Loper et al. MMPI studies, are about the clinical alcoholic personality. To determine what, if anything, is characteristic of the prealcoholic personality, longitudinal studies that follow a population sample from childhood through adulthood are needed. Such studies permit examination of the childhood characteristics of people who later become alcoholic. There are few such studies. Besides the MMPI studies, there are essentially four: (1) the McCord and McCord (1960) study of Cambridge, Massachusetts, blue-collar boys; (2) Robbins, Bates, and O'Neill's (1962) study of child guidance clinic clients; (3) Jones's (1968, 1971) Oakland Growth Study, which is more middle-class and includes girls; and (4) Vaillant's (1983) study of Harvard graduates and Cambridge working-class men. The Danish, Swedish, and

Iowa adoption studies discussed earlier are also longitudinal in design, but deal only with high risk subjects.

For the most part, these studies have shown that prealcoholics, those who later become alcoholic, were outwardly confident, nonconformist, rebellious, acting-out children and adolescents. Their personality profiles are similar to those of predelinquent or mildly delinquent youngsters. They tended to be restless, active (perhaps hyperactively so), and quite possibly angry. This is true of the Loper et al.'s (1973) psychopathically deviant, hypomanic middle-class college students, of McCord and McCord's working-class boys, of Jones's lower-middle and middle-middle-class junior high school boys and girls, of Robbins et al.'s child guidance clinic clients, and of Vaillant's blue-collar New England boys. In short, all of these prealcoholics resembled Blane's counterdependent alcoholics, Winokur's psychopathic alcoholics, and, to a lesser extent, Cloninger's male limited type 2, rather than the depressed, anxious, dependent clinical alcoholics lacking in self-esteem found in so many other studies. The picture also lends support to Tarter's (1981) retrospective study that found a high correlation of childhood hyperactivity with adult alcoholism. What does all of this mean? Vaillant thought and vehemently argues that these results vitiated the dependency conflict theory (see McCord & McCord, below) of the etiology of alcoholism. Most of the other authors of these studies thought otherwise; they believed that the childhood profiles of their alcoholic subjects reflected a "reaction formation" against a deepseated dependency conflict. In light of the open dependence and neediness of many adult alcoholics, this view is plausible. It is well known that mild and severe juvenile delinquency, as well as "acting out" in general, may be a symptom of masked depression. It may also be an expression of and a defense against underlying anxiety. The hyperactivity (Tarter, 1981), the hypomania (Loperet al., 1973), and the psychopathic deviance (Loper et al., 1973) found in alcoholics can be seen as manifestations of a "manic defense" against massive underlying depression. The hyperactive, hypomanic, unrestrained, shallow lifestyle these researchers found to be characteristic of prealcoholics is pathognomonic of a narcissistic personality disorder.

Seen in the light of the longitudinal data, Blane's (1968) counterdependent–openly dependent distinction is seen as a result of cross-sectional sampling. If Blane had followed his subjects longitudinally, he might have found many instances of early counterdependency as a manifestation of a manic defense against underlying depression, which then breaks down under the psychophysiological assault on the integrity of the organism and its defenses by uncontrolled alcohol consumption. Eventually the defense fails; more general deterioration occurs; and depression, helplessness, and open dependence result. At least that is one way to explain the data. Let us look briefly at the individual studies.

McCord and McCord

McCord and McCord (1960) followed a population of white, predominantly Irish Catholic working-class boys who were at risk for delinquency from childhood into their 30s. They collected data from the boys' latency years in the 1930s through their early adulthoods in the 1950s. McCord and McCord (1962) described the childhood personalities of those who later became alcoholic as "outwardly self-confident, undisturbed by abnormal fears, indifferent toward their siblings, and disapproving of their mothers, . . . [They] evidenced unrestrained aggression, sadism, sexual anxiety, and activity rather than passivity" (p. 427). The McCords found that these active and aggressive children became dependent, passive, self-pitying, and grandiose after they developed alcoholism and that they also felt victimized by society. A combination of aggressivity and shyness made for the greatest risk of alcoholism. McCord and McCord theorized that this childhood pattern is a reaction formation to an intense unresolved *dependency conflict* resulting from inconsistent, erratic satisfaction of their childhood dependency needs by their parents. Vaillant (1983) felt that the McCords explained away their actual findings on the basis of a theory. In his book *The Natural History of Alcoholism* Vaillant strongly argued that the McCords had no evidence of a dependency conflict. The point is important because it relates to the whole issue of the role of emotional factors in the etiology of alcoholism. I do not find Vaillant's criticisms convincing. The McCords did not have an antecedent theory into which they attempted to force their data, and they did have a great deal of highly specific data (gathered by "blind" interviewers, that is, interviewers who did not know the purpose of the study) on the home life of the children, which supported their interpretation of their findings.

Robbins, Bates, and O'Neil

Robbins, Bates, and O'Neil's (1962) study was based on a population of child guidance clinic clients, many of whom were referred for antisocial behavior. As such, it is a highly biased sample, and not surprisingly Robbins et al.'s findings on the childhood personalities of future alcoholics were very similar to those of the McCords. The boys who later became alcoholic were more active (or hyperactive), more acting out, and more aggressive than her population as a whole but less so than those who later became sociopathic. This was also true of the few girls in the study who later became alcoholic. Robbins et al. found that low family status, parental inadequacy, antisocial fathers, and antisocial childhoods all increased the likelihood of adult alcoholism.

Jones

Jones (1968, 1971) followed Oakland, California, students from junior high school into adulthood. Hers is the only longitudinal study that includes a significant number of women. Although Jones's sample size was very small, it is probably no accident that her findings on the boys who later became alcoholic were virtually identical to those of the McCords and Robbins et al. The girls who later became heavy social drinkers were "expressive, attractive, . . . and buoyant" (p. 62); that is, they tended to have high levels of activity, but the girls who became alcoholic were "self-defeating, pessimistic, withdrawn, guilty, and depressive" (p. 62). Jones's findings are especially significant because her subjects were more middle class and they were not at risk for delinquency or in trouble at the time they were initially studied.

Vaillant

The most recent longitudinal study, which is based on the largest samples, is that of Vaillant (1983). Using *multiple regression research methodology* Vaillant sought to determine what antecedent variables determined what *percentage of the variance* in adult alcoholism. Percentage of variance is the square of the correlation between two variables, such as, disturbed childhood environment and alcoholism. Correlation is measured in terms of a correlation coefficient that can vary from negative one (a perfect inverse correlation) to zero (no correlation) to positive one (a perfect correlation). The order in which variables are fed into the regression analysis influences the results since variables entered later can only account for a percentage of the remaining variance. That is, if all of the alcoholism is accounted for by the first four variables entered then nothing is left over to be accounted for by a fifth variable for even though it might have accounted for a percentage of the variance if entered first in the analysis. The researcher can also calculate a "regression equation," in which the coefficients, called *beta weights*, of each variable determine how much that variable contributes to the value of the dependent variable, in this case alcoholism. Beta weights do not depend on the order in which the variables enter the analysis. The point of all this statistical detail is that the methodological problems facing longitudinal researchers are formidable and that the data analysis chosen influences the results.

Vaillant reported on two relatively large research samples. One consisted of Harvard University students chosen for their mental health who were followed from their sophomore years into their 50s, and the other consisted of normal core-city working-class subjects who were followed from their childhoods into their 40s. Vaillant found that childhood and adolescent emotional problems and overtly disturbed childhoods did not predict (correlate with) adult alcoholism in either sample, although such disturbed childhoods did predict adult mental illness. Vaillant found that *ethnicity* (Irish or northern European ancestry) and *parental alcoholism* did predict adult alcoholism. He argued that the clinical alcoholic personality is the result of drinking, not of premorbid personality factors. Vaillant also argued that adult alcoholics retrospectively falsify the degree of pathology in their childhood environments in order to rationalize their drinking. I have found that retrospective idealization of their childhoods is at least as characteristic of adult alcoholic patients as is retrospective devaluation or denial of whatever may have been positive in their childhoods; this, however, is a clinical not a research finding. Vaillant's data cannot be dismissed, but his interpretation of them is not entirely persuasive.

Zucker and Gomberg (1986) argue that methodological artifacts are responsible for Vaillant's conclusion that childhood experience and antecedent psychopathology play no role, or at least account for no variance, in adult alcoholism. They also suggest that he was looking for the wrong stuff, pathological dependency and negative affect, while if he had looked for Cox's stuff—nonconformity, impulsivity, and reward seeking at high enough levels to constitute an antisocial trend—he would have found it. In fact, they reanalyzed Vaillant's data (by changing the order of regression of his variables) and did find such childhood antecedents, including disturbed homes and psychopathology as they defined it, of alcoholism.

Interestingly, although Vaillant didn't find a correlation between disruptive childhood environment and alcoholism, he did find a correlation between disruptive childhood environment and early onset and severity of alcoholism. On the surface, this looks like Cloninger's type 2 (male limited) alcoholism, while Vaillant's data suggest an environment etiology for the severity since he controlled for parental alcoholism. However, Vaillant's analysis didn't support the type 1–type 2 distinction. It is a puzzlement.

Vaillant basically argues that culture (as manifested by ethnicity in his study) and parental alcoholism (seen as primarily contributing to inherited biological vulnerability) are far more powerful determinants of (male) alcoholism than psychological, let alone antecedent psychopathological, factors. But since parental alcoholism is almost certainly a determinant of Vaillant's variables—boyhood competence (ego strength), child-hood environmental strengths, childhood emotional problems, and childhood environmental weaknesses—their effect is already factored in by the variable parental alcoholism and add no independent proportion of variance when they are entered into the regression analysis. Another way of saying this is to say that Vaillant's independent variables are not actually independent of one another, rather they manifest what statisticians call *collinearity*.

Vaillant comes to other important conclusions including support for the notion that alcoholism is a unitary phenomenon. He reaches this conclusion because measures of alcoholism drawn from sociological models and measures of alcoholism drawn from medical-disease models are congruent. Noting that it is the number of alcohol-related problems, not their severity, that determines when problem drinking progresses into alcoholism, he concludes that Jellinek's model of progression poorly fits his and others' longitudinal data, but in spite of this, he thinks that alcoholism is usefully conceptualized as a disease. He compares it to hypertension, which also has a fluctuating course, is powerfully influenced by behavioral and situational variables, and is often treatable by wise self care. His data also show that problem drinking, particularly in adolescents and young adults, does not necessarily progress to alcoholism. In fact, many "problem drinkers" return to asymptomatic social drinking. However, for those who are most symptomatic there is no going back; they have the disease. In both his samples, alcoholism took a long time to develop, and his data do not support Cloninger's distinction between type 1 and type 2 alcoholics. Further, those who did manifest antisocial behavior had just as high a recovery rate, in fact at a younger average age, as the population as a whole.

One of Vaillant's most intriguing, albeit incidental, findings was that *heavy cigarette smoking* in adolescence was an excellent predictor of (that is, it had a high correlation with) adult alcoholism. This suggests some sort of nonspecific (to any particular drug) addictive factor, constitutional or acquired, in those "prealcoholics." Problem drinking tended to remit (if it did) in the late twenties after marriage had changed the problem drinker's peer groups and self concepts ("Those wedding bells are breaking up that old gang of mine"), while alcoholism, if it went into remission, did so at a much later age. The rates of spontaneous remission were 2 to 3% per year. The most common reason alcoholics became abstinent was ill health. Looking at all the data available, Vaillant notes the early morbidity of alcoholics (average age 52) and concludes that half of alcoholics either die of complications of alcoholism or become severely socially impaired, while the rest either become abstinent or in a small percentage of cases return to asymptomatic, or at least "controlled," drinking. Although advocating it, he questions the effectiveness of professional treatment, seeing AA as the single most efficacious "treatment."

Vaillant is undoubtedly right in his most salient conclusion that significant portions of the clinical alcoholic personality are caused by the drinking and remit with sobriety. However, he notes that full psychosocial recovery is slow and must be measured in years, not months. Clinicians and AA members would agree.

SPECIAL POPULATIONS

There is a growing literature on *special alcoholic populations*: women, Blacks, Hispanics, Native American, ghetto dwellers, professionals, teen-agers, and the elderly. However, little is actually known about these groups and alcoholism. Several of my alcoholism counseling classes have criti-cized my use of the term "special populations," particularly as applied to women, who constitute fully a third of alcoholics, an enormous number of people. I considered dropping it, but the term is so firmly ensconced in the literature that I have retained it in this edition.

Alcoholism in Women

The largest body of literature on special populations concerns women. At one time alcoholism was considered an almost exclusively male disease; it is now known that this is certainly not the case. It is also known that alcoholic women are more likely to suffer from depression than are alco-holic men. That is, women are *more* likely than men to be Winokurian depressive secondary alcoholics, and they are also *less* likely than men to be Winokurian secondary sociopathic alcoholics. In other words, they are far more likely to be MacAndrew secondary alcoholics. Women are more likely to drink to alleviate intolerable feelings of worthlessness—that is, they suffer more than male alcoholics from devastating low levels of self-esteem. Blane (1968) thought that women drink to deal with feelings of inferiority and that men drink to deal with repressed dependency needs. The research data, although fragmentary, supports him. Wilsnack (1973) thought that women drink to alleviate sex role conflicts and to feel more feminine. There is considerable research evidence (Wilsack, 1991) that female alco-holics have a higher than average rate of gynecological problems, but it is not clear if this increases sex role conflict, makes them feel less feminine, or is an etiological factor in their alcoholism. It is also known that, at least until recently, women were more likely to become iatrogenically cross-addicted to minor tranquilizers. Winokur's data on the relatively high inci-dence of depression in alcoholic women is compelling; the other findings are more questionable. Women do appear to have more difficulty maintain-ing self-esteem in our society; it is not known, however, whether this struggle is commonly self-medicated with alcohol or whether such self-medication is an important factor in the etiology of female alcoholism. Given Winokur's data, it may be. It has consistently been found that women suffer *more somatic damage* from lower doses of alcohol consumed for shorter periods of time than do men. They are particularly vulnerable to liver damage. There is no question that women suffer early and more severe physical, emotional, and social consequences of their drinking.

More women are being diagnosed and treated for alcoholism than in the past. Whether this means that female alcoholism is more common or that it is simply "coming out of the closet" is not clear. Young women are drinking more, and heavy drinking by women in their twenties is reported in the recent prevalence literature. Whether this will eventuate in an "epidemic" of female alcoholism remains to be seen.

Women more often than men report a precipitating event (such as loss of a loved one or failure to conceive a child) for their alcoholism. Similarly, they are more likely to report traumatic childhoods. Whether this actually reflects the prevalence of these events in the lives of alcoholic men and women, or whether it is an artifact of the greater social shame associated with alcoholism in women and their concomitant need to find a "reason" and of men's greater reluctance to self-disclose is not clear. However, there is evidence (Wilsnack & Beckman, 1984) of high rates of childhood incest (sexual abuse) in alcoholic women. They are more likely than male alcoholics to have an alcoholic spouse. Black women are far more likely to be abstinent than White women, although there are indications that Black women who do drink are at higher risk to develop problem drinking than White women who drink . There is fragmentary evidence that Lesbian women have high rates of problem drinking and alcoholism.

Wilsnack's (1973, 1984) research using the *Thematic Apperception Test* (TAT), a projective technique in which subjects are asked to make up stories in response to a picture on a stimulus card, demonstrated that women who drank heavily in a simulated social situation drank to feel more feminine, or at least their stories, which were assumed to be projections of their inner feelings, dealt with "feminine" material and themes. Wilsnack hypothesized that problem drinking in women is correlated with sex role conflict. Although there are other studies that tend to confirm her hypothesis, Wilsnack's data are too fragmentary to permit any broad conclusions. One wonders if this finding would be replicated today.

Whether or not treatment of female alcoholism should be distinct from treatment of male alcoholism is a vexed question. I have had several female alcoholic patients reject AA, seeing it as a male oriented ideology. In particular, they objected to the notion of "surrender" and admitting they are "powerless" (see chapters 9 and 12), saying that while that may have been just the thing for male alcoholics, they had spent their lives in a state of powerlessness and were not about to surrender the power they had fought so hard to acquire (Nancy Roberts, personal communication, March, 1993). A recent issue of the *AA Grapevine* was largely devoted to letters for and against revising the AA "Big Book," *Alcoholics Anonymous* (Alcoholics Anonymous World Services, 1955), to remove sexist language and outlook.

Adolescent Problem Drinking

The data on adolescents show that problem drinking by youths is extremely common and that it is not predictive of adult alcoholism. Although this manifestation of rebellious acting out can have serious consequences, as when kids drive and drink, it does not in itself mean very
much. However, those who have a family history of alcoholism *do* increase their risk of adult alcoholism if they drink heavily as teenagers.
For this reason, alcohol education can help prevent alcoholism in this
population. On the other hand, diagnosing problem drinking adolescents
as having a "disease" tends not to be helpful and is mainly untrue. Vaillant
(1983) advocates teaching young people how to drink in a socially controlled and acceptable manner as the best prophylactic against problem
drinking. Moderate drinking, rather than abstinence, is frequently the treatment goal with this population.

Alcoholism in Minorities

Plantation owners supplied their slaves with alcoholic beverages and encouraged holiday drinking as a cheap form of pacification. How, if at all,
this influences contemporary Black drinking practices is unknown. Many
black churches preach abstinence and this is reflected in the high abstinence rates among blacks.

The data on Blacks show that Black males have a lower rate of alcoholism than do White males, but that Black women, if they drink, have
higher rates of alcoholism than do White women. Since many Black women
have been forced to be the breadwinners in single-parent homes, this finding is consistent with Wilsnack's hypothesis. It is possible that Black women
forced into traditionally male roles drink to feel more feminine. There can
be no doubt that alcoholism among poor urban Blacks and demoralized
populations such as Native Americans is connected with feelings of hope-
lessness and helplessness. It is anomic drinking. Alcoholism serves as a
passive-aggressive expression of rage and as a means of anesthetizing that
rage.

Blacks suffer more than Whites from the medical complications of
alcoholism. This is especially true of cirrhosis. Whether this difference is
genetic-biological or economic-social is not known, but the differential
rate is well established (Lex, 1985). Middle-class Blacks are often "top
shelf" drinkers and the social status so accrued may contribute to denial if
they develop alcoholism. Hispanic males, who have high rates of alcoholism, are postulated to have a unique drinking pattern related to machismo,
but there is little research evidence for this, so the degree of truth, if any,
in this stereotype is not known. Hispanic women tend to abstain.

Alcoholism in the Elderly

The most important finding about alcoholism in the elderly is that it exists. Most elderly alcoholics are survivors of a lifelong career of alcohol abuse, but some are newly recruited to the ranks of the alcoholic because of their inability to handle the losses of later life and the narcissistic blow inflicted by retirement. Thirty percent of the residents of one Florida retirement community drank daily, but it was not clear if this was detrimental, or to how many it was detrimental. Since relatively small quantities of alcohol can cause serious physical damage in the elderly, it is especially important that this syndrome be recognized and treated. I once treated a retired woman librarian in her 70s who had developed late-onset alcoholism when she could not adjust to retirement. She was a classic "old maid," prim, proper, and rather supercilious. She responded to treatment, became sober and joined AA, where she met a hell-raising retired sailor who had been in more beds, in more ports, than she had books in her library. They fell in love, married, and lived happily for eight years until he died of a heart attack. She is still sober and active in AA.

Alcoholism in the Disabled

Another population that has been underserved both in terms of treatment and in terms of investigation by researchers is the disabled. Although the scientific evidence is lacking, it would appear from the reports of clinicians and administrators of chronic care facilities and rehabilitation agencies that the prevalence of alcoholism among the disabled is high. The alcoholic disabled population is bimodal, consisting of those whose disabilities have been caused by or are related to their drinking and those who turned to alcohol in a futile attempt to cope with their disabilities. Recently, this population has finally begun to receive alcoholism treatment, as witnessed by the New York University Department of Rehabilitation Counseling's initiating a combined master's degree in rehabilitation and alcoholism counseling.

Alcoholism in the Mentally Ill

In recent years there has been much emphasis on treatment of *dual diagnosis* patients, those who suffer from both alcoholism and mental illness. The prevalence rates of alcoholism in those suffering from major psychiatric illness has been estimated as high as 50 percent (Richards, 1993). Undoubtedly, part of this is attributable to unwise, poorly managed deinstitutionalization of psychiatric patients who lack the inner resources to cope with life on the "outside" and turn to alcohol and other drugs as both self-medication and as *prostheses* to provide what they cannot provide for themselves (such as self-esteem, inner calm, the ability to be aggressive) because of some inner, perhaps developmental, perhaps biochemical, deficiency. The drinking fails as both self-medication and as prosthesis and their condition worsens. The causal vector between mental illness and alcoholism may go in either direction, or in both directions, or the two conditions may be independent diseases. In any case, treatment must address *both* disorders or the prognosis is poor.

Although it is an advance that the coexistence of alcoholism and major mental illnesses such as schizophrenia is now widely recognized and addressed, I wonder if the high prevalence of dual-diagnosis disorder is not partly an artifact of face saving by an alcoholism treatment community that, in response to a long history of ineffectual treatment based on resolution of underlying psychological conflict, had come to deny, or at least minimize, antecedent psychopathology in alcoholics. Having a formidable array of research as well as a clinical rationale on their side, they are reluctant to give up their hard won insight that "it's the booze that does it, stupid," and as we have seen, there is much truth in that viewpoint. However, the current focus on dual diagnosis now allows us to speak of anxiety disorders, obsessive-compulsive neurosis, depression, and personality disorders co-morbid with, and even perhaps antecedent to, alcoholism, without altering a basic, and tenuously held, conceptual framework.

We are appallingly ignorant about female, gay-Lesbian, Hispanic, and African American drinking practices and about alcoholism in these populations. The literature is scant and not very illuminating. Unfortunately, it also is not very helpful clinically. Its main contribution has been to make alcoholism counselors and mental health workers aware that alcoholism is not exclusively a disease of middle-aged, red-nosed, Irish men and of social outcasts. Sensitivity to culture, gender, age, environmental stress, and the effects of economic deprivation and racial discrimination is essential if a counselor or psychotherapist is to be effective. This is part of empathic listening.

APPENDIX 6A
MMPI Psychopathetic Deviate (Pd) Scale (50 Items)

	Response	Item
8	F	My daily life is full of things that keep me interested.
16	T	I am sure I get a raw deal from life.
20	F	My sex life is satisfactory.
21	T	At times I have very much wanted to leave home.
24	T	No one seems to understand me.
32	T	I find it hard to keep my mind on a task or job.
33	T	I have had very peculiar and strange experiences.
35	T	If people had not had it in for me, I would have been much more successful.
37	F	I have never been in trouble because of my sex behavior.
38	T	During one period when I was a youngster I engaged in petty thievery.
42	T	My family does not like the work I have chosen (or the work I tend to choose for my life work).
61	T	I have not lived the right kind of life.
67	T	I wish I could be as happy as others seem to be.
82	F	I am easily downed in an argument.
84	T	These days I find it hard not to give up hope of amounting to something.
91	F	I do not mind being made fun of.
94	T	I do many things which I regret afterwards (I regret things more and more often than others seem to).
96	F	I have very few quarrels with members of my family.
102	T	My hardest battles are with myself.
106	T	Much of the time I feel as if I have done something wrong or evil.
107	F	I am happy most of the time.
110	T	Someone has it in for me.
118	T	In school I was sometimes sent to the principal for cutting up.
127	T	I know who is responsible for most of my troubles.
134	F	At times my thoughts have raced ahead faster than I could speak them.
137	F	I believe that my home life is as pleasant as that of most people I know.
141	F	My conduct is largely controlled by the customs of those about me.
155	F	I am neither gaining nor losing weight.
170	F	What others think of me does not bother me.
171	F	It makes me uncomfortable to put on a stunt at a party even when others are doing the same sort of things.
173	F	I liked school.

180 F   I find it hard to make talk when I meet new people.
183 F   I am against giving money to beggars.
201 F   I wish I were not so shy.
215 T   I have used alcohol excessively.
216 T   There is very little love and companionship in my family as compared to other homes.
224 T   My parents have often objected to the kind of people I went around with.
231 F   I like to talk about sex.
235 F   I have been quite independent and free from family rule.
237 F   My relatives are nearly all in sympathy with me.
239 T   I have been disappointed in love.
244 T   My way of doing things is apt to be misunderstood by others.
245 T   My parents and family find more fault with me than they should.
248 F   Sometimes without any reason or even when things are going wrong I feel excitedly happy, "on top of the world."
267 F   When in a group of people I have trouble thinking of the right thing to talk about.
248 T   I am sure I am being talked about.
287 F   I have very few fears compared to my friends.
289 F   I am always disgusted with the law when a criminal is freed through the arguments of a smart lawyer.
294 F   I have never been in trouble with the law.
296 F   I have periods in which I feel unusually cheerful without any special reason.

APPENDIX 6B
MacAndrew Alcoholism Scale (MAC)

Response   **Item**
1   T   I have used alcohol excessively.*
2   F   I have used alcohol moderately (or not at all).*
3   T   I have had periods in which I carried on activities without knowing later what I had been doing.
4   F   I have never been in trouble with the law.
5   T   I have not lived the right kind of life.
6   T   I like to cook.
7   T   I sweat very easily even on cool days.

Reprinted by permission from "The differentiation of male alcoholic outpatients from non-alcoholic psychiatric out-patients by means of the MMPI," by C. MacAndrew, 1965, *Quarterly Journal of Studies on Alcohol, 26,* pp. 238–246.

8	T	My parents have often objected to the kind of people I went around with.
9	T	I played hooky from school quite often as a youngster.
10	T	I would like to wear expensive clothes.
11	T	As a youngster I was suspended from school one or more times for cutting up.
12	T	While in trains, buses, etc., I often talk to strangers.
13	T	I pray several times every week.
14	T	I deserve severe punishment for my sins.
15	T	I have had blank spells in which my activities were interrupted and I did not know what was going on around me.
16	T	I have a cough most of the time.
17	F	I do not like to see women smoke.
18	F	My table manners are not quite as good at home as when I am out in company.
19	T	I have few or no pains.
20	T	I do many things which I regret afterwards (I regret things more or more often than others seem to).
21	T	I like to read newspaper articles on crime.
22	F	I am worried about sex matters.
23	T	My soul sometimes leaves my body.
24	T	Christ performed miracles such as changing water into wine.
25	T	I know who is responsible for most of my troubles.
26	T	The sight of blood neither frightens me nor makes me sick.
27	F	I cannot keep my mind on one thing.
28	T	In school I was sometimes sent to the principal for cutting up.
29	T	The one to whom I was most attached and whom I most admired as a child was a woman (mother, sister, aunt, or other woman).
30	F	I have more trouble concentrating than others seem to have.
31	T	I am a good mixer.
32	T	I enjoy a race or game better when I bet on it.
33	T	I enjoy gambling for small stakes.
34	T	I frequently notice my hand shakes when I try to do something.
35	T	Everything is turning out just like the prophets of the Bible said it would.
36	T	If I were in trouble with several friends who were equally to blame, I would rather take the whole blame than to give them away.
37	T	I was fond of excitement when I was young (or in childhood).
38	T	I have at times had to be rough with people who were rude or annoying.
39	T	If I were a reporter I would very much like to report sporting news.
40	F	I am certainly lacking in self-confidence.
41	T	I have frequently worked under people who seem to have things arranged so that they get credit for good work but are able to pass off mistakes onto those under them.
42	T	I readily become one hundred percent sold on a good idea.
43	T	I think I would like the work a forest ranger does.
44	T	Evil spirits possess me at times.

45 F Many of my dreams are about sex matters.
46 F I liked school.
47 T I have been quite independent and free from family rule.
48 F I have often felt that strangers were looking at me critically.
49 F I used to keep a diary.
50 T I seem to make friends about as quickly as others do.
51 F I have never vomited blood or coughed up blood.

*Not included in the MacAndrew Alcoholism Scale

Part Two

Theoretical

Chapter 7

Psychodynamic Theories About Alcoholism

There are many theories about the etiology of alcoholism, ranging from the conviction that it results from sin to the belief that it is the result of a biochemical flaw. Recent evidence supports the belief that alcoholism results from a complex interaction of neurophysiological, psychological, sociological, pharmacological, cultural, political, and economic factors. This chapter examines some of the psychological theories of the etiology and *psychodynamics* of alcoholism. Psychodynamics is the science—or theory—of the contending forces in the inner world—the mind. It deals with mental and emotional conflict—conscious or unconscious—and its resolution or lack of it. Some of the older psychodynamic theories may be dated as explanations of the *cause* of alcoholism, but they can help the alcoholism counselor understand the inner experience of the alcoholic and how the disease manifests itself psychologically. In other words, a psychodynamic theory is not necessarily a theory of causality, although it may be; rather it is an attempt to describe the inner world and the forces, conscious and unconscious, contending within it.

PSYCHOANALYTIC THEORIES

Psychoanalytic theory has evolved over the past hundred years from Freud's realization that repressed feelings, or *affects*, as analysts like to call them, and repressed instinctual drives, sexual or otherwise, cause people all sorts of grief while managing to find expression in indirect ways as symptoms or slips of the tongue, to contemporary psychoanalytic accounts of the formation of the self and the ways in which that formation can go awry. Freud's first (1900/1953) model of the mind was the *topographical* model which understood mental activity as taking place in three realms: consciousness, preconsciousness, and unconsciousness. Another way of saying this is that the mind has three regions: the *conscious mind*, the *preconscious mind*, and the *unconscious mind*. The conscious mind is everything that we are aware of at a particular moment; the unconscious mind comprises those metnal contents of which we are not currently aware; and the preconscious mind is that part of the unconscious that we can call to consciousness by a simple effort of will. The "dynamic" unconscious is that part of our thoughts and feelings that is both out of awareness and not accessible by a simple effort of recall. These thoughts and feelings are kept from consciousness by *repression*, a defense mechanism that keeps the unpleasant and unacceptable out of view. Freud's term for the preconscious plus the dynamic unconscious was the *descriptive* unconscious, which is all of the mind's contents of which we are unaware. Freud envisioned a "censor" between the dynamic unconscious and the rest of the mind that guards against the emergence into consciousness of forbidden or otherwise threaten-ing thoughts (such as the knowledge that one's drinking is suicidal).

Freud's other (1923/1956) model of the mind is the *structural model*. It conceptualizes the mind as *tripartite*, consisting of three "mental organs" defined by their functions. The first organ is the *id*, which literally means the "it." The id is the repository of instinctual drives seeking, indeed pressing for, immediate gratification. Libidinal (sexual), aggressive, and perhaps other biologically determined drives restlessly assert their claims on the organism. The id works by *primary process*, a form of thought devoid of logic or structure. The contents of the id are unconscious, although they may be represented in consciousness by derivatives, including symbols.

The *ego*, which literally means the I, is the executive organ of the mind. Its functions include both defending against threats from the external environment and prohibiting emergence into consciousness of the forbidden or unacceptable, as well as judgment, motility, memory, logical or *secondary process* thinking, perception, reality testing, and delay of gratification. Parts of the ego are conscious, and other parts, especially defenses such as projection onto others of one's own stuff, are unconscious.

The *superego*, literally the "super I," is that part of the mind formed through identification with and internalization of one's parents and other representatives of culture. It contains the conscience and the *ego ideal*, that which one would like to be. The superego is also partly conscious and partly unconscious. Unconscious guilt leading to self-punishment is a common unconscious superego activity. It may lead alcoholics to continue drinking to punish themselves for their past drinking behavior.

Freud said that the ego—the rational part of the mind—is frail and beleaguered. It has to mediate between the claims of the id, the claims of the superego, and the demands of external reality. Freud saw the major function of therapy as the strengthening of the ego. Ego weakness may contribute to alcoholism, but whatever its etiological role there is no question that alcoholism weakens the ego and that alcoholism counselors must seek to strengthen it.

The concepts of *regression* and *fixation* are important in psychoanalysis, as is the concept of *narcissism*. The regression/fixation hypothesis states that psychopathology reflects either a regression to or a fixation at an early stage of development. Illness is immaturity. One may never have developed beyond a certain point and thus be fixated there, or one may have achieved normal adult levels of functioning but gone backwards, regressed to an earlier stage in the face of some event such as the development of an addiction in adulthood.

Narcissism means love of oneself. It has both healthy and pathological forms. Healthy self-esteem involves self-love, while morbid preoccupation with self is pathological. Most observers agree that alcohol addiction leads to narcissistic regression, returning to an immature and pathological form of narcissism characterized by self-absorption and self-centeredness.

Early psychoanalysis, which emphasized making conscious unconscious mental contents, particularly those of a sexual nature, was known as *id psychology*. It sought to make people aware of the incestuous, murderous, and otherwise unlovely impulses within them. Later psychoanalysis emphasized strengthening the ego and making unconscious defenses conscious. It was therefore called *ego psychology*. More recently, psychoanalysis has turned to the study of interpersonal relations, particularly those of infancy and early childhood, and their internal representations, an area known as *object relation theory*, and to an examination of the self: its development, vicissitudes, and pathology. This aspect of psychoanalytic theory and practice is called *self-psychology*. Heinz Kohut (1971, 1977a) was its principal developer.

The psychoanalytic theories surveyed here do not necessarily tell us the cause of alcoholism; they do help illuminate the dynamics—the interplay of conflicting forces—found in alcoholics, regardless of whether those dynamics are etiological to the illness. As such they are useful to the alcoholism counselor.

Sigmund Freud

The earliest psychoanalytic insight into addiction of all kinds is contained in a letter from Sigmund Freud (1897/1985) to his friend Wilhelm Fleiss. Freud wrote, "It has occurred to me that masturbation is the one great habit that is a 'primary addiction,' and that the other addictions, for alcohol, morphine, etc., only enter into life as a substitute and replacement for it" (p. 287). Thus, in Freud's view, masturbation is the "model" addiction. All later addictions are modeled after it. They are substitutes for and reenactments of the addiction to masturbation. According to Freud, infantile masturbation is both compelling and guilt inducing. Often it is forbidden by parents or other caretakers, and the child comes to internalize the prohibition. A struggle ensues between a wish for instinctual gratification and the internalized prohibition. The struggle not to masturbate is almost always lost; the pleasures of genital, or pregenital (oral and anal), masturbation are too great. However, the return to masturbation is accompanied by guilt and the fall in self-esteem that accompanies the failure to carry through a resolution. Masturbation can then be used as a way of assuaging the anxiety, and a vicious cycle is set up. This certainly sounds familiar and is indeed the pattern of much addictive behavior. From this point of view, later addictions are not only displacements and reenactments of the original addiction to masturbation but also are attempts to master, through repetition, the traumatic loss of self-esteem that followed the failure to live up to the resolution not to masturbate. Here Freud was being very much a man of the 19th century, which was obsessed with masturbation and the alleged damage it caused. Exactly why is not clear, but perhaps masturbation represented an escape from social control that an increasingly bureaucratized and rationalized society could not tolerate. It is now believed that infantile masturbation plays an important role in the process of separation-individualization and that it is a vehicle through which the child establishes autonomy and confirms the cohesion of self. If this is the case and later addictions are symbolic reenactments of the first addiction, then all addiction must serve the same purposes. The fact that addiction to alcohol fails in these purposes is not relevant to the present argument.

Freud returned to this theory of addiction many years later in *Dostoevsky and Parricide* (1928/1957). There he analyzed the great Russian novelist's compulsive (addictive) gambling. Playing on the word play Freud traced Dostoevsky's compulsion back to an addiction to masturbation, but he added the insight that the addiction also served as a means of *self-punishment* for the original forbidden wish. The "payoff," for Dostoevsky, his conscious wishes not withstanding, was losing at the gaming table. There can be a condensation of guilts: masturbatory, Oedipal (for incestuous wishes toward parents), and for the addiction itself all of which are "punished" by the nega-tive consequences of the addiction. Thus, it is the *conflict* around masturbation that is reenacted in the addictive behavior and the conflict around it. This use of an addiction for self-punishment is certainly widespread.

Freud's insight into the self-punishing potential of addition has more than a little validity, as do Freud's other insights. Alcohol addiction is indeed a dead-end path, as is masturbation as an exclusive form of adult sexual activity. Freud's theory has the additional merit of highlighting the narcissistic nature of addiction. In masturbation, one's love object is oneself, one's genitals, or at best one's fantasy of another object, but it is not another person. Similarly, in addictions, including alcoholism, there is a regression (or fixation) to a state in which there is no human object. The love object of the addict becomes the abused substance itself, which is experienced as either an extension of the self or as an omnipotent substance with which the addict merges.

Freud's theory also highlights another aspect of the narcissistic pathology inherent in addictions: the loss of self-esteem that the masturbator or alcohol addict experiences when he or she gives in to the addiction. This loss of self-esteem in turn requires more of the addictive substance or activity to attempt to raise the lowered self-esteem, and an addictive cycle is thus established. Freud's (1920/1955) late theory of the *repetition compulsion* also sheds light on addictions. In this theory he postulates the existence of an innate "death instinct" which drives all organic being to seek the quietus of the inorganic. Life is a struggle between *Eros*, the force that makes for integration, union, and growth, and *Thanatos*, the force that makes for dissolution, disassociation, and regression. Comparing his vision to that of the Greek pre-Socratic philosopher Empedocles, who wrote of the eternal war between Love and Strife, Freud thought that some sort of innate destructive drive had to exist to account for such phenomena as self-mutilation, suicide, and addiction. He also cited the *negative therapeutic reaction*, in which the better the therapy patient does in treatment, the worse he or she feels, and the compulsive reenactment of destructive relationships as evidence for the innateness of Thanatos. Most analysts have rejected Freud's theory of the indwellingness of a self-destructive drive, but they have thought him correct descriptively; that is, human beings do hold on to and repeat the familiar no matter how pernicious the experience, and this built-in conservatism—resistance to change—is a datum with which the alcoholism counselors must contend.

Karl Abraham

Karl Abraham (1908/1979), one of Freud's early students, published the first psychoanalytic paper on alcoholism in 1908. In it he stated that "alcoholism is a nervous and sexual perversion" (p. 87). By perversion he meant oral regressive and homoerotic tendencies. Abraham based his theory on an analysis of male alcoholics and on his observation that homophobic men become openly physically affectionate in the camaraderie of the beer hall. He inferred that heavy drinking allows the expression of forbidden homosexual wishes and postulated that alcohol addicts have especially intense conflicts about *repressed* homosexuality. In emphasizing the regression to orality in alcoholism, he not only calls attention to the oral ingestion of the drink but also points out the parallel between drunken stupor and the warmth and security felt by the satiated infant. In his view, it is this state of satiation that the alcohol addict craves. Abraham highlights the psychological and emotional regression brought about by the drinking itself irrespective of the underlying developmental fixation. His paper is prescient in its integration of the dynamic and the sociological aspects of alcoholism.

Edward Glover

Edward Glover (1928), an English analyst, emphasized the *aggression* in alcoholism. Writing from the viewpoint of classical analysis, he spoke of "oral rage" and "anal sadism," by which he meant drinking *at* somebody, using one's alcoholism as a weapon to hurt others. This is common in addictions. Alcoholic rage is partly in defense of the addiction, partly self-hatred projected outward, partly a response to narcissistic vulnerability (that is, ego weakness that sets one up to be easily hurt), partly pharmacologically induced, and partly Glover's regressive oral and anal fury. In any case the management of anger is crucial in alcoholism counseling. Most "slips" are rage responses. Glover also cites alcohol's antianxiety properties, in particular its use to quell *castration anxiety*, that is, fear of retaliation by the father for murderous wishes toward him.

Sandor Rado

Sandor Rado (1933) was the first to point to the similarity between alcoholism and manic-depressive psychosis, with the cycle of elation during the alcoholic high and depression during the hangover paralleling the manic-depressive cycle. Rado related both the mood alterations of manic-depressive illness and the alcoholic pattern of highs and lows to the cycle of infantile hunger and satiation. He movingly captures the alcoholic's futile attempt to chemically relieve "tense depression" and turn it into elation, only to fall into an even deeper depression, necessitating more alcohol intake. As the addiction proceeds the periods of elation become briefer and briefer and in the end there is nothing but unrelieved depression. This exacerbation of the condition that is being self-medicated by drinking is characteristic of all attempts to use alcohol for this purpose. Much alcoholic drinking is just such self-medication. It is an important dynamic in alcohol addiction even when the dysphoria being medicated is caused by the drinking itself. Rado saw the key issue in addictions, including alcoholism, as a disturbance in the regulation of *self-esteem*. What the drinker seeks in the alcohol elation is the elevation of self-esteem. Few alcoholism counselors would question the centrality of the necessity to raise self-esteem if sobriety is to be maintained.

Robert Knight

Robert Knight (1937, 1938), whose typology of alcoholism was discussed in chapter 5, emphasizes the *depressive* aspects of the alcoholic personality. Frustrated orality results in repressed rage and hence in depression. Knight was the first to highlight the severity of alcoholic psychopathology. The depression he spoke of is both an "empty" depression and an "angry" depression with rage turned against the self. Such depression is certainly found in clinical alcoholic populations, and Knight's dynamic is operative in some of those depressed alcoholics.

Otto Fenichel

Otto Fenichel, whose book *The Psychoanalytic Theory of the Neurosis* (1945) is almost canonical, also thought that oral dependence and frustration result in chronic depression in the alcoholic. He saw alcoholism as a maladaptive defense mechanism used to resolve neurotic conflicts, especially conflict between dependence and the expression of anger. It is to Fenichel that we owe the observation that "the superego has been defined as that part of the mind which is soluble in alcohol," (p. 379) making it possible for the drinker to use alcohol to indulge in forbidden impulses and resolve id-superego conflicts. Fenichel was the first to explicitly refer to narcissistic regression in alcoholism. He highlighted the deepening self-involvement that accompanies alcoholic regression.

Karl Menninger

Karl Menninger (1938), one of the few American analysts who subscribe to Freud's theory of a death instinct, put more emphasis on the self-destructiveness of alcoholism than did the other theorists considered here.

He called alcoholism a form of *chronic suicide*. It is a destructive aggression against the self as punishment for hostile, aggressive feelings that are unacceptable to the self. In his view alcohol makes manageable the conflict between passive erotic dependence on and resentment of the father, who the drinker experiences ambivalently.

There is no question that alcoholics engage in self-destructive behavior. Their addiction costs them dearly in terms of health, career success, relationships, emotional tranquility, and sometimes life itself. The question is, is that self destruction sought on if not a conscious then an unconscious level? Analytic writers like Menninger cite clinical material as evidence that alcoholics do deliberately seek self-destruction, whether they realize it or not, while researchers and behaviorally oriented clinicians believe that alcoholics initially sought "positive affect" (elation) and only later, after alcohol itself had produced dysphoria, drank to alleviate "negative affect" (tense depression), and that in both cases the "self destruction" is a side effect, not a desired outcome at any level. The analysts, with their notion of a "dynamic unconscious," ask why was the elation sought in the first place if there wasn't an underlying depression to start with? I cannot help but observe that drinking can simultaneously serve as an act of forbidden aggression and as a punishment for that aggression, a "double hook" that is indeed powerful. Obviously I am not going to solve this vexed controversy in this book, so I invite the reader to keep an open mind and to view the phenomena of alcoholism from many perspectives. In my experience, they are all useful clinically.

Ernst Simmel

Ernst Simmel (1948) pioneered the psychoanalytic treatment of alcoholism first in a sanitorium, Schloss Tegel, in Berlin, which he founded for the express purpose of treating alcoholism, and later in New York. In creating what was really the first alcoholism rehabilitation unit, he ingeniously integrated milieu therapy—that is, the use of the entire hospital environment as part of the treatment—and psychoanalytic therapy. He analyzed his patients' unconscious motivations for drinking and the unconscious symbolic meanings of that drinking. Following in Abraham's path he examined the relationship between the alcoholic's outer world, the cultural and sociological milieu, and inner world, of emotions, beliefs and thoughts. He forecast an upsurge of addiction, including alcohol addiction, as an aftermath of World War II. He proved to be right. In his paper, written as he was dying, he recognized the potential of AA, tried to understand the unacknowledged psychological insights that made it effective, and urged cooperation between AA and psychiatry as the most hopeful means of "curing" alcoholics.

EGO PSYCHOLOGY AND SELF PSYCHOLOGY APPROACHES TO ALCOHOLISM

More recent psychoanalytic theorists, including Szasz (1958), Hartocollis (1968), Krystal and Raskin (1970), Kernberg (1975), Wurmser (1978), Kohut (1977b), Khantzian (1981), and Levin (1981, 1987), emphasize impairments in ego functioning, lack of affect tolerance, and the use of primitive ("borderline") defense mechanisms, including "splitting," into all good and all bad and denial. These theorists stress the adaptive function of the addiction—what alcohol does for the person or what the person believes it is doing. Kohut and Levin believe that the psychological dimension of alcoholism is a futile attempt to remediate deficits in the self. Alcohol is experienced as an all-powerful mother with whom the drinker merges in order to raise self-esteem, quell anxiety, feel soothed, feel cohesive or whole, feel full as opposed to empty, feel companioned as opposed to alone, and feel safe. Since alcohol cannot do any of these things for very long and in fact exacerbates the very deficits it is used to ameliorate, an addictive cycle is set up. The theories of Szasz, Krystal and Raskin, Khantzian, Wurmser, Hartocollis, Fromm, Kernberg, and Kohut are summarized below.

Thomas Szasz

Thomas Szasz (1958) views addictions as *counterphobic* activities. The drinker drinks to confront and master intolerable fears, including the fear of being addicted. The drinker's basic motivation is to prove that he or she is in control, that he or she has ego mastery. A defiance of fate is implicit in this counterphobic behavior. Szasz's theory is insightful. In my view, the phobia is a fear of psychic annihilation and oblivion, of both regressive fragmentation of the self and engulfment of the self by the symbiotic mother. Experientially, both outcomes are death. Alcoholics therefore self-inflict death in order to master their fear of death. Seen in this way, alcoholics are mythic heroes who descend to the underworld and emerge intact—at least that is their hope. The alcoholic's defensive grandiosity is fed by participation in this unconscious drama.

Henry Krystal and Herbert Raskin

Henry Krystal and Herbert Raskin (1970) offer a theory of affect development in which the infant starts out with global, undifferentiated feelings, including a kind of *ur*-affect (primitive undifferentiated emotion) of dysphoria, which will later differentiate into anxiety, tension, and depression in many gradations and with many fine discriminations. They postulate that alcoholics suffer *affect regression* to a stage in which affects are massive, primitive, and overwhelming. Such regression may be pharmacological or it may be psychodynamic, particularly if the alcoholic has been deprived of the kind of early experience, the *labeling of affects* by loving parents, that facilitates affect development, a deprivation resulting in a fixation to an early stage of affect development. In either case, the alcoholic literally doesn't know what he or she is feeling. Krystal and Raskin's global dysphoria is reminiscent of Rado's tense depression. One also wonders how this theory may related to alcoholic stimulus augmentation (discussed in chapter 6). Is that augmentation partly a result of failed socialization and/or affect regression?

Krystal and Raskin's theory has important clinical implications. Verbalization is a crucial developmental task involving both maturation and object relations. Whatever the original socialization experience of the alcoholic client, the counselor must facilitate affect progression by giving the alcoholic words for what he or she is feeling. This *affect labeling* provides cognitive structure, starts the process of affect (re)differentiation, and reduces the terror of the experientially primitive, unfamiliar, and chaotic emerging feelings. Affect labeling is a way station on the road from feelings experienced as mysterious happenings, as lightning bolts from above, inflicted on the alcoholic, to feelings experienced as consciously owned aspects of the self. To recur to a classic metaphor, a little territory has been gained for the ego from the id. Initially, affect labeling must be done by the counselor. "You are angry" or "You are sad," and so on. Although these are interpretations, the feelings are usually near the surface and are transparent to a trained and experienced counselor. It is always those feelings that are close to consciousness that are interpreted, with the exception of sobriety-threatening feelings, such as rage, which must be made conscious. The idea is not to raise too much conflict in early sobriety, rather to dose interventions on a "need to know" basis. Counseling techniques are discussed in Part III. Krystal and Raskin's theory of affect regression makes sense of the ubiquity in early sobriety of automatic, maladaptive defenses, including drinking, against strong feelings.

Edward Khantzian

Edward Khantzian (1981) emphasis ego and self deficits in the areas of *self-care* and *regulation of feelings*. Khantzian, unlike Menninger, sees alcoholic self-destruction as resulting from a deficit rather than as a self punishment. The alcoholic is unable to take better care of himself or herself because something is missing inside. There is a "basic fault" (Balint,

1968). This deficit also precludes normal affect regulation and tolerance, resulting in maladaptive defenses including pathological drinking.
Khantzian reinterprets alcoholic dependency not as a form of orality, but
rather as a necessary consequence of deficiency. He recommends a combination of psychotherapy addressing to remediation of deficits (rather
than interpretation of conflicts) and psychopharmacology as the treatment
of choice in alcoholism.

Leon Wurmser

Although he writes about drug addiction in general, Leon Wurmser (1978)
has a psychodynamic model that applies to alcoholism. He sees the addict
as caught in a seven-stage vicious cycle. In stage one, there is a sudden
plummeting of already tenuous self-esteem, usually following a disappointment in reality or in fantasy, which leads to a *narcissistic crisis* (stage
2). This crisis leads to a breakdown of *affect defense* (stage 3) in which
feelings become overwhelming, global, generalized, archaic, and in-
capable of being expressed in words. This experience is intolerable and
leads to repression and denial of inner reality, leaving only a vague tension and restlessness (stage 4). In the process, the self is split and de-
personalized. The addict experiences an urgent need to act; since the inner
world is denied and externalized, it is logical to look for the answer exter-
nally and concretely in the drug—in the case of the alcoholic, alcohol. At
this point aggression is mobilized, and it may be turned against the self
(stage 5). In the next stage (6), the superego is split so that it won't be
an impediment to action, and feelings of entitlement and grandiosity lead
to a consummation in the binge. The narcissistic crisis ends in pleasure,
but it isn't quite successful. Wurmser quotes Rado (1933): "The elation
had augmented the ego (self) to gigantic dimensions and had almost eliminated reality; now just the reverse state appears, sharpened by the contrast. The ego (self) is shrunken, and reality appears exaggerated in its
dimensions" (p. 10). The drinker is in worse shape than ever, with even
lower self-esteem (stage 7). Wurmser's model suffers from overcompli-
cation and is derived from work with a population that is more psychopathological (he believes that the psychopathology is antecedent to
the drug use) than the typical alcoholic population, yet it has much to
offer alcoholism counseling. His emphasis on maladaptive defenses—
particularly the defenses of *splitting* of self, superego, and reality into
incommunicable parts; of *denial* not only of the addiction but of the inner
world of fantasy and feelings, and of *externalization* of inner deficit, conflict, and possibility of resolution—provides a means of understanding what is going on and a guide to what to look for in counseling
sessions.

Peter Hartocollis

Peter Hartocollis (1968) stresses the use of alcohol to bolster defenses. Defenses are ego functions, and the use of alcohol to shore them up implies ego weakness. The defense most in need of bolstering is *denial*, which Hartcollis sees as repudiation of the need for help. His formulation is thus a variation on the counter-dependency hypothesis of the dynamics of alcoholism. In a later paper (Hartocollis & Hartocollis, 1980), he presents evidence from his extensive experience in analyzing alcoholic patients that this denial originated in a disturbed mother-infant relationship, postulating that the difficulty frequently started in the *rapprochement* substage of the separation-individualization process. Hartocollis is here drawing on the developmental theory of Margaret Mahler (Mahler, Pine, and Bergman, 1975), who traced how the human infant evolves out of a symbiosis with the mother into an autonomous person with a unique and separate sense of self. During this evolution, there is a period in which the toddler, now exploring the world, needs the assurance that he or she can safely regress to symbiosis. Mahler calls the child's gesture rapprochement. If the mother either cannot permit separation or rejects rapprochement, the stage is set for borderline personality disorder. Hartocollis hypothesizes that not only do these developmental vicissitudes predispose people to borderline and narcissistic personality disorders but that these disorders in turn predispose people to alcoholism. To account for the research evidence of lack of "psychopathology" in prealcoholics he points to the relatively smooth surface functioning of some narcissists who compensate for inner emptiness and emotional shallowness by acting "as if". He further suggests that as their compensation falters, they turn to alcohol to maintain their as if personality (Deutsch, 1965), and as in all the other uses of alcohol as a self-medication, they ultimately fail. AA agrees with Hartocollis in its emphasis on the centrality of admitting the need for help as a prerequisite to recovery.

Erich Fromm

Erich Fromm was an unusual analyst who synthesized Freudian and Marxist thought into a unique amalgamation with a strongly existential flavor. Interested in the intersection of the political and the personal, Fromm's interest was only tangentially in addiction yet he elucidated one of the most powerful dynamics driving addictive behavior, including alcoholism: "escape from freedom." In his 1941 book of that title, Fromm convincingly demonstrated that one of the social dynamics behind the rise of fascism and other forms of totalitarianism is a desire to escape from what the Danish philosopher Søren Kierkegaard (1849/1944) called the "dizziness of freedom"—the anxiety ineluctably concomitant with the realization that I am responsible for—indeed in a sense I *am*—my choices.

The philosopher-theologian Paul Tillich (1952) delineated a distinction between neurotic anxiety and ontological anxiety. *Neurotic anxiety*, on the one hand, is anxiety caused by inner conflict—the sort of conflict Freud described and understood as being between desire and conscience, each or both of which can be unconscious. *Ontological anxiety*, on the other hand, is not based on conflict. It is the anxiety intrinsic to being human. Tillich saw ontological anxiety as having three forms: anxiety over fate and death; anxiety over guilt and condemnation; and anxiety over emptiness and meaninglessness. Tillich believed that the last source of ontological anxiety, the dread of emptiness and meaninglessness, is particularly characteristic of our time. An addiction provides meaning and structure to a life, and the loss of meaning and structure in recovery provokes ontological anxiety. Twelve-step programs intuitively address this anxiety and help recovering alcoholics deal with this form of dread by providing them with meaningful activities, goals, and values. The dizziness of freedom and the flight from freedom are both ontological in Tillich's sense.

Fromm saw not only social, but individual psychopathology as derivative from a desire to flee the anxiety of being free. A neurosis, a psychosis, or an addiction is a constriction, a narrowing of possibility. The history of any addiction is a history of progressive enslavement. Seen from this point of view, alcoholism with its progressive impoverishment of the self and loss of potentiality is clearly an escape from freedom and its burdens. The achievement of sobriety is a reclamation of freedom. Fear is always concomitant with this newfound freedom, with its choices, decisions, and responsibilities. The result is a sort of ontological agoraphobia, which can arouse such intense anxiety that sobriety is jeopardized. The dizziness of freedom has caused many a slip. The intense anxiety that accompanies the realization that one has choices occurs in relation to all life areas. This is one reason that AA advises its members not to make major decisions during the first year of sobriety. This waiting postpones the eventual necessity of dealing with this particular kind of anxiety until more stable sobriety is attained.

Fromm's existential understanding of the dynamics of alcoholism has great clinical utility. An exploration of the choices the client needed to flee often opens unexpected vistas that provide insight and strengthen sobriety. (Fromm's influence on an empirial study of alcoholism in a Mexican village, which draws on a different aspect of his thought, is discussed on page 71.)

Otto Kernberg

Otto Kernberg has written extensively on borderline and narcissistic personality disorders, which he treats with a variant of psychoanalysis that emphasizes interpretation of the transference in a context of setting limits including restrictions on drinking. He too sees alcoholism as a symptom of underlying personality disorder. He stresses disturbed *object relations*, by which he means abnormalities in the inner, representational world; that is, each of us has conscious, preconscious, and unconscious representations of ourselves and others, which he calls *self-representations* and *object representations*. In human development, the internal world is initially undifferentiated. There is nothing but a global, undifferentiated representation that does not distinguish between self and other. Kernberg calls this a *self-object representation*. In response to experiences of gratification and frustration, this global representation is split into good and bad self-objects. If development goes no further, reality testing is never developed since self and world are confused. At the next stage, good and bad self-objects are differentiated into good self, bad self, good object, and bad object representations. This is the inner reality of the borderline who oscillates wildly in terms of self evaluation and relations to others. In AA language, this is the world of "the great I Am and Poor Me." According to Kernberg, pathological narcissists confuse their ideal selves (ego ideals), real selves, and ideal others, forming an abnormal amalgamated representation in which these three are fused. In a healthy person, the good and bad self and object representations are integrated, with goodness predominating over badness, and the internal world becomes one of complex, differentiated, more or less realistic self and object representations. Kernberg theorizes that the inner world of the alcoholic lacks such integration and is either characterized by the borderline lack of preintegration of good and bad representations, or by the abnormal fusion of real and ideal of the pathological narcissist. His treatment is aimed at modification of this internal world.

Heinz Kohut

Heinz Kohut was a classical analyst who came to see that classical theory could not account for what went on in some of his analyses. He realized that certain patients, whom he later identified as having narcissistic personality disorders, did not relate to him as a separate person; rather they related to him as if he was an extension of themselves. He built a whole developmental theory from this analysis of the *transference*. Transference is the unconscious repetition of an early object relation in which the reality of a present relationship is distorted by projections of the internal images of childhood loves and hates. Transference is part of human life and plays a large role in interpersonal difficulties of all kinds. In psychoanalytic treatment, it is maximized and used therapeutically. Kohut called these ways in which certain patients related to him as part of themselves *narcissistic transferences.* Later, he called them *self-object transferences.* He distinguished between two kinds of such transferences: *mirror transferences* and *idealizing transferences.* In the mirror transference, the analyst's only function is to reflect back (mirror) the patient's wonderfulness. What the patient seeks is affirmation of archaic (infantile) grandiosity. In the idealizing transference, the patient puts all the wonderfulness—omnipotence and omniscience—in the analyst and then fuses with him or her. I would suggest that *the alcoholic's relationship to alcohol can usefully be understood as a combined mirror and idealizing transference.* Kohut also spoke of a type of mirror transference which he called a *twinship transference,* in which the patient sees the analyst as an identical twin.

Kohut spoke of the *transmuting internalization* of *psychic structure.* By transmuting internalization he meant the gradual taking into the self, so to speak, a grain at a time, of the functions once performed by self-objects, by which Kohut meant not the internal representations referred to by Kernberg but people to whom one relates in a special undifferentiated way. Each nontraumatic failure of the self-object to meet a psychological need results in acquisition of some capacity to meet that need oneself, for example, tension regulation. Kohut's notion was one of "optimal frustration": no frustration, no internalization, no need for it; too much frustration, no internalization—what is absent can't be taken in. As Donald Winnicott puts it, parents and counselors "succeed by failing." Kohut would have been more accurate had he referred to psychic structure as psychic *capacity,* for that is what he meant. He conceptualized most psychopathology, and certainly narcissistic pathology, as a deficit state—something is missing inside. It is missing inside because something went wrong developmentally. Some crucial phase of early object relations went awry. Of course, it makes perfect sense to take something in—alcohol for instance—to remedy an internal lack. The only trouble is that what is missing can only come from people, from a certain kind of relationship, not from a chemical, so the treatment of alcoholism must be, in some sense, a replacement of rum with relationship. That is what self-help groups and professional counseling are all about. Kohut compared an addiction to a futile attempt to cure a gastric fistula by eating. The food may taste good, but it falls right out the hole without either nourishing or repairing the hole. As Kohut put it, "no psychic structure is built."

The Kohutian notion of *narcissistic rage* illuminates much alcoholic behavior. Narcissistic rage, unlike mature aggression, is not instrumental in the service of a reality based goal; rather it is the response of the unmirrored self to narcissistic injury (see Levin, 1993), injury to the core self, which is characterized by deep pain, intense feelings of shame, a precipitous fall in self-esteem, and an unquenchable desire for revenge. It is the response of the offended monarch, "Off with their heads." Kohut used as an example Captain Ahab in *Moby Dick*. Ahab's insane desire for revenge on a "dumb brute," the white whale, destroys him and all but one of his crew.

Narcissistic rage turned against the self can result in suicide. Alcoholic rage is multidetermined: part of it is pharmacological, the result of ethanol's effect on central nervous system tissue; part of it is in defense of the addiction; part of it comes from the accumulation of unexpressed anger (alcoholics have a lot of bluster, but rarely are effectively communicative or assertive); part of it is self-hatred projected outward; part of it is historical (that is, unconscious rage over childhood injury); and part of it is narcissistic rage as a consequence of narcissistic vulnerability (that is, lack of the resources to process the "slings and arrows of outrageous fortune," not to mention everyday disappointments and slights), and feelings of entitlement of the archaic grandiose self (see chapter 10 for a more detailed discussion). Since most slips (relapses) are rage responses, helping the client recognize, contain, and appropriately express rather than act out narcissistic rage is of the essence of alcoholism counseling.

Chapter 8

Other Etiological Theories
of Alcoholism

In addition to the psychodynamic theories examined in chapter 7, there are many other theories, spiritual, psychological, and neurochemical, that purport to account for alcoholism, that is, to give an etiological explanation for it, or that illuminate some aspect of the inner world, the experience of the alcoholic. This chapter examines some of the most important of these theories ranging from Carl Jung's spiritual account to conflict theories to learning theories to Robert Cloninger's neurochemical tridimensional personality theory to stages-of-change theories. Complex, sometimes competing, sometimes complementary, this array of primarily psychological theory is fascinating. It also has profound clinical implications. As you read, think about ways, if it is possible, to integrate the various theories and consider how you might apply them to clinical work.

CARL JUNG: ALCOHLISM AND SPIRITUALITY

Carl Jung, who broke with Freud and is not usually considered an analyst, had an important, albeit indirect, role in the foundation of Alcoholics Anonymous (AA) and a strong influence on one of its founders, Bill Wilson. It seems highly improbable that Jung, a Swiss psychiatrist whose writings are often obscure, would have influenced an American self-help organization, but he did. It is an interesting story that has become part of the AA mythology. Jung had treated a patient known in AA literature as Roland H. He was a successful American businessman who had come to Jung for help with alcoholism. He had undergone a seemingly successful analysis with the master himself and left Zurich certain that he had been cured. Roland believed that he had such a deep self-understanding that he would never have trouble with alcohol again. In a short time, however, he returned to Jung drunk and in despair. Jung told him that there was no hope. Roland asked if there really was none at all, and Jung replied that only a major personality reorganization driven by a powerful emotion, in essence a "conversion experience," could save him. Roland left in deep despair, but Jung's words touched something deep inside him and he did what AA would later call "hitting bottom." In his despair he reached out for help and did indeed have a conversion experience, joining the Oxford Movement, which was an upper-middle-class revival movement popular in the 1920s and 1930s. He became and remained sober. The Oxford Movement had a set of spiritual steps that their members followed. These steps became the basis of the famous Twelve Steps of Alcoholics Anonymous. Roland spread the good word to his friend and fellow drunk Ebby Thacker, who also became sober. Ebby in turn went to visit his buddy, Bill Wilson, who was drunk. Ebby told Bill the story of his meeting Roland and joining the Oxford Movement. Bill entered a hospital to dry out. There he experienced some sort of "peak" or mystical experience. When he left the hospital, he too joined the Oxford Movement, and he remained sober. Bill gradually pulled away from the Oxford Movement, although he borrowed a great deal from it. He began to work with drunks on his own. Shortly thereafter, he joined with another drunk, Bob Smith, whom he helped to get sober, and thus Alcoholics Anonymous was born. Ebby did not make it; he died in Rockland State Hospital of alcoholism. Many years later, Bill Wilson wrote to Jung to tell him the story, and Jung (1961/1973) replied that Roland's "craving for alcohol was the equivalent on a low level of the spiritual thirst of our being for wholeness, expressed in medieval language: the union with God. . . . You see, 'alcohol' in Latin is 'spiritus' and you use the same word for the highest religious experience as well as for the most depraving poison. The helpful formula therefore is: *spiritus contra spiritum*."[1]

CONFLICT THEORIES

The three major conflict theories of the dynamics of alcoholism are (a) the *dependency conflict theory*, (b) the *need-for-power theory*, and (c) the

[1]From Jung (1961/1973). Reprinted by permission of publisher.

epistemological error theory. The first theory overlaps and is implicit in the work of most of the psychoanalytic writers discussed in chapter 7. The second was created by a social-psychologically oriented personality theorist. The third is a *cybernetic* theory in which alcoholism is seen as a disturbance in information flow. (Cybernetics is the study of automatic communication and control systems. It is also known as information theory.)

Dependency Conflict Theory

The dependency conflict theory of alcoholism states that alcoholics are people who have not succeeded in establishing or at least maintaining healthy patterns of *interdependence*. This is certainly true. However, this theory also states that alcoholics' failure to establish such forms of adult mutuality is the principal etiological factor behind their alcoholism. This tenet is more controversial. In its naive form, the theory states that alcoholics are socially, psychologically, and often economically dependent people. Holders of this form of the theory cite the openly dependent behavior of many alcoholics. Many alcoholics, however, are not openly dependent, so the naive form of the theory is contrary to fact. It also runs afoul of the fact that the open dependence of some alcoholics might be a consequence of their disease. The more sophisticated form of the theory states that alcoholics are people who suffer particularly acute conflict over how to meet their dependency needs and who have turned to alcohol in an attempt to resolve this largely or entirely unconscious conflict. Holders of this form of the theory believe that dependency needs and the necessity of meeting them in psychologically and socially acceptable ways are inherent in the human condition. It is not dependence per se that is pathological but rather certain ways of being dependent. In this tenet, the dependency conflict theorists are certainly right. As discussed previously, the more sophisticated form of the theory, or a variation of it, has been held by many students of alcoholism, including Blane (1968), Child et al. (1965), Knight (1937, 1938), the McCords (1960), and Menninger (1938). The more psychodynamic of these theorists twist the screw a turn by pointing out that the conflict is exacerbated by the fact that the alcoholic is often enraged at those on whom he or she depends.

   The dependency conflict theory of the etiology of alcoholism is largely based on the observation that alcohol provides a socially acceptable way of meeting dependency needs without appearing to do so. It concludes that people who cannot openly acknowledge their dependency needs, who suppress or repress them, are particularly prone to meet those needs in a veiled manner through alcohol consumption. If they belong to a culture or subculture that sanctions heavy drinking, this is even more likely to occur. In our society, at least until recently, such a denial of the need for the support and love of others has been more characteristic of men than of women. Our society also has tended to be more approving, or at least less censorious, of heavy drinking and even drunkenness in men. Therefore, the dependency conflict theory of alcoholism is essentially a theory of male alcoholism. From the perspective of this theory, alcoholism is a form of *pseudo-self-sufficiency*.

Empirical evidence for the dependency conflict theory has three sources: clinical studies, anthropological studies, and longitudinal studies. The overt social dependence of many alcoholics is often cited as evidence for this theory, but as noted earlier there are difficulties in using this evidence to support the theory. Clinical evidence is of two kinds: statistical studies using objective measures of various sorts and case studies. Evidence from objective studies is mixed. Most of the psychoanalytic theorists who stress the centrality of dependency conflicts in the dynamics of alcoholism base their conclusions on in-depth case studies. Certainly, such conflicts are often powerfully revealed in the analysis of alcoholics. The clinical works of Blane, Knight, and others support the belief that very intense dependency conflicts are common in alcoholics. Whether such conflicts are etiological is not clear. The anthropological work of Child et al. has already been discussed. As they interpret their data, societies that drink heavily are those that frustrate dependency needs. Whether it can be inferred from their evidence that a similar dynamic is etiological in alcoholism in our culture is problematic. The McCords interpreted the data from their longitudinal study of alcoholism as supporting the dependency conflict theory. Others have interpreted the McCords' data differently. The hypothesis most consistent with their data and with the evidence of rebellious and undercontrolled behavior in prealcoholics is that alcoholism is one outcome of a reaction formation against unacceptable dependency needs, but that not all alcoholism is so motivated. Altogether, evidence for the dependency conflict theory of alcoholism is sufficiently compelling that it cannot be ignored. Apparently there is something about dependence and the conflict about it that is implicated in alcoholism, but exactly what this might be is not quite clear.

Need-for-Power Theory

McClelland et al. (1972) theorized that men drink to feel powerful and that male alcoholics have a particularly strong need to feel powerful. McClelland et al. further specified that the kind of power men seek in alcohol is personal (egoistic) and not socialized; that is, the power is sought for the satisfaction of purely personal needs. McClelland is a professor with Harvard University's Department of Social Relations and has done much interdisciplinary work on the relationship between culture and personality; he is particularly known for his study of achievement motivation. He and his associates have also studied why men drink and the psychological motives for drinking. Their studies cut across cultures and social classes and range from examination of anthropological data to carefully controlled experimental studies. McClelland studied under the personality theorist Henry Murray (1938), who developed a theory of personality that has two main structural components: *need* and *press*. Needs are internal to the organism and may be biological or psychological. Presses are external and come from the environment.

In Murray's theory, the dynamic interplay of needs and presses determines personality. Murray also developed the *Thematic Apperception Test* (TAT), which is a series of pictures about which subjects are asked to tell stories. In response to each stimulus card, the subject tells a story about what happened, what is happening, and what is going to happen. As is the case for all projective techniques of personality assessment, the underlying assumption of the TAT is that the subject projects aspects of self into the production, be it a drawing as in the Draw-a-Person test, a perception as in the Rorschach, or a story as in the TAT. In Murray's original formulation of the TAT technique, subjects' stories were evaluated in terms of the needs and presses expressed, which were assumed to be characteristic of the personality of the storyteller. The first card on the TAT shows a dreamy boy with a violin. The subject is asked to tell what has preceded the scene depicted, what is happening now, and what will happen. It is assumed that the storyteller identifies with the protagonist and projects his or her conscious and unconscious thoughts, fantasies, feelings, and wishes onto that protagonist. To give a perhaps over-obvious example, the subject who reacts to card 1 by saying, "That boy is a genius. He always loved his violin and his parents sacrificed everything to give him lessons. He grew up and had a brilliant debut at Carnegie Hall. He married his childhood sweetheart and went on to world fame," is different from the subject who responds to the same card by saying, "That boy hated the violin. His mother beat him savagely when he didn't practice. When he grew up, he murdered her. She didn't see the gun because he hid it in his violin case. He was raped in prison and killed himself."

McClelland took over much of Murray's theory and has made extensive use of the TAT in his research. He has studied the need for achievement and the need for power, breaking down the latter into the need for *socialized power* and the need for *personal (egoistic) power*. An example of a story of socialized power would be, "He [the protagonist in the TAT or folk tale story] went into business and was very successful. In fact, he made millions of dollars and used it to endow a research foundation to find a cure for AIDS." An example of a story of egoistic power would be, "He went into business and was very successful. In fact, he made millions of dollars and used it to put out contracts on all his enemies." The heavy drinkers studied by McClelland tended to tell stories of the second type. McClelland therefore concluded that men drink to feel powerful. More explicitly, they drink to feel enhanced feelings of personal power. These findings are based on an analysis of the folktales of many cultures and on a series of experiments in which subjects were asked to tell stories about TAT cards while sober. They were then offered alcohol and were asked to tell another set of stories after having drunk.

In his analysis of folktales from an extensive compilation of anthropological research, McClelland found a correlation between tribal cultures that drink heavily and cultures that tell stories with personal power themes. In the cultures that had high levels of drunkenness McClelland found that tribesmen experienced conflict between obedience and achievement or autonomy and that the enhanced feelings of personal power induced by alcohol allowed them to resolve this conflict.

His experimental evidence showed that men who told TAT stories of personalized power while sober were men who drank the most during the experiment and that consumption of alcohol increased the incidence of themes of personal power with a concomitant decrease in themes of socialized power in both moderate and heavy drinkers. On the basis of this evidence—the absence of dependency or oral themes in the sober stories of the heavy drinkers and the absence of an increase in oral or oral-dependent themes with alcohol consumption—McClelland concluded that the dependency conflict theory of alcoholism is wrong, and he proposed a counter theory that men drink to feel personally powerful and that alcoholics are men with a particularly strong need to feel powerful.

McClelland's power theory and the dependency conflict theory are not so far apart. After all, the intense need to feel powerful suggests underlying feelings of powerlessness and to be powerless is necessarily to be dependent. Its ultimate source is infantile helplessness. It is of some interest that Bill Wilson, cofounder of Alcoholics Anonymous, in discussing the "proper form of dependence" used the example of being dependent on electrical *power* as an example of healthy dependence. It is also noteworthy that the AA "cure" turns on the admission of powerlessness (over alcohol), which would seem to undercut the very motivation for heavy drinking that McClelland hypothesizes.

Epistemological Error Theory

Gregory Bateson was an anthropologist interested in mental illness who advanced an interesting theory of alcoholism. Bateson, who has also written on schizophrenia, sees mental illness as disturbed communication. In his view, this disturbance in communication is both a cause of mental illness and the essential quality of the illness itself. Communication is essentially the exchange of information, and Bateson was vitally interested in and profoundly influenced by scientific information theory, or *cybernetics*. His principal work on mental illness is titled *Communication: The Social Matrix of Psychiatry* (1951). Bateson was the principal author of the "double bind" theory of the etiology of schizophrenia. The double bind theory asserts that the continuous immersion in "damned if you do and damned if you don't" environments in which covert messages contradict overt ones leads to madness (schizophrenia). Since he drew so heavily on information theory in his studies of psychopathological conditions, it is not surprising that his essay on alcoholism is titled "The Cybernetics of 'Self': A Theory of Alcoholism" (1971).

Bateson believed that the experience of the self as a thing rather than as a process and as set in opposition to a disjunctive world is an illusion or, as he would prefer to put it, an *epistemological error*. There is no substantial self apart from its world; rather the self is interrelational, the pattern of its communications with its world. Bateson believed that Western culture in particular makes this kind of cognitive or epistemological error in its understanding of self, world, and their interrelationship and that the alcoholic is caught in a particularly intense form of this error. Bateson was interested in the unreflective assumptions, sometimes conscious but mostly unconscious, that people use to "construe" a world. In this view, the human mind is constitutive of its experiences of the world, although one is usually unaware of one's role in shaping that experience. According to Bateson, these largely unconscious assumptions are a cognitive structure that one imposes on experience in an effort to organize and make sense of that experience. This cognitive structure consists of a person's unspoken ontologies and epistemologies (that is, one's understandings of and assumptions about the nature of reality and how one knows that reality). There is a dialectical relationship between one's assumptions about the nature of reality and how one comes to know that reality and how one actually experiences it. Cognitive structures tend to be self-validating, even though they may be wrong; that is, they may distort the data that filter through them.

Here Bateson echoes the philosopher Immanuel Kant (1787/1929), who taught that we are not passive recipients of sense data and information about the world but, rather, active organizers of sense data and data from the "inner" sense. Knowing is an active not a passive act, and we can only know the world as we experience it, filtered through perceptual "categories of the understanding," rather than as it may be apart from our knowing it. We construct our experience of both self and world. The poet William Wordsworth put it somewhat differently when he said, "The world is half perceived and half created," but he was making the same point. For Kant, the action of the human mind in constituting knowledge is invariant; it is the same for all people. Bateson, however, believed that one's ontology-epistemology is personally and culturally determined. Bateson used the word *epistemology* to denote the whole automatic, reflexive process of understanding experience. Different cognitive structures or epistemologies result in different ways of construing the world. For Bateson the alcoholic suffers from *cognitive error*, from a false epistemology. Instead of being part of a (feedback) loop, the alcoholic gets looped.

What is the nature of this epistemological error? It is the error, first promulgated by the 17th century philosopher Rene Descartes, that there is a subject, the "self," that knows an object or objects "out there." It is a radically disjunctive way of viewing human experience. In Bateson's view, this error leads to a disjunction between self and world that does not really exist. For him the "real" reality is a feedback loop in which information, or in his words, "transformations of differences," flows, and self and object are nodal points in that flow, mutually interactive and mutually interdependent. The radical disjunction of self and world predisposes one who lives by this epistemology to *objectify* (that is, to treat as objects) both the world and the people in it. This results in an attempt to totally control the world and the objects in it, as if destruction of the objects would have no effect on the destroyer since they have nothing to do with him or her. This leads to a kind of sadomasochistic relationship with the world. It is also a kind of pseudo-self-sufficiency.

An interactional, information-flow model of reality simultaneously connects knower and known and makes the known a center of independent, or better interdependent, initiative and does not lend itself to efforts at omnipotent control. It contains less epistemological error. According to Bateson, the sober alcoholic does not construe the world in this way, and alcohol offers a corrective to his or her epistemological error. Alcohol breaks down the barriers between self and world, here experienced as an object to be exploited, and reestablishes the alcoholic's interconnection with and interdependence on that object. In other words, alcohol dedifferentiates self and object representations. If such differentiations are too rigid, if the ego boundaries are too impermeable, the alcohol will be corrective. In Bateson's view, no matter how regressive the psychological consequences of this pharmacological process are, they result in a world picture that in some sense is more true or correct in that it allows the alcoholic to experience him or herself as "a part of" rather than "apart from" the world. Alcoholism is then an attempt to correct an epistemological error. Unfortunately, the pharmacological qualities of alcohol are such that the attempt is doomed to failure. Like all other attempts to self-medicate with alcohol, the "cure" ultimately exacerbates the "illness" and the alcoholic winds up more disjunctive, more cut off from world and fellows than he or she was before drinking.

Bateson is fascinated with AA and its Twelve Steps, which he sees as a noninjurious mode of correction of the alcoholic's false epistemology. Since drinking is here seen as a corrective to a deficient sobriety, the state of being of the sober alcoholic must be modified if that sobriety is to endure. Bateson argues that AA does just that by inducing an epistemological shift toward *complementarity* (the state of being in which disjunctive power relations are replaced by communicative interactions) through the "surrender experience" and the AA ideology in general.

LEARNING THEORIES

Learning theory asserts that alcoholism, like all human behavior, is learned. It is one of the more "scientific" parts of psychology, its principles are empirically based and have been verified many times. It is a "hard" science in ways that the more speculative parts of psychology are not. Learning theory teaches that people learn in three principal ways: by *classical conditioning*, by *instrumental* or *operant conditioning*, and by *social learning*, or *modeling*.

Classical Conditioning

Classical conditioning is the pairing of an *unconditioned stimulus* with a *conditioned stimulus* to produce a *conditioned response*. An unconditioned stimulus produces an unconditioned response; for example, in dogs the smell of meat, an unconditioned stimulus, is followed by salivation, which is an *unconditioned response*. The connection between an unconditioned stimulus and an unconditioned response is biological. It is prewired. If we pair another stimulus, say the sound of a bell, with the meat, after many such pairings a dog will salivate when the bell is rung, even in the absence of the meat. The bell thus becomes a conditioned stimulus and the salivation following it a conditioned response. The connection between a conditioned stimulus and a conditioned response is not innate or biological; it is learned.

This famous example of classical conditioning was first demonstrated by the Russian psychologist Ivan Pavlov (1927) whose experimental work led him to discover classical conditioning and its laws. Since unconditioned responses are built-in biological givens and since drinking alcohol is not an unconditioned response, it is probable that classical conditioning does not play a central role in the development of alcoholism, although animals that salivate at the sound of a cocktail shaker are not unknown. Drinking alcohol can, however, be paired with an unconditioned stimulus (say, food) and become a conditioned stimulus for consummatory behavior, which is an unconditioned response of a hungry animal to food. Now alcohol acts as a conditioned stimulus, and drinking has become a conditioned response. In other words, the drinker has learned to drink when hungry.

Classical conditioning is used in a form of treatment for alcoholism known as aversive conditioning or *aversion therapy*. This treatment pairs a punishment, such as an electric shock, with drinking, and alcohol becomes the conditioned stimulus for the anticipation of pain. As long as the association holds, it is unlikely that the alcoholic will drink.

Instrumental Conditioning

Instrumental, or operant, conditioning is different from classical conditioning in that it does play a central role in the acquisition of excessive appetite for alcohol. Operant learning is based on the fact that actions that are pleasurable tend to be repeated. If an action is reinforced (that is, rewarded in some way), its frequency will increase; if it is punished, its frequency will decrease. As learning theorists say, behavior is controlled by its consequences. Consequences that lead to greater frequency of a behavior are *reinforcers*. Behavior that is instrumental in producing reinforcement is said to be reinforced—hence the term *instrumental learning*. An operant is a spontaneous behavior. It is what is operated on by reinforcement or its absence—hence the term *operant conditioning*. Just as classical conditioning theory is associated with Pavlov, operant conditioning theory is associated with B. F. Skinner (1938). Skinner is best known for his experimental work on learning, particularly on the relationship of different schedules of reinforcement to changes in behavior.

Anxiety reduction is reinforcing, and for some people, alcohol is particularly effective as an anxiety reducer. For them, drinking alcohol is highly reinforced. *Avoidance learning*, or learning to escape from a painful situation, is particularly persistent; that is, it is very well learned. An action (operant) that leads to escape from an aversive situation such as tension is said to be *negatively reinforced*. Cessation of pain or discomfort is a negative reinforcer. A negative reinforcer is not a *punisher*, which increases rather than decreases discomfort; the two terms are often confused. Punishment reduces the frequency of a behavior, but the punishment—the adverse effect—must follow immediately for the punishment to be maximally effective in reducing the frequency of the behavior. The punishing sides of drinking—the hangovers, the adverse health consequences, the social disapproval—are delayed, to the next day, the next month, or even the next decade. Quick pleasure and remote pain make for increased frequency of an action. This is exactly what can happen to drinking behavior.

All kinds of events can be paired with anxiety or another adverse state and thus become occasions to drink. Both classical conditioning and what is called *stimulus generalization* play a role here. For example, first you reach for a drink only when the boss yells at you (anxiety followed by anxiety reduction); then you drink when anybody yells at you; then you drink if there is an increase in volume in any verbal exchange; then you drink if the boss walks into the room; then you drink if you *think* about the boss coming into the room. In this way, many things can become *drink signals*. Alcoholics are usually unaware of the events that serve as drink signals for them. Consequently, an important function of the alcoholism counselor is to help make the alcoholic aware of environmental and inner drink signals so that other, less harmful actions can be taken to reduce the dysphoria induced by the drink signal.

Another principle of instrumental learning theory is the notion that *intermittent reinforcement* leads to persistence of a behavior. If a rat is randomly reinforced by a food pellet for pressing a bar, the rat will go on pressing the bar long after the last reinforcement. Psychologists say that behaviors that have been intermittently reinforced are highly resistant to *extinction*. Just as the intermittently reinforced rat goes on pressing the bar, the intermittently reinforced alcoholic goes on drinking at the bar. For the alcoholic, drinking may once have been highly and regularly reinforced—it always felt good, it reduced guilt, it raised self-esteem. Then drinking became only irregularly (intermittently) reinforced, and finally, not reinforced at all; for the alcoholic, there is no longer cessation of pain, let alone more positive pleasure in drinking, yet the drinking continues. The expectation of positive pleasure or anxiety reduction from the glass dies hard; it had been intermittently reinforced both positively (it felt good) and negatively (it was an avoidance behavior). Both the intermittence and the avoidance make it highly resistant to extinction. This explains much seemingly senseless alcoholic behavior.

Whether alcohol is reinforcing, exactly what is reinforced, for whom it is reinforcing, and under what circumstances it is reinforcing are far from clear. There is much controversy among learning theorists about these issues, including the effectiveness of alcohol as a tension reducer. It may be that alcohol reduces self-awareness, which can be extremely painful, and that this reduction is the reinforcer, or that it reduces tension in a conflict situation but not in others. In a famous experiment, Masserman and Yum (1946) gave cats a shock when the cats approached their food boxes. This induced an intense approach-avoidance conflict; it made the cats neurotic, crazy. The experimenters then laced the cats' milk with gin and continued to shock them when they tried to eat. The "high" cats approached the food box with much less conflict than they had when sober.

It has become increasingly clear that thoughts, expectations, beliefs, and labels play an important part in learning. Behavior is not just a matter of stimulus and response. Intervening events, cognitive events that are mental contents, play an important part in human learning. If a person believes that alcohol gives pleasure, reduces pain, or increases status, he or she is likely to drink it. How one labels an event is important. If drinking is labeled sinful, a different behavior results than if it is labeled "cool" or, at the very least, the same behavior will arouse different feelings.

Modeling

Social learning theory teaches that other people's behavior is a powerful influence on us. We model our behavior after them. Social learning theory was elaborated by Bandura and Walters (1963). Our culture, the media included, provides numerous models for drinking, including excessive drinking. People model their behavior accordingly. Sobriety can be modeled too, and one reason that self-help groups such as AA are so effective is that they provide models of sobriety. AA also changes expectations (beliefs) about alcohol. Research validates that a change in social surround powerfully affects drinking behavior. Joining a self help group radically shifts one's social surround, one's reference group, and the effect of doing so is potent.

Tension Reduction and Self-Awareness Theories

The *tension reduction model* of the motivation for drinking was one of the earliest attempts to account for alcohol consumption. It was congruent with popular beliefs and had the support of learning theory. Drive reduction (with anxiety or tension here conceptualized as a drive) is highly reinforcing and therefore a powerful motivator. Early research (Conger, 1956) seemed to support the notion that alcohol was tension reducing, but later research showed that that was not always the case (Cappell & Herman, 1972). Tension reduction as a single factor theory of why people drink, let alone why they drink alcoholically, proved untenable. Whether or not ethanol is tension (anxiety) reducing is dependent on many factors: expectations (if you believe a drink will reduce tension, it probably will); individual differences; dosage (alcohol in low doses reduces anxiety, high doses increase it); whether blood alcohol levels are rising or falling; social setting, and stage of drinking career (there is evidence that alcohol actually increases tension in alcoholics, at least in an experimental hospital setting). A further difficulty with the theory lies in the fact that for many, the chief motivation for drinking is the anticipation of the initial euphoria (positive affect motivation), not tension reduction (negative affect motivation). Nevertheless, there is no question that ethanol can be tension reducing and that many drink for that effect whether or not their tension comes from prior drinking. Cloninger's (1983, 1987) notion of increased somatic anxiety (body tension) in type 2 male limited alcoholism and increased cognitive anxiety (guilt and obsessive worry) in type 1 milieu limited alcoholics which he believes to be antecedent to the alcoholism suggests that those who later become alcoholic may have that individual variation which accentuates the tension reducing properties of ethanol. This theory goes against the research evidence that alcoholics initially drank for the positive affect. Reality, however, is complex, and the contradiction may be more apparent than real. People drink for many reasons and some who drink for tension reduction may be prealcoholics, so may some who drink for euphoria, and so may some who drink for both reasons.

The difficulties with the tension reduction hypothesis have led to a sophisticated reformulation of it known as the *stress response dampening* (SRD) theory (Sher, 1987). It states that alcohol dampens the biological stress response and that that is highly reinforcing, increasing the likelihood that the individual will drink if stressed. This will be particularly true if the person sees no alternative way of dealing with the stress. Sher, who does not see his model as a univariate (having only one variable) explanation of drinking behavior, reviews some possible biochemical path-ways by which alcohol may dampen the adrenal-pituitary-hypothalamic stress response and concludes that—social-cognitive factors and the initial increase in heart rate notwithstanding—stress response dampening is a major motivating factor in both social and alcoholic drinking.

Jay Hull (1981) has formulated an interesting theory of motivation for drinking, including pathological drinking, which he calls the *self-awareness model*. He postulates that one pharmacological effect of ethanol is impairment of cognitive functioning, including information storage, and that that impairment decreases self-awareness. Therefore, in situations in which self-awareness is painful, such as the aftermath of failure, drinking alcohol will be highly reinforcing. Hull concludes that empirical studies support the self-awareness hypothesis as one pathway to drinking. It is easy to see how self-awareness obliviation could lead to a vicious cycle in which a failure results in drinking to blot out painful self-awareness, which in turn results in further failures "necessitating" more drinking *ad infinitum* until alcoholism develops.

Self-Handicapping and Opponent Process Theories

Steven Berglas (1985) has formulated an ingenious hypothesis to explain problem drinking in successful people called the *self-handicapping model*.

It states that a successful person who wishes to maintain his reputation for competence and positive self-regard but who anticipates possible failure may drink so that if the anticipated failure should occur it will not have been his fault. After all, what can be expected from a man who happened to drink too much? However, if success rather than failure occurs, then people will say, "What an extraordinary person—he pulled that off half-looped." So the drinking sets up a win-win situation. Unfortunately, the potential for a vicious cycle in this scenario is not hard to imagine; failure becomes more likely as of previous self-handicapping leads to more self-handicapping by drinking and what started as a "game" can easily end in addiction. (According to Berglas, women do not self-handicap with alcohol since it "won't wash," although they self-handicap by other means, such as premenstrual syndrome [PMS]).

Literary critic Alfred Kazin (1976) has also written of alcoholism among the highly successful, pointing out that five of the seven American Nobel Prize winners in literature have been alcoholic. He relates the American writers' penchant for alcoholism to narcissistic conflict, pointing out the tension between the pursuit of success, the "bitch goddess," and the pursuit of aesthetic excellence.

Opponent process theory (Shipley, 1982; Solomon, 1977) states that any emotional arousal or hedonistic process (such as drinking for pleasure) will engender opposing affects, or an *opponent response*. It is sort of an action-reaction model. Further, opponent process theory postulates that in time the opponent response to the psychic event will become stronger and an opponent process will come to predominate. This model has been applied to many behaviors. In terms of alcoholism, it essentially says that with continued drinking, euphoria decreases and dysphoria (the opponent response) increases. Hangovers become whoppers and drinking to avoid withdrawal symptoms (the opponent process) replaces drinking for pleasure. The opponent process learning theory is a restatement of Rado's (1933) description of the addictive trap (see discussion in chapter 7) buttressed by a neurological-physiological account of the underlying process. According to its adherents, there is empirical support for opponent process theory. It is one more way of accounting for the vicious cycle that is alcoholism.

TRIDIMENSIONAL PERSONALITY THEORY

C. Robert Cloninger (1987a) has developed a theory of personality that postulates "three independently inherited dimensions of personality that reflect variation in underlying neurogenetic systems" (p. 410). These neurogenetic systems which involve neurological tracts in the brain that use differing neurotransmitters (the levels of which are genetically determined) to mediate synaptic transmission are postulated to mediate novel, appetive, and aversive stimuli. Although the three systems are independently inherited, they influence one another through negative feedback loops so that the level of one affects the significance of the inherited levels of the others. Cloninger does not suggest that personality is totally determined by genetically controlled neurotransmitter levels; on the contrary, he recognizes the influence of learning and environment on behavior and the expression of personality. Rather, his emphasis is on the inheritability of certain tendencies.

Cloninger's three dimensions are: *novelty seeking, harm avoidance, and reward dependence*. The relationship between these dimensions, their biological function, their behavioral manifestations, and their mediating neurotransmitters is summarized in Table 8.1 as is their relationship to drinking behavior.

Cloninger interprets the Oakland Growth Study (Jones, 1968) discussed in chapter 6 as demonstrating two types of prealcoholic personality, antisocial (type 2) and passive-dependent (oral, type 1), and goes on to cite other data supporting this hypothesis. In terms of his three-dimensions, *type 1*, milieu-limited alcoholics are characterized by low novelty-seeking, high harm avoidance, and high reward dependence, while *type 2*, male limited alcoholics are characterized by high novelty-seeking, low harm avoidance, and low reward dependence. (See chapter 5 for a more detailed discussion of type 1 and type 2 alcoholics.) The neurotransmitters thought to be responsible for these characteristics are identified in Table 8.1.

In a 1988 study, Cloninger and his colleagues hypothesized that this same tridimensional structure of personality would be found in children. They devised measuring instruments that operationalized these dimensions and their presumed relationship to inherited levels of neurotransmitter activity and predicted that deviations from the mean on any of the dimensions would be correlated with (that is, they would predict) adult drinking problems. Using Swedish children who had been put up for adoption but not all of whom were actually adopted and whose ratings on the three personality scales were done by their teachers at age 11, Cloninger et al. found strong correlations on all three scales between deviation from the mean and development of alcohol problems, as manifested in public records of social difficulties and treatment for alcohol problems or both by age 27. The risk for alcoholism was *exponentially*, not linearly, related to deviation from the mean on the three variables. Those severely high in novelty seeking and severely low in harm avoidance were at the greatest risk of alcoholism. Statistical analysis confirmed the existence of the two types of alcoholism and the model proved to have predictive value, although the level of predictability was low. Cloninger attributes this result to the only 50% inheritability of these traits and to small sample size and low

Table 8.1 Cloninger's Tridimensional Model

Dimension	Biological function	Behavioral manifestations	Relation to drinking
Novelty seeking	Behavioral activation	Impulsivity, exploration, curiosity, fickleness, excitability, quick temper, extravagence, disorderliness, and distractability	High novelty seeking is correlated wi... alcohol-seeking behavior, both of wh... are correlated with high levels of dopamine
		Mediating neurotransmitter—dopamine (high)	
Harm avoidance	Behavioral inhibition	Caution, fearfulness, inhibition, shyness, pessimism, fatigability, and apprehensive worry	High harm avoidance is correlated with low alcohol-seeking behavior but with accelerated development of tolerance for and psychological dependence on alcohol, all of which are correlated with levels of serotonin. (High levels of serotonin decrease dopamine activity levels.)
		Mediating neurotransmitter—serotonin (high)	
Reward dependence	Behavioral maintenance	Sentimentality, sensitivity to social cues, helpfulness to others, "people-pleasing," sympatheticness, industriousness, and persistence	High reward dependence is correlated with separation anxiety and vulnerability to abandonment depression and greater release of norepinephrine upon drinking, both of which are correlated with low basal noradrenergic (norepinephrine) activity levels. Norepinephrine circuits are involved in tolerance to the sedating effects of ETOH.
		Mediating neurotransmitter—norepinephrine (low)	

rate of alcoholism in the sample, rather than to a flaw in the model. He suggests that risk for alcoholism is a continuous rather than a dichotomous variable so that studies set up as high risk-low risk analyses are inadequate.

Cloninger's model is intriguing. Unlike the serotonin deficiency hypothesis that was discussed in chapter 6, which was derived primarily from findings of low platelet MAO levels in high-risk children of alcoholics and which is unifactorial and hard to interpret because low platelet MAO is associated with a wide variety of psychopathologies, the tridimensional theory is sophisticated, multifactorial, and closely linked to drinking behaviors. However, its low predictability, with the exception of the high novelty seeking/low harm avoidance cluster, precludes its acceptance as an explanation of alcoholism. At best it suggests some behavioral and neurochemical antecedents, which interact with social, cultural, cognitive, and psychodynamic factors to eventuate in alcoholism. In fairness to Cloninger, he knows this and he deserves credit for conceptualizing the most encompassing neurochemical model we have of the antecedent risks for alcoholism.

STAGE THEORY

It has become clear during the past decade that talking about addiction and recovery as simple processes does violence to what is actually an extremely complex progression in which people first become addicted and then "decide," if that is the right word, to change their behavior and enter recovery. The realization that people do not just change one day but that fairly predictable sequence of events precedes "hitting bottom" (as AA would put it) has definite treatment implications. The stages-of-change literature grew out of the longitudinal studies of the development and antecedents of adolescent problem behavior by theorists like Jessor (1987), whose work was discussed in chapter 4. Working in the same tradition, Kandel (1975, Kandel, Yamaguchi, and Chen, 1992) traced the development of adolescent drug use and showed that cigarette smoking and beer drinking preceded the use of marijuana, which in turn preceded heroin and cocaine use. Cigarette smoking best predicted illegal drug use in girls and alcohol consumption in boys. Kandel's data seem to affirm the "reefer madness" approach of the U.S. Department of Narcotics in the 1940s and 1950s, which taught that pot smoking ineluctably led to drug addiction. Kandel's data, don't explicitly demonstrate that, of course, but the correlation is there. What Kandel showed was that the use of "gateway" drugs precedes use of "hard" drugs, which does *not* mean that all, or even a large percentage, of gateway drug users go on to hard drugs. The earlier the children smoked and/or drank, the greater was the likelihood that they would go on to illegal drug use. Parental smoking, drinking, and drug use were highly correlated with those behaviors in their children, again demonstrating the saliency of modeling. Interestingly, Kandel found that the highest correlation of adolescent smoking was with maternal smoking, which suggested to Kandel that a prenatal effect might be present.

The stages-of-change literature evolved out of these developmental, epidemiological studies. The pioneering works were by Prochaska, DiClemente, and Norcross (1992) and Prochaska and DiClemente (1984). They conceptualized change as taking place in five stages: *precontemplation, contemplation, preparation, action,* and *maintenance.* In the first stage, the pleasurable effects of using the drug predominate and the user or drinker does not even entertain the thought of quitting. Why should he or she? After all, he is not crazy and his use is a source of pleasure without pain, or at least any pain experienced is tolerable and nonconsequential. Expectancies play a role here. Thus, if hangovers are accepted as "part of the game" and are experienced as honorific their onset will not lead to change.

In the next stage, contemplation, the aversive consequences have become too insistent to be completely ignored and discounted and the thought of stopping or at least cutting back is now allowed to enter into consciousness. Although no action is yet actually contemplated, it is at least a cognitive possibility. Retaining clients in the pre-contemplative stage is extremely difficult. Most of the time they are enjoying their drinking and not considering stopping or changing it. The best the clinician can do is to recognize where the client is and not get into a power struggle.

In the contemplative stage, the pleasure-pain ratio has changed, perhaps even reversed, and the client is seriously considering behavioral change (that is, ceasing to drink or drug); however, there is intense ambivalence. The pleasures of use are still highly salient and the client, although willing to consider change, is not yet ready to actually change. The counselor must acknowledge and reflect back the client's ambivalence and minimize his or her (countertransferential) frustration and rage by understanding where the client is at.

In the preparation stage, the client actually considers a concrete plan of action but does not yet carry it out. Then, finally the action stage is reached and change occurs. Unlike the AA model, which tends to envision "hitting bottom" and "surrender" as sudden moments of illumination, the stages of change model sees a long developmental process preceding eventual action. Even AA founder Bill Wilson makes a distinction between Damascus conversion experiences (an allusion to St. Paul's illumination on the road to Damascus), which are sudden moments of insight, and educational conversion experiences which are gradual and culminative. Wilson, who took the distinction between these experiences from William James's *Varieties of Religious Experience* (1902), suggested that sobriety could come about either way. Prochaska and DiClemente stressed that the action stage involves more than stopping drug use or drinking and that action must include changes that will help maintain sobriety such as a change in peer group or in attitude and expectancies or both. The change process ends in the *maintenance stage*, where the emphasis is on relapse prevention.

Although I have alluded to counselor interventions in the various stages, Prochaska and DiClemente recognized that many alcoholics go through the stages of change without professional contact or treatment. They also point out that *recycling*, with its return to earlier stages, is more common than linear progress and usually occurs before action is taken and the maintenance stage is reached.

Prochaska and his colleagues also have formulated a mathematical model in which perceived pleasure in the use of the drug (such as alcohol) is graphed against time, and so are the perceived aversive consequences of drug use. At the point where the two lines intersect, action will occur. This model is illustrated in Figure 8.1. As neat and compelling as this theory is, it is a little too rationalistic for my taste. I am not so sure that people work so clearly in terms of pleasure-pain evaluation, that they use what the 18th century utilitarian philosopher Jeremy Bentham (1789/ 1939) called a *felicity calculus*. I have the same reservation about such models as Berglas's (1985) self-handicapping hypothesis of problem drinking by the successful. I doubt that people are that deliberate and I wonder if some sort of factor or force beyond the felicity calculus, such as Freud's (1920) innate self-destructive drive, isn't necessary to account for human, including addictive, behavior. Somehow the unconscious and the self-destructive must be given their place in the sun, or should I say in the darkness. Be that as it may, the Prochaska-DiClemente stages-of-change model does provide us with some conceptual tools for moving away from black-and-white dichotomous thinking to multidimensional process think-

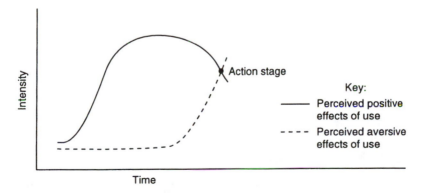

Figure 8.1 Prochaska-DiClemente Stages-of-Change Model.

ing about addiction and recovery, which has the nontrivial advantage of being more congruent with reality. As noted above, the model has numerous clinical implications.

Howard Shaffer (1992, 1994) elaborated and fine-tuned the stages of change model. Shaffer's *Stage 1: the emergence of addiction* has three phases: (a) *Initiation: beginning drug use* (he points out that you can't get addicted unless you start, but that the vast majority of initiators do not become addicted); (b) *The substance use produces positive consequences*, which may be pharmacological, psychological, or social; and (c) *Adverse consequences develop but remain out of awareness* [as he says, "Addictive behaviors serve while they destroy" (p. 324)].

His *Stage 2: the evaluation of quitting* also has three phases: (a) *Turning points*, in which the user first realizes the connection between use and abuse and profound negative consequences, although this may not lead to any immediate action but rather will begin a dynamic process that may eventuate in action; (b) *Active quitting begins* either by tapered quitting or cold turkey quitting as the end result of the dynamic process begun by the turning points; and (c) *Relapse prevention*. Shaffer stresses the clinical utility of his model especially in reducing countertransferential hate induced by client ambivalence and denial. *Countertransference* has two meanings: in the narrow, technical sense it refers to the counselor's unconscious projection of archaic object relations onto the client (see the earlier discussion of transference); and in the more contemporary usage it refers to all of the counselor's feelings toward the client regardless of their source. I use the term in the latter sense. But this brings us to treatment issues, which are the subject of the next chapter.

Part Three

Clinical

Chapter 9

Treatment Methods for Alcoholism

Treatment of alcoholism must be multifaceted because alcoholism is a *biopsychosocial* disorder. Treatment must be aimed at every known facet of the disease. Alcoholics and their particular alcoholisms have great commonality, but they are also unique; therefore, treatment must be aimed at both the commonality or universality of each alcoholic's alcoholism and the uniqueness or individuality of the way in which the disease affects the person seeking help. Treatment strategies can have medical, educational, psychological, and social components. Detoxification and treatment of alcohol-induced anemia are examples of medical components of a treatment plan. Lectures on the effect of alcohol on the brain and nutritional counseling are examples of educational components. Group therapy and individual counseling are psychological components. Use of a structured or semistructured environment (such as, a halfway house) and participation in a self-help program are social components. Self-help groups work in complex ways and are both psychological and social modalities of treatment.

Treatment can be conceptualized as tripartite: treatment of the active alcoholic, treatment of the early-sobriety alcoholic, and treatment of the stably sober alcoholic. Alcoholism counselors usually handle the first two parts. Since this book is written for counselors and counseling students, its emphasis is on psychological treatment methods, or interventions. The word *intervention* is used in two senses. A *psychological intervention* is an action taken by a counselor or therapist does in the course of treatment (for instance, confronting an alcoholic about his or her alcoholism). Psychological intervention refers both to individual events—the particular things said by the counselor—and to categories or types of interventions. "Your blacking out last night is a symptom of alcoholism" is an intervention. It is both *confrontational* and *educational*. Other categories of psychological intervention are *clarification* ("Tell me more about that"); *labeling of affects* ("You are angry"); and *interpretation* ("Your drinking, whatever else it means, is an act of rebellion," "an identification with your father," or "a means of self punishment"). In alcoholism counseling, intervention also means a planned confrontation of an alcoholic about his or her alcoholism by family, friends, and sometimes an employer for the purpose of getting the alcoholic to enter a treatment program. Such an *alcoholism intervention* is usually arranged and managed by a professional interventionist who is likely to be an alcoholism counselor.

TREATMENT OF THE ACTIVE ALCOHOLIC

Psychological treatment of the active alcoholic has three principal components: *diagnosis, confrontation,* and *education*. Psychological treatment alone is often insufficient; medical, nutritional, and social treatment also may be needed. In any case, the first step is diagnosis. Diagnosis is sometimes obvious, as in the case of a man in delirium tremens who has cirrhosis and who was fired from his last three jobs for excessive drinking. Sometimes it is far from obvious, as in the case of the brain surgeon who drinks four martinis and a bottle of wine each night but who is otherwise functional and healthy and seemingly relates satisfactorily to others. Alcoholics are diagnosed in many different ways by many different kinds of people. Alcoholics Anonymous says that alcoholism is a self-diagnosed disease, and in a sense it is: unless the alcoholic accepts the diagnosis, treatment is futile. Alcoholism is often diagnosed by spouses, other relatives, friends, employers, clergy, physicians or other professionals, or even by acquaintances long before self-diagnosis occurs. Alcoholism is "the disease that tells you that you don't have it," and denial is intrinsic to it— hence the need for diagnosis by others.

Although alcoholism counselors often deal with people who have already been diagnosed as alcoholic, they are also asked to evaluate, or *assess*, persons whose drinking behavior or the meaning of whose drinking behavior is unknown. Although structured interview techniques may be used, a careful and systematic history taking will elicit considerable information about a person's drinking behavior and its consequences. Such diverse behavior and objective signs as Monday morning absences from work, morning shakes, blackouts, interpersonal conflicts, *spider angioma* (the characteristic patch of red lines seen on the faces of heavy drinkers), elevated liver enzymes, depression that does not remit with appropriate treatment, increasing and inexplicable fears, neglect of personal hygiene, and otherwise unexplained social withdrawal can be symptoms of alcoholism. Of course, they can also be symptoms of other disorders. What the counselor looks for is a pattern. The more symptoms a person shows, the more likely that alcoholism is present. A family history of alcoholism greatly increases its probability, and the closer the alcoholic relative, the greater the risk factor.

Building trust is important; clients who trust their counselors and patients who trust their therapists tell them their secrets, and in doing so they often tell themselves what they knew yet did not know—that they were drinking alcoholically.

Research on biological markers for alcoholism may eventually yield laboratory tests to diagnose some forms of alcoholism, perhaps before they become manifest, so that preventive measures can be taken. But for now, careful assessment by a physician, therapist, or counselor is necessary for diagnosis. Once the diagnosis is made, treatment follows. Since alcoholism entails the ingestion of a highly toxic substance over an extended period of time, a comprehensive medical examination is always in order. A medical examination will indicate whether detoxification is necessary. If so, the physician must decide whether it is best accomplished on an outpatient or an inpatient basis. This should *always* be a medical decision and should never be made by a nonmedical counselor or therapist.

DETOXIFICATION

Detoxification is the medical management of withdrawal from a depressant drug with the fewest possible adverse consequences. It is not in itself a treatment for alcoholism. Detoxification can be accomplished in many different ways, but, as noted in chapter 3, all involve the substitution of another sedative-hypnotic drug for alcohol and then gradual reduction of the dosage of the substituted drug to zero. This is done over a period ranging from three to ten days, with four or five being the usual.

Detoxification can be accomplished on an outpatient or inpatient basis. Many people can withdraw from alcohol without medication; they are uncomfortable but not in danger. Getting over a bad hangover, is a familiar example of nonmedical withdrawal, although a hangover results from alcohol's toxicity as well as its withdrawal. Some people can be safely detoxified with medication and social support; others require the facilities of a hospital.

Librium is the drug most commonly used for detoxification. Pentobarbital, paraldehyde, and other sedative-hypnotic drugs also are used. In addition to Librium, patients are sometimes given anticonvulsive agents such as Dilantin, shots of vitamin B_{12}, other nutritional supplements, and sleeping medicines such as Chloral Hydrate. Librium is an anxiolytic, or antianxiety, drug. Librium has addictive potential and should not be prescribed for alcoholics after they have withdrawn. The same is true for other minor tranquilizers such as Valium, Miltown, and Xanax. Cross-addiction between alcohol and antianxiety drugs is common.

The medical and psychiatric complications of alcoholism are often diagnosed during inpatient detoxification and their treatment is then begun. Depression is often caused by alcoholism, and it should not be treated psychopharmacologically until the alcohol has been cleared from the alcoholic's mind and body. Depression usually remits with abstinence. As soon as the patient is well enough, education about alcoholism should be initiated. At the same time, the detoxifying patient's denial should be empathically confronted, and a plan to sustain recovery should be worked out with the patient. If possible, exposure to AA should be arranged. Even if the patient decides not to affiliate with the "program," acquaintance with it gives the patient an important option. Social support is important during detoxification, and reassurance is certainly indicated especially for someone experiencing severe withdrawal symptoms. Patients experiencing DTs may need to be restrained to prevent injury to themselves or others.

Outpatient detoxification is best for a patient whose alcoholism is not too severe and who has an intact support system. Inpatient detoxification is indicated if the patient has been drinking heavily, especially if for a long time. If the patient is known to have medical complications or is otherwise debilitated, inpatient detoxification is clearly best. An alcoholic with a history of seizures or DTs should be hospitalized. Another factor in favor of hospitalization is its provision of external control. This is sometimes necessary to get a patient to stop drinking. While the alcoholic is an inpatient, he or she cannot drink, and thereby time is bought in which to initiate a recovery program; this time can be used for therapeutic interventions.

USE OF ANTABUSE AND NALTREXONE

Antabuse is the trade name of the drug *disulfiram*. Disulfiram blocks the conversion of acetaldehyde into acetate (see discussion in chapter 1), and the blood level of acetaldehyde, the highly toxic first metabolite of alcohol, rises. This quickly makes the drinker acutely, and possibly seriously, ill. Although there can be side effects with Antabuse, they are unusual and in most cases, the alcoholic on Antabuse feels no effect of the drug unless he or she drinks. Nevertheless, disulfiram use must be carefully monitored. It inhibits a variety of enzymes including dopamine beta-hydroxylase, possibly resulting in increased dopamine activity which can precipitate a psychotic episode. There are many medical and psychiatric conditions in which disulfiram is counterindicated. The intensity of the Antabuse-alcohol reaction depends on the dosages of both, but even minute amounts of alcohol will make the drinker taking Antabuse ill. Reactions include sweating, dizziness, feelings of impending doom, chest pain, vomiting, shortness of breath, and falling blood pressure. If the Antabuse level is high enough, severe cardiovascular symptoms and even death may ensue. Doses lower than those prescribed in the past are now used, and dangerous reactions are thus much less common.

Alcoholics put on Antabuse are thoroughly instructed on the alcohol-Antabuse reaction and told to take their medicine each morning. Sometimes the Antabuse is administered by a nurse or other health care worker in a facility such as a halfway house. Other times it is self-administered, usually by an alcoholic who is motivated to become abstinent but who fears his or her lack of impulse control. If the alcoholic wishes to resume drinking, he or she must go off Antabuse and wait three to seven days, depending on the dosage, before he or she can drink without becoming ill. This prevents impulse-driven lapses of abstinence. The success rate of Antabuse therapy is unknown. A recent NIAAA (1988) study showed that patients on Antabuse did no better than a control group, but like all such studies, this does not indicate which alcoholics in the sample benefited or how to select those most likely to benefit from the treatment. Obviously, patients on Antabuse can plan slips and stop taking their medicine and some do. For others it serves as an external control until internal ones can be established. It would seem to be a treatment of choice for the medically intact drinker who is motivated to stop but who has, or fears, poor impulse control. Since Antabuse is usually used with patients who have been unable to achieve stable sobriety any other way, it is not to be expected that the success rate will be high. Patients usually stay on Antabuse for six months to a year, and some use it during times of stress even after years of sobriety.

Antabuse therapy should not be used alone; it should be an adjunct to counseling and to participation in a self-help program. The counselor needs to explore with the patient the meaning of taking the drug. Is the drug experienced as an impingement or violation; as a self-protective action, like securing a safety belt in a car; as a magical talisman, a security blanket that is not part of the self; as an internal punitive, withholding parent; or as an internal loving, limit-setting parent? Both sides of the alcoholic's ambivalence toward Antabuse need to be uncovered. The decision to take Antabuse may be as important as its actual ingestion; it constitutes a considerable commitment on the part of the drinker.

Naltrexone, an opiate antagonist that blocks highs, has long been used in the treatment of heroin addiction. More recently, it has been adapted to the treatment of alcoholism. Early results have been promising, suggesting that Naltrexone, which is said to reduce cravings, is a useful adjunctive treatment as one component of a comprehensive rehabilitation plan for alcoholics.

ABSTINENCE VERSUS CONTROLLED DRINKING AS A TREATMENT GOAL

The longer an alcoholic has been drinking, the less likely it is that he or she can return to social drinking. Many alcoholics have never been normal social drinkers. Few people are able to move from problem drinking of any duration and severity to normal social drinking. The goal of therapy with the vast majority of alcoholics must therefore be abstinence. There are some exceptions. Total abstinence is not a realistic goal with some adolescent substance abusers, who are not necessarily prealcoholic, nor is it a realistic goal with some late middle-aged alcoholics who have been abusing alcohol for many years but who have reached a relatively stable intrapsychic and interpersonal adjustment and whose relationship to alcohol is also relatively stable. Abstinence remains the treatment of choice with these patients too. If abstinence proves to be untenable, then helping the adolescent deal with developmental issues or helping the aging drinker minimize binges and express feelings, especially rage, in a more adaptive way may be the best that can be done. These are exceptions, however; complete abstinence must be the treatment goal with the overwhelming majority of active alcoholics.

Some behavioral psychologists (Sobell & Sobell, 1978; Marlatt & Gordon, 1985) disagree with this, opting instead to attempt to recondition their clients to drink normally by using a variety of classical conditioning, instrumental conditioning, social learning, and cognitive-behavioral techniques. The research evidence does not support the use of this approach, except with a few carefully selected patients. The problem is that we do not know how to predict reliably which alcoholics can be successfully treated with these methods. Problem drinkers who may not be alcoholic are better candidates for behavioral treatments with controlled drinking as their goal. (See Levin, 1991, for a discussion of problem drinking as distinguished from alcoholism.) The Sobells (1993) have now made a clear distinction between alcoholics and problem drinkers. In their view, 5% of the adult population is alcoholic (severely dependent on alcohol), while

20% of the population are problem drinkers. Citing the survey research findings that alcohol problems come and go (see chapter 4), they deny that alcohol problems are progressive and have devised a social psychological-cognitive behavioral treatment for problem drinking, which they call a "self-management approach." This approach uses self-monitoring forms, behavioral logs, and homework assignments.

Risk Management, also known as *least harm* theory, holds that any treatment that reduces the harm addicts, including alcoholics, do to themselves is worth doing. From this point of view, convincing intravenous cocaine users to smoke crack would be seen as a positive outcome. Although this paradigm is usually applied to multiaddicted populations, there are alcoholism specialists who view reducing the client's intake as a highly worthwhile goal. The therapeutic goal of controlling drinking can be seen as a form of risk management treatment.

Some behavioral therapists use various forms of *aversive conditioning*, in which drinking is paired with punishment in a classical conditioning paradigm, with the goal of abstinence. The research evidence is not conclusive on the efficacy of aversive conditioning in treating alcoholism, but it clearly takes extraordinarily motivated patients to subject themselves to this treatment.

Some psychoanalysts believe that an alcoholic should be able to drink normally after a successful analysis. It is now known that there are both innate biological factors, at least in some cases of alcoholism, and acquired biological factors, such as changes in brain chemistry, that mitigate against such an outcome, and that analysis will not change either. Besides, it is amazing how unimportant, or even undesirable, drinking becomes to most successfully rehabilitated alcoholics.

What about the alcoholic for whom alcohol meets vital psychological needs and who does not do well in sobriety? It is the purpose of psychological treatment, including counseling, to change this state of affairs, and it usually does. Very few alcoholics are worse off when they are sober, and those who are tend to be near-psychotic or overtly psychotic drinkers who need psychotropic medication to do what they hoped alcohol would do. With these exceptions, if the counselor helps the alcoholic mourn the loss of alcohol and find alternative and more adaptive means of satisfying emotional needs, the alcoholic will not feel worse when sober. Quite the contrary, overcoming an addiction increases self-esteem and inevitably raises the recovering alcoholic's level of functioning. If depression persists after several months of sobriety, the answer is not to return to drinking (although the alcoholic usually thinks so), but instead the depression must be treated psychologically, psychopharmacologically, or both. In these cases depression is not caused by drinking and must itself be treated before the alcoholic can enjoy sobriety.

Chapter 10

A Theoretical Model
and Case Study

This chapter presents my own (Levin, 1987) model of the psychodynamic correlative of alcoholism, and of addiction in general, as a regression or fixation to *pathological narcissism* in a special sense. Drawing on the work of Heinz Kohut (1971, 1977a, 1977b) on the development of the self and its pathological vicissitudes, I define pathological narcissism as regression or fixation to Kohut's stage of the archaic nuclear self. The model may at first seem overly abstract and remote from the concerns of the counselor, but when you have given it a little thought, it will make a lot of sense to connect the internal psychological and emotional consequences of developmental difficulties with adult vulnerability to addiction. You will also see the model as quite practical when I spell out its clinical implications following the case example. So don't let Kohut's often forbidding terminology throw you. Kohut's ideas are also discussed in Chapter 7 and you may find it worthwhile to review that section before proceeding in this one.

Since the model speaks of regression or fixation it is not necessarily etiological; rather, it is descriptive of the alcoholic's inner world. For those alcoholics who are fixated at (have never grown beyond) the stage of the archaic self, their pathological narcissism is one of the causes of their alcohol addition; for them the model is etiological. For those who have regressed in the course of their drinking to the stage of the archaic self, their pathological narcissism is a consequence of their addition. In either case the alcoholism counselor has to deal with clients who lack a healthy, mature self. Since this presentation combines theory with a case and with treatment recommendations, it could just as well have gone in the treatment chapter, but since it is a psychoanalytic conceptualization, I decided to place it here.

Kohut sees narcissistic disturbance as central to the psychopathology of the addict. The core difficult of narcissistic personalities is the absence of internal structure; that is, there are deficits in the self's capacities for tension regulation, self-soothing, and self-esteem regulation. The alcoholic's pathological drinking is an attempt to make up for this missing structure; that is, the drinking serves to reduce tension and regulate self-esteem in the absence of adequate intrapsychic resources to achieve such regulation. Thus, in early sobriety these deficits in the structure of the self, with their concomitant psychological dysfunctions, will continue to disable the alcoholic until psychic structure can be built.

THE SELF

Kohut defines the self as a unit cohesive in space and enduring in time, a center of initiative and a recipient of impressions. It can be regarded either as a mental structure superordinate to the agencies of the mind (the id, ego, and superego) or as a content of those agencies. Although Kohut believed that these two conceptualizations were complementary rather than mutually exclusive, in his later work he emphasized the self as a central or superordinate principle. It is, so to speak, the organized and organizing center of human experience and is itself experienced as cohesive and enduring. How does this sense of a self that coheres in space and endures in time develop? According to Kohut, the infant develops a primitive (fragmented) sense of self very early. That is, each body part, each sensation, each mental content is experienced as belonging to a self, to me, as mine; however, there is no synthesis of these experiences as yet. There are selves, but no unitary self. Nor are there clear boundaries between self and world. Kohut designates this the stage of the *fragmented self*; it is the developmental stage at which psychotic persons are fixated or to which they regress. Although there are important differences, Kohut's stage of the fragmented self corresponds to Freud's stage of autoeroticism; it is another way of understanding the stage of human development that precedes the integration of the infant's experienced world.

At the next stage of development, an *archaic nuclear self* arises from the infant's experience of being related to as a self, rather than as a collection of parts and sensations, by empathic caretakers. This self is cohesive and enduring, but it is not yet securely established. Hence, it is prone to *regressive fragmentation*. It is nuclear in the sense of having a center, or nucleus, and it is archaic in the sense of being a primitive (that is, grandiose and undifferentiated) precursor of the mature self. The archaic nuclear self is bipolar in that it comprises two structures: the *grandiose self* and the idealized *self-object*. The grandiose self is a differentiated self that is experienced as omnipotent, but there are no truly differentiated objects. Objects are still experienced as extensions of the self, as self-objects. At this stage, the child's grandiose self attempts to exercise omnipotent control of his self-objects, including the people who care for him. In healthy maturity, all loved objects have a self-object aspect. However, in maturity the experience of the object as a self-object is a reversible regression in the service of the ego that lacks the rigidity that characterizes the experience of objects as self-objects in pathological narcissism.

The internalization of psychic structure (albeit in rudimentary form) is codeterminous with the formation of the nuclear self. As Kohut (1977a) put it, "The rudiments of the nuclear self are laid down by simultaneously or consecutively occurring processes of selective inclusion and exclusion of psychological structure" (p. 183). Failure to adequately internalize functions originally performed for the child by self-objects results in deficits in the self. Addiction is a futile attempt to compensate for this failure in internalization.

To paraphrase Kohut: it is the inner emptiness, the missing parts of the self experienced as a void, that addicts try to fill with food, with alcohol, with drugs, or with compulsive sexuality. It cannot be done. Whatever is compulsively taken in goes right through and no psychic structure is built; that can only be done by internalization of relationships. It is abysmally low self-esteem, doubts about being real or of existing at all, and terror of fragmentation that addicts, including alcohol addicts, try to remediate by their addictions. They always fail.

PATHOLOGICAL NARCISSISM

Pathological narcissism is the regression or fixation to the stage of the archaic self. It is characterized by the presence of a cohesive, but insecure, self that is threatened by regressive fragmentation; grandiosity of less than psychotic proportions, which manifests itself in the form of arrogance, isolation, and unrealistic goals; feelings of entitlement; the need for omnipotent control; poor differentiation of self and object; and deficits in the self-regulating capacities of the ego. Further, affect tolerance is poor. The tenuousness of the cohesion of the self makes the narcissistically regressed individual subject to massive anxiety, which is in reality fear of annihilation (that is, fear of fragmentation of the self). Narcissistic personality disorders are also subject to *empty depression*, which reflects the relative emptiness of the self, or the paucity of psychic structure and good internal objects. In the condition of pathological narcissism, these manifestations of the grandiose self or the idealized self-object or both may be either blatantly apparent or deeply repressed or denied, with a resulting facade of *pseudo-self-sufficiency*, but they are never smoothly integrated into a mature self, as they are in healthy narcissism.

In Kohut's formulation, the overtly grandiose self is the result of merger with (or lack of differentiation from) a mother who used the child to gratify her own narcissistic needs. It is a *false self* in the terminology of Winnicott (1960). Kohut envisions this false self as insulated by a vertical split in the personality. The reality ego is in turn impoverished as a result of the repression of the unfulfilled archaic narcissistic demands by a horizontal split (repression barrier) in the personality (see Figure 10.1). For our purposes, the salient point to be derived from Kohut's and Winnicott's theories is an understanding of the overt grandiosity of the alcoholic as a manifestation of a "false self," which is isolated, both affectively and cognitively, from the more mature reality ego, which is itself enfeebled by its inability to integrate the archaic self. Hence, some sense can be made of the coexistence of haughty arrogance and near-zero self-esteem so frequently seen in alcoholics.

Regression or fixation to the stage of the archaic nuclear self makes sense of and gives a coherent account of the empirically determined psy-

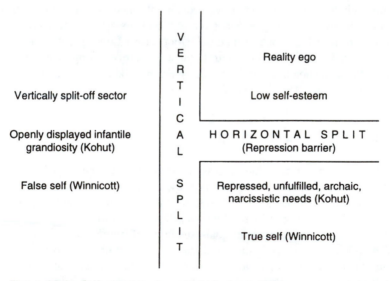

Figure 10.1 Self structure in pathological narcissism.

chological correlatives of alcoholism discussed in chapter 6 (elevated Pd, field dependency, ego weakness, and stimulus augmentation). It also integrates such competing psychodynamic theories as the dependency conflict model, the need-for-power model, and the epistemological error model (see chapters 7 and 8), all of which can be reformulated in terms of characteristics of the archaic nuclear self. The theory has the additional virtue of applying, as few other theories do, to both male and female alcoholism.

It is of some interest to note that the AA literature sees the attitudinal component of alcoholism ("Alcoholism is a disease of the attitudes") as pathological narcissism. Bill Wilson quotes Freud's phrase "His [or her] Majesty the Baby" from Freud's essay *On Narcissism* (1914), which Wilson learned from his psychiatrist Henry Tiebout. AA addresses this issue in a cognitive, didactic way in its slogans, "Alcoholism is self-will run wild"; "Get out of the driver's seat"; and "Let go and let God." It is also noteworthy that both narcissism and narcotic have the same Greek root, *narke*, which means to *deaden*, so pathological narcissism deadens, while healthy narcissism vivifies.

Alcoholics as a group have received exceedingly bad press and I do not wish to add to the popular notion of alcoholics as self-centered SOBs, although active addiction is necessarily self-centered. The DSM-III-R definition of narcissistic personality disorder stresses emotional shallowness, exploitiveness, and feelings of entitlement. Kernberg (1975) sees pathological narcissism similarly (see chapter 7). Although these traits frequently characterize the clinical alcoholic personality, they are at least partly consequences of the alcoholism. To suggest that the majority of alcoholics are DSM-III-R narcissistic personality disorders is contrary to fact, and narcissistic conflicts and difficulties are intrinsic to the human condition; nevertheless, it is my observation, which has much research support, that alcoholics suffer particularly acute forms of narcissistic difficulties and narcissistic deficits. My application of Kohut's formulation seems to account for the research and clinical data (see chapter 6).

THE THEORY AND THE "FACTS"

Elevation in the *Psychopathic deviate* (Pd) scale of the Minnesota Multiphasic Personality Inventory (MMPI) in both active and recovering alcoholics is the most consistent finding in the literature on the alcoholic personality and can be understood as a manifestation of the overtly grandiose self, with its arrogance, isolation, and lack of realistic goals. The elevation of the Depression (D) scale on the MMPI, which is also a consistent finding in advanced active alcoholism and early recovery, reflects both the psychopharmacological consequences of active alcoholism (depletion of available catecholamines) and the impoverishment of the self, riddled with structural deficits and impaired in its capacity for self-esteem regulation, that is found in pathological narcissism.

Developmentally, the depression reflects the disappointment that results from inadequate phase-appropriate *mirroring*, or approving confirmation, of the child's grandiose self by self-objects. Additionally, active alcoholism gives one much to be realistically depressed about. Empirical findings, using adjective checklists and self-reports, of impoverishment of the self can be understood in the same way. The structurally deficient self of pathological narcissism is experienced as an empty depression, and it is reported as lack of interest in people, activities, and goals. Even the self is uninteresting to itself. The regression to pathological narcissism that is concomitant with the alcoholic process progressively strips the already enfeebled ego of its investments in objects and activities, leaving an empty self, an empty world, and an empty bottle.

Another consistent finding in alcoholics is *field dependence* (see discussion in chapter 6). Field dependence entails a relative inability to utilize internal resources, as well as impairments in the differentiations of body image, of figure and ground, and of self and world. By definition, the field-dependent person experiences the environment as a self-object—which is precisely the way in which the person who has fixated or regressed to pathological narcissism experiences the world. My hypothesis accounts well for this datum.

Confused gender identity is a frequent finding in alcoholic populations. This confusion also can be understood in terms of pathological narcissism. (Conflict over sex roles, a related finding, has both sociological and psychological determinants.) Developmentally, the archaic self arises before the establishment of firm gender identity. Hence, regression or fixation to the stage of the archaic self entails a blurring of gender identity. The failure to adequately internalize (identify with) the ideal self-object of the same sex, which is postulated as etiological in person's vulnerable to pathological narcissism, renders difficult the establishment of a firm gender identity. The early psychoanalytic findings of latent homosexuality in male alcoholics may also reflect failure to internalize ideal self-objects, although these findings are expressed in terms of libido theory and the psychosexual stages.

Ego weakness is a construct that integrates several empirically confirmed characteristics of active and early-sobriety alcoholics: impulsivity, lack of frustration tolerance, lack of affect tolerance, and lack of differentiation of the self-concept. It overlaps many of the findings just discussed: confused gender identity, conflicts over sex roles, psychopathic deviancy, and impoverishment of the self. In terms of pathological narcissism, ego weakness in the alcoholic is understood as encompassing the structural deficits in the self. In other words, the failure to internalize by a process of selective and depersonified identification (which Kohut [1971] calls *transmuting internalization*) the functions of affect regulation once performed from the outside by the mother and other caretakers results in ego weakness. In the case of weak or incomplete internalization, the self is subject to regression to pathological narcissism, with its accompanying ego weakness.

Stimulus augmentation, which has been found to be characteristic of alcoholics and which contributes to their ego weakness, can also be understood in terms of pathological narcissism as a failure to internalize the mother's function as an auxiliary to the innate (biologically given) stimulus barrier. Although constitutional factors certainly play a role in the alcoholic's stimulus augmentation, failures in internalization and structuralization just as certainly play their role.

SALLY: A CASE STUDY

Sally came to me for treatment of a posttraumatic stress reaction. She had been in an automobile accident and was badly shaken. Her face had been scarred and she was deeply depressed. Plastic surgery later restored her face, leaving little evidence of the accident, but when she first came to my office she didn't know that that was going to happen. Sally was young and very appealing. She had been referred by her attorney, who had not mentioned alcohol, so I was surprised when she told me that she was an alcoholic. She said that she had been alcoholic since the age of 12 and had "hit bottom" four years ago. I asked her how old she was. She said, "Twenty-five." My next question was, "How did you get sober?" She replied, "The part about getting sober wouldn't make sense unless I told you about my drinking too: should I do that?" I said, "Sure."

> Well, I don't know where to start. I come from an alcoholic family. Both my parents died of alcoholism. Well, I think my father died of alcoholism; he deserted us when I was four. I remember the last time I saw him. We were eating in a diner and I spilled my food. He screamed at me and said I was disgusting. I always felt that he left because I was so disgusting. I feel like a pig; I'm a compulsive overeater, too. I know in my head that he didn't leave because of the way I ate, but I don't know it in my heart. I still believe it.
>
> Things got worse then. My mother drank more and more and we had very little money. Sometimes there was no toilet paper in the house, but there was always beer. Later we moved to my grandfather's. He was rich, but he grabbed my pussy sometimes and I didn't know what to do. I think he was senile, but he drank too, so maybe that was it. After I grew up, my mother told me she knew what he did to me, but she was afraid to do anything about it because he might have thrown us out. She was drunk when she told me that.

Why did she have to tell me? I hate her for letting it happen, and I hate her for telling me that she let it happen. How could a mother do that? I have a daughter. I'd cut off his balls, if a man did that to my daughter. How could she? My grandfather got more senile and I don't know exactly what happened after that.

My mother was like two people. When she was sober she was wonderful—beautiful and interested in me. But very snobby and up-tight. Then I didn't think she was a snob, I thought that she was a great lady—perfectly dressed and so elegant. I loved her so much. Then there was Mother when she was drunk. Sloppy and falling down, she'd sit with her legs spread with no panties and you could see everything. She'd curse and then try to play the great lady, "Oh, my dear," and all that shit. I hated her then.

I was around ten when I started having sex play with my cousins and some of the neighborhood kids. Mostly with the boys, but some-times with the girls too. Do you think I'm a lesbian? I loved sex—it felt so good and it made me feel good about myself. Somebody wanted me. Maybe I felt guilty underneath. Later I hated myself and maybe all that sex play had something to do with it. I was raised a strict Catholic, sort of. Once I was naked—I had just gotten out of the tub and I did an imitation of the Virgin Mary—I was about six—and my mother really whaled my ass with a ruler.

When I was about ten my mother met my stepfather. Eddy was a complete asshole. He drank all the time, too. Can you imagine marry-ing a fucking drunk like him? Then Mother really dropped me. She was more interested in drinking with Eddy. I started getting in trou-ble in school—at 11 I got fucked for the first time. And I mean got fucked, not made love to, by some 20-year-old pervert. Can you imagine an 11-year-old getting fucked? I loved it, or thought that I did. I hung out with all the older boys. They had cars and liquor and pot. I can't tell you how many cocks I had in me. Big ones, small ones, white ones, black ones. And you know I was never sober once. Every one of those guys had something to get high on—beer, pot, hard stuff. I loved pot from the first time I smoked it. It was even better than sex. And I drank a lot. Any boy or man who gave me something to get high on could have me. Sometimes I really liked it, but I liked fool-ing around with other girls even more. I think I was really turned on by myself when I played with the other girls. My mother and step-father raised hell when they weren't too drunk to care, and finally my mother had me put away. Can you imagine that? What kind of fucking mother would put a kid in the places she put me? For God's sake, one place had bars and I was locked in. I hate her for doing that. Mental hospitals, homes for delinquent girls, the House of the Good Shepherd, the whole ball of wax. Finally I got out—I wasn't actually in any of those places for very long, it's just the idea: how could you do that to a kid?—and I met Calvin.

What a bastard he was. Oh, I forgot to tell you that when I was 15 I was team banged by a gang who pulled me into an alley and fucked me until my thing was raw and bloody. They beat me real hard too, but not as hard as Calvin did later. Oh yeah, Calvin beat me all the time. I must have been crazy but I loved him. He took me away from my hometown and my mother didn't bother me anymore. He sort of made a prisoner out of me—if I even went to the grocery store without his permission he beat me. He had a big one, the biggest I ever saw and I had seen plenty, so I thought he was a great lover. He always had beer and weed and other stuff and I stayed high most of the time. He's the father of my child. When I went into labor he was stoned. He slapped me and called me a rotten whore. He wouldn't go to the hospital with me. Do you know what it's like for a 16-year-old kid to have a baby alone? Forget it.

I never cheated on Calvin but he never stopped accusing me of being with other men and hitting me. Sometimes he hit me with a wooden plank. I thought I deserved it—that I needed to be punished for all the things I had done. I needed Calvin to beat me. As long as he supplied drugs and alcohol and beat me, I would have stayed. It was the way he acted around the baby that made me leave. One day when he wasn't home and the baby was about two, I ran away. I couldn't stand his insane jealousy anymore; he was even jealous of the baby. A guy crazy enough to be jealous of his own kid, that's sick. He was real sick; sick in his head. I couldn't stand any more so I ran away and went to a town in the mountains where my older sisters and brother lived. Something in me said *enough*, you've been punished enough. Of course I kept on drinking. There wasn't any more sex, not then, just falling down drunk every day. I went on welfare and sometimes I worked off the books. I was sort of dead—no, not *sort of*, just plain *dead*. That went on for a few years and I hated myself more and more. I tried to be a good mother through it all and I don't think I did too badly, but God, was I depressed!

My stepfather was dead by then and my mother was far gone. I think I saw it in her before I saw it in me. My brother was in the Program—AA, that is. I thought he was a jerk, a real ass, an uptight loser. Who else would join those holy rollers? What I couldn't figure out was how such a raving asshole could be happy, and the damn jerk *was* happy. Even I could see that. He did something really smart; he didn't lecture me. In fact, he never even mentioned my drinking. Damn good thing he didn't, because the way I rebelled against everything and everybody I would never have listened. What he did do was tell me what had happened to him—ran his story, as they say in AA. I didn't want to hear that shit and I told him so, but I did hear it in spite of myself. I was getting worse; I was more and more terrified that Calvin would come back and kill me—I guess I thought that he should because of the way I was living, but I didn't know that then, I was just scared. I was getting sicker and sicker from all the drinking and I never had any money; it got to the point where I couldn't stand any more. If it wasn't for my daughter, I would have killed myself. I don't know why, but one day I asked my brother to take me to a meeting. An AA meeting, that is. I think it was the guilt; once I didn't have Calvin to beat me I couldn't stand the guilt. I *knew*, I mean I really knew what it's like to have alcoholic parents. I loved my daughter—she has such a sick fuck for a father, so I wanted her to have at least one parent with her head screwed on straight. So I went to that fucking meeting. I loved it—I mean, I *loved* it—like I never loved anything. For Christ's sake, I even identified with the coffee cups. When I do something I *do* it—I went all the way, the whole nine yards. I was sick—sick, sick, sick from my crotch to my toes, not to mention my head. I was so scared; I hadn't had a sober day in years, but I've made it one day at a time. I haven't made it any too swiftly. I still can't stand the guilt and the rage; you wouldn't believe how angry I get, and the crying. I cry all the fucking time, but I don't drink, I don't drug, and I don't care if my ass falls off, I'm not going to. At least not today.

I didn't want to be like my mother. I *won't* be like her. She's dead now. I couldn't stand it when she died; she died from her drinking. She had an accident while drunk; it was kind of a suicide. I knew she was dead, but I didn't know it. I couldn't let her go—not the awful way it was. If she was sober and I was sober, I could have let her die, but she wasn't, so I knew but I didn't know she was dead. I never accepted it; she couldn't forgive me dead, nor I her. Then one day I went to the cemetery. I looked at her grave for a long time. I couldn't believe she was dead. I started screaming, "Move the fucking grass, move the fucking grass, Mother." I screamed and screamed but she didn't move the fucking grass and I finally knew she was gone. I went to my home group meeting hysterical. All I said was she couldn't move the fucking grass, and I cried the rest of the meeting. Nobody said a word, they just let me be me; they didn't try to take away my pain, and I didn't want or need anybody to take it away. What I needed was somebody to be with me in that pain, and they were.

I love the fucking program and all the crazy screwed-up people there. They're like me; I'm crazy too, but I'm sober. For God's sake, can you imagine what it would have been like if I was drinking when she died? Thank God I wasn't. I hate her—I love her—I still can't let go of her although I know she's dead. I hate alcohol. I hate drinking; look what it did to her, to my father, to me. How did I get sober? I don't really know. I sort of had two bottoms: a beaten bottom and an alcohol bottom. In that first bottom, I sort of saw myself and saw I couldn't go on exposing my daughter to that stuff; the second was luck or something. No, not exactly luck or not only luck. I had something to do with willingness—I became willing to go to that meeting. Maybe I had just had enough; I didn't want any more pain for me or for the baby; she's not a baby anymore. They say, "Why me?" in the program. When you're drinking, you have the "poor me's," so you're always asking, "Why me?" If you recover, you say it differently. I don't know why me. The way I lived, I should be dead, but I'm not. I don't know if I deserve it or not, but I'll take it.

Sally is a very clear example of an attempted self cure of narcissistic deficit and narcissistic injury by substance abuse. All such attempts at self cure are futile, eventually leading to further narcissistic injury. This was true for Sally. Although alcohol and drugs turned out to be the wrong medicine, Sally had found another way to heal herself or start to heal herself before she came for therapy, and I largely stayed out of her way and was nonimpinging as she continued to heal herself. My relative inactivity allowed identification and transmuting internalization to take place. This led to structure building, firmer self cohesion, and greater ego strength. Most alcoholics and substance abusers do not have Sally's powerful drive for health and they require more active interventions on the part of the counselor.

PRACTICAL IMPLICATIONS OF THE MODEL

Self psychology has a number of powerful interventions to suggest for use in working with alcoholics. In their respective ways these interventions address what theory understands as narcissistic deficit and narcissistic injury and their attempted self-cure through drinking; the attempt to fill inner emptiness due to failures in transmuting internalization; the acting out of and turning against the self of narcissistic rage; *idealizing* and *mirror transferences* to alcohol (that is, experiencing alcohol as an ideal object or as a source of affirmation of one's grandiosity or both); attempts at omnipotent control through substance use and abuse; attempts to boost abysmally low self-esteem through the use of alcohol; and shame experiences that are both antecedents to and consequences of alcohol and drug abuse. The following 11 ways of translating theory into concrete interventions need to be modified so that each particular patient can hear them, but they are models of great utility in working with alcoholics.

Most of these interventions are addressed to "actives," those still drinking; yet their maximum effectiveness is with the "recovering," particularly those in early sobriety. By varying the tense from "you were" to "you are," they can be used with both groups. As you read, think how you might use them with Sally or with another person with whom you have worked.

1 This intervention addresses the narcissistic wound inflicted by not being able to drink "like other people." The admission that one is powerless over alcohol, as AA puts it, or that one can not drink without the possibility of losing control, as I would put it, is extremely painful. It is experienced as a defect in the self, which is intolerable for those who are as perfectionistic as alcoholics usually are. The self must not be so damaged and deficient. Additionally, to be able to "drink like a man" or "like a lady" may be a central component of the alcoholic's self-concept—his or her identity. This is particularly so for "macho" men, but is by no means restricted to them. The counselor must recognize and articulate the conflict between the client's wish to stop drinking and the client's feeling that to do so entails admitting that he or she is flawed in a fundamental way. The counselor does this by saying, "You don't so much want *to* drink as not want *not* to be able to drink." This intervention makes the client conscious of the conflict in an empathic way and allows him or her to struggle with this issue, and often opens the way for the patient to achieve a more comfortable stable sobriety.

2   All addictions, including alcoholism, are one long experience of narcissistic injury. Failure usually stalks the alcoholic like a shadow. As one of my patients put it, "When I drink, everything turns to shit." It sure does: career setbacks, job losses, rejection by loved ones, humiliations of various sorts, ill health, economic decline, accidental injury, and enduring bad luck are the all too frequent concomitants of alcoholism. Each negative experience is a narcissistic wound. Cumulatively they constitute one massive narcissistic wound. Even if outward blows have not yet come, the inner blows—self-hatred and low self-regard—are always there. The alcoholic has all too frequently heard "It's all your fault" in one guise or another. The counselor must empathize with the alcoholic's suffering. "Your disease has cost you so much," "You have lost so much," and "Your self-respect is gone" are some ways the counselor can make contact with the alcoholic's pain and facilitate his experiencing this pain instead of denying, acting out, or anesthetizing it.

3   Alcoholics feel empty. Either they have never had much good stuff inside or they have long ago flushed the good stuff out with alcohol. "You drink so much because you felt empty" makes the connection as well as brings into awareness the horrible experience of an inner void. After sobriety has been achieved, the historical (that is, childhood) determinants of the paucity of psychic structure that is experienced as emptiness can also be interpreted.

4   Alcoholics lack a firm sense of identity. How can you know who you are if your experience of self is tenuous and its partially unconscious inner representation lacks consistent cohesion? The counselor can comment on this and point out that being an alcoholic is at least something definite—having an identity of sorts. When an AA member says, "My name is _____ and I am an alcoholic," he or she is affirming that he or she exists and has at least one attribute. With sobriety many more attributes will accrue—the self will enrich and cohere. A way of conveying this to the client is to say, "You are confused and not quite sure who you are. That is partly because of your drinking. Acknowledging your alcoholism will lessen your confusion as to who you are and give you a base on which to build a firm and positive identity."

5 Many people drink because they cannot stand to be alone. They drink to enjoy someone's companionship. They have not developed what Winnicott (1958) calls the *capacity to be alone*. Winnicott thinks that this ability comes from the experience of being alone in the presence of another—from having been a small child in the presence of an empathic, nonimpinging other who one has internalized so that one is not really alone when one is by oneself. Being alone in this sense is very different from defensive isolation driven by fear. Presumably, those who drink for companionship have never acquired the capacity to be alone. This, too, should be interpreted. "You drink so much because you can't bear to be alone and drinking gives you the illusion of having company, of being with a friend. After you stop drinking, it will be important for us to discover why it is so painful for you to be alone."

6 Alcoholics form self-object (narcissistic) transferences to alcohol, as do other drug abusers to their drug of choice. Relating to alcohol as a friend can be regarded as forming a *twinship transference* (Kohut, 1977a) to alcohol. Alcoholics also form idealizing and mirror transferences to alcohol. The image of the archaic idealized parent is projected onto alcohol and it is regarded as an all-powerful, all-good object with which alcoholic drinkers merge in order to participate in this omnipotence. "Alcohol will deliver the goods and give me love, power, and whatever else I desire" is the drinker's unconscious fantasy. The counselor should interpret this thus: "Alcohol has felt like a good, wise, and powerful parent who protected you and made you feel wonderful, and that is why you have loved it so much. In reality, it is a depressant drug, not all the things you thought it was." The counselor can go on to say, "Now that drinking isn't working for you anymore, you are disillusioned, furious, and afraid. Let's talk about those feelings."

7 One of the reasons that alcoholics are so devoted to the consumption of alcohol is that it confirms their grandiosity—in other words, they form a mirror transference. I once had an alcoholic patient who told me that he felt thrilled when he read that a sixth Nobel prize was to be added to the original five. He read this while drinking in a bar at 8:00 a.m. His not-so-unconscious fantasy was to win all six.

The counselor should make the mirror transference conscious by interpreting it. "When you drink, you feel that you can do anything, be anything, achieve anything, and that feels wonderful. No wonder you don't want to give it up."

8 Alcoholics, without exception, have abysmally low self-esteem no matter how well-covered-over by bluster and bravado it may be. Self psychology understands this as an impoverishment of the reality ego that is a consequence of failure to integrate archaic grandiosity, which is instead split off by what Kohut (1971) calls the "vertical split" and which manifests itself as unrealistic reactive grandiosity. This low self-esteem persists well into sobriety. At some point the counselor needs to say, "You feel like shit, and that you are shit, and all your claims to greatness are ways to avoid knowing that you feel that way. You don't know it, but way down somewhere inside you feel genuinely special. We need to put you in touch with the real stuff so you don't need alcohol or illusions to help you believe that the phony stuff is real." The particular reasons, which are both antecedents to and consequences of the alcoholism, that the client values himself or herself so little, need to be elucidated and worked through.

9 Sometimes the client's crazy grandiosity is simultaneously a defense against and an acting out of the narcissistic cathexis of (that is, mental and emotional investment in) the client by a parent. In other words, the client is attempting to fulfill the parent's dreams in fantasy while making sure not to fulfill them in reality. This is especially likely to be the case if the client is an adult child of an alcoholic. Heavy drinking makes such a defense or acting out easy. If the recovering client's grandiosity does seem to be a response to being treated by either parent as an extension of themselves, the counselor can say, "One reason you feel so rotten about yourself is that you're always doing it for Mom or Dad and not for yourself. You resent this and spite them by undermining yourself by drinking."

10 Many alcoholics have a pathological need for *omnipotent control*. Alcohol is simultaneously experienced as an object they believe they can totally control and coerce into doing their will and as an object which they believe gives them total control of their subjective states and of the environment. This can be seen as a manifestation of their mirror and idealizing transferences to substances. Alcoholics frequently treat people, including the counselor, as extensions of themselves. The AA slogans, "Get out of the driver's seat" and "Let God and let go" are cognitive-behavioral ways of loosening the need to control. Counselors should interpret this need to control in the client's relationships to alcohol, in the client's relationship with other people, and in the client's relationship with the counselor—for example, "You think that when you drink, you can feel any way you wish," "You go into a rage and drink whenever your wife doesn't do as you wish," or "You thought of drinking because you were upset with me when I didn't respond as you thought I would."

11 Alcoholics and their children suffer greatly from shame experiences. Alcoholic clients are ashamed of having been shamed and often use alcohol to obliterate feelings of shame. Counselors need to help alcoholic clients experience rather than repress their feelings of shame now that they no longer anesthetize them. One way to do this is to identify feelings of shame that are not recognized as such. For example, "You felt so much shame when you realized that you were alcoholic that you kept on drinking so you wouldn't feel your shame."

Sally's story amply exemplifies the relationship between narcissistic deficit, narcissistic injury, and the futile attempt to remediate the former and heal the latter through the addictive use of substances—alcohol and food—and compulsive actions—sex and excitement. Sally suffered massive failures of internalization, leaving her with gaping structural deficits. She also felt dead, doubting both her aliveness and her existence, and sought out stimulation of any kind, even beatings, to feel alive. Lacking idealizable parents she found Calvin; having had little phase-appropriate mirroring of her archaic grandiosity, she found alcohol. In addition to mirroring her, alcohol gave her the illusion of cohesiveness. The amazing strength she did display may have been possible because her mother very early on was "good enough." Sally's capacity for splitting also helped her preserve a good mother from whom she could draw some sustenance in face of all the badness of her later, and by then overtly alcoholic, mother. Sally had not integrated the two mothers. Her "bad" mother became Sally's split-off grandiosity and denial. So split off from any kind of reality testing was this side of Sally's vertical split that her unassimilated grandiosity came very close to killing Sally. Sally's mother was not so fortunate, her mother's grandiosity did kill her.

On the other side of the vertical split, Sally's reality ego was impoverished, depressed, empty, fragile, and never far from fragmentation. The phase-appropriate grandiosity of the stage of the archaic nuclear self had never been integrated into her reality ego; it couldn't be because it had never been adequately mirrored. In Winnicott's (1960) terms, her true self was buried for safekeeping from a dangerous, treacherous environment. Whether this is understood in Kohut's or in Winnicott's terms, it is clear that her defensive system made survival possible, *and* that it was now an encumbrance, and that a major aim of treatment had to be its modification.

The child of an alcoholic carries a special kind of narcissistic injury. Humiliation and shame are recurrent and the wounds go deep. Sally's narcissistic injuries were denied, repressed, and acted out as was the narcissistic rage that is a natural reaction to these injuries. Sally's delinquency was an attempt at self-cure. As Winnicott says, when there is an antisocial tendency, there is hope. Sally found some kind of solace, responsiveness, and, in however distorted a form, mirroring in her acting out. It also allowed her to externalize her rage. However, what saved Sally was her ability to love and to seek love. She never gave up her search for good objects that she could idealize and internalize. Alcohol was one such object—one that traumatically failed her, but she didn't give up. Abandonment depression and abandonment rage were central to Sally's psychopathology, but they could be worked through in the transference, because she did transfer, because she was still searching for relationship. Her love for her baby, probably an identification with the early good mother, got her away from Calvin, and her ability to enter into a twinship relationship with her brother allowed her to identify with him and join AA. The AA program then became an idealized object. She formed the same kind of transference with me, and the working through of her predominantly idealizing transference, which also had mirror aspects, enabled her to build psychic structure. Of course, she was sober by then or this would not have been possible.

The scene in the cemetery was crucial to Sally's recovery. As long as she couldn't let go of the bad mother or of just plain *Mother*, there was no way that she could internalize a good object. Bad Mother was a pathological introject, the content of the vertical split. Only by letting her die and then mourning her could Sally reclaim the energy to love a new object and by transmuting internalization, acquire the psychic structure she lacked. *Mourning is not possible during active addiction to alcohol* or to other substances. I have found in case after case that facilitating mourning must take priority in the therapy of the stable sober alcoholic. Only then can the work proceed as one hopes it will.

Kohutian analysis is not the treatment of choice for most recovering alcoholics. Rather, what is indicated is once- or twice-weekly intensive, insight-oriented psychodynamic psychotherapy that is informed by Kohut's insights into the vicissitudes of narcissism. Alcoholics have an intense need for mirroring as well as a need to idealize the counselor. They are also particularly narcissistically vulnerable. The treatment should therefore focus on alcoholism's blows to the substance abuser's already low self-esteem, failures of the childhood environment to supply sufficient phase-appropriate mirroring and opportunities for idealization, and the alcoholic's experience of much of the world as an extension of self. Anxiety is usually understood and interpreted as panic-fear of psychic death, rather than as a manifestation of intrapsychic conflict, and rage is usually understood and interpreted as narcissistic rage, fury at the failure of the self-object to perfectly mirror or protect, rather than as a manifestation of mature aggression.

Much seemingly irrational behavior can be understood in terms of both the alcoholic's need for omnipotent control and the rage that follows failure to so control. The grandiosity and primitive idealization of the archaic nuclear self also explain the perfectionism of alcoholics and the unrealistic standards that they set for themselves. Most recovering alcoholics have not developed realistic ambitions or livable ideals—these are characteristics of the mature self. The alcoholic's depression can be understood in terms of the paucity of psychic structure, which was never built up through the normal process of transmuting internalization. This empty depression also reflects the repression, rather than the integration, of the archaic nuclear self and the failure to integrate archaic grandiosity. This emptiness does not abate with sobriety. Further, the narcissistic rage to which the alcoholic is so prone can be turned against the self, resulting in intensely angry depression, sometimes of suicidal proportions. Failure to internalize the stimulus barrier and poor resources for self-soothing render the alcoholic especially vulnerable to psychic injury. Therefore, the ordinary events in daily life long continue to threaten the alcoholic's already tenuous self-esteem.

The insights of self psychology into the dynamics of pathological narcissism are relevant and helpful in working with stably sober alcoholics. Further, Kohut's approach can be used in a modified form in which the narcissistic transferences are allowed to unfold, the client's need to control and to participate in greatness is accepted, and a slow working through of issues is used to help integrate components of the archaic nuclear self into the reality ego.

The empirical psychological and the learning theory literatures both suggest that hyperactivity, learning difficulties, and neurochemical vulnerabilities may characterize the prealcoholic but are loath to take seriously psychodynamic conceptualizations of antecedent psychopathology. The "pink cloud" of early sobriety, during which, much of the research finds, all or most of the negative affect (depression, anxiety, and self-hatred) has been lifted, distorts the picture. So does the absence in this literature of a notion of the dynamic unconscious. Most certainly, alcohol causes an awful lot of pain, and cessation of self-poisoning radically improves the alcoholic's life and inner experience, yet much remains to be done. In common with many clinicians, I treat many alcoholics who return to therapy after extended periods of sobriety. Now the pink cloud is gone and the developmental issues and deficits suggested by Kohut are all too apparent. Of course this is a biased sample and many recovering alcoholics simply stop drinking and do just fine. Further, I see many adult children of alcoholics (ACOAs) and women, so my picture is necessarily different from the predominantly male clinic and rehabilitation population on which most researchers build their picture of alcoholism.

As I have said, this model applies both to cases in which it is etiological and to cases where it is not, so the issue of antecedent psychopathology is not so acute. Nevertheless, it is a *deficit model* (as are many of the genetic and biochemical theories) that is, it sees alcoholism as an attempt to provide something lacking. Whether as cause or as consequence the inner world and style of relating postulated by the Kohut-Levin model is what must be dealt with in the active and early recovery alcoholic.

Readers interested in psychoanalytic approaches to alcoholism will find the classical papers and contemporary formulations anthologized in Levin and Weiss (1994).

Chapter 11

"God Is in the Quiet Room": One Patient's Experience on the "Flight Deck"

Before the growth of rehabilitation units, known as "rehabs," alcoholics who needed extended treatment went to psychiatric hospitals or wards. In the language of AA, they were "on the flight deck." Some alcoholics are still treated in psychiatric wards and we may see more of this in the future. For this reason, I have included one patient's account of his experience in a psychiatric hospital for the treatment of alcoholism. Since he is an AA member, his story gives insight into the dynamics of AA. His vicissitudes in the hospital are not unlike what patients in rehabs go through and the issues of recovery and early sobriety raised by his story are those commonly dealt with by alcoholism counselors.

As you read, evaluate the narrator, the hospital, and the treatment given. What issues does the narrator raise? Is he an alcoholic? What is your guess at the mix of pharmacology, genetics, psychodynamics, personality, and environment that brought him to the hospital? What is his diagnosis? Does he have a psychiatric illness or personality disorder in addition to his drinking problem? What do you think of the psychiatrist and other hospital staff? Would you do things differently? What do you think his prognosis is? How will he do in life beyond the hospital? If you were counseling him at the point I did, how would you proceed?

The patient initiated psychotherapy after four years of sobriety, primarily because he was unhappy in his career choice and felt trapped. Like so many recovering alcoholics, he had wished to become an alcoholism counselor. But it had been a wrong choice for him: he hated it. As a result of psychotherapy, he entered a graduate program in business administration and is now happily employed in a stock brokerage firm. Some of his other problems proved more recalcitrant, but on the whole he did well. During therapy, he recounted his experience in the psychiatric hospital that had served as his rehab. Having been in the field, he "spoke the language"; his story appears here as he reported it during the first weeks of his therapy.

Doctor, I'm coming to you because I'm not getting as much out of my sobriety as I would like, but my present unhappiness is paradise compared to what it was like when I was drinking. I've been thinking about that a lot since I called to make this appointment. It's just about four years to the day since I entered the University Hospital psychiatric clinic. I was a drinker and a failure at many things as far back as I can remember. After many years of drinking, I really fell apart and went to AA. It wasn't easy, but I managed to stay sober for two and a half years. Then I had a fight with my girlfriend and picked up a drink. I'm sure you've heard that alcoholism is a progressive disease; believe me, it is. It was sheer hell once I picked up that drink. I would go on a binge, either not go to work or go to work with the shakes, not go home, sleep in fleabag hotels, wake up shaking in the middle of the night, reach for the bottle or run past the other bums to find an open bar; then I would go to a few AA meetings, get sober for a while, make some excuses, and go back to work. After a few days I would pick up a drink again and it would be worse than ever. It—or maybe I should say *I*—was crazy; I had been in AA and I knew what to do, but I couldn't do it; I had a place to live, a house with some friends, but I didn't go there. Instead I went to those lower-depths hotels when I was drinking.

Things got worse; the sober periods became shorter and the drinking became almost constant. I just couldn't get my feet on the ground. I wanted to stay sober but I just couldn't do it. Finally I became desperately ill, physically and mentally. I went to my regular doctor—the kind who takes your temperature instead of showing you the dirty pictures, the Rorschach cards. That's supposed to be funny; don't you ever smile, Doctor? I told the internist I was going mad. He arranged for me to enter the hospital. First I got drunk and went to my job, where I resigned with a melodramatic flourish. I drank some more and blacked out.

The next thing I remember I was in an office signing myself into the mental hospital. I had taken only nine months to change from a somewhat dissatisfied, somewhat anxious, but functional human being into a stumbling wreck of a zombie who couldn't even remember how he got to the funny farm. I had managed to find a new girlfriend during that period. I did that by staying away from her when I was drinking heavily; that meant she hadn't been seeing much of me. Fortunately, she had known me during my sober years, and I guess she had some hope that I would stop drinking. I asked the admitting doctor if I could call her before I went up to my floor. The resident looked disapproving, but he gave me permission. When two attendants appeared, I really started shaking. What the hell had I done? I had signed myself into a bughouse. I wanted a drink; I wanted a thousand drinks; I wanted to leave. It was too late! I had signed away my freedom. The attendants, who looked preppy, started to lead me to the elevator. I told them that I had permission to make a call, and they let me. Permission to make a call! Jesus Christ, what had I gotten myself into? I called my girlfriend and told her I had signed myself into the "flight deck," as the bughouse is called in AA. She said, "Wonderful; that's the best thing you could have done." I knew she meant it supportively, but her comment didn't feel supportive. I gathered that she had been less than delighted with my condition during the past few months. I thought of saying, "Gee, thanks"; instead I said, "I love you"—we're still together—and stumbled somewhat tearfully toward the elevator.

The tweedy attendants were firm although friendly, but somehow they looked like concentration camp guards to me. One of them took out his key to open the elevator door, and as that door shut behind me, I heard the clang of all the dungeon doors that have ever closed upon a previously free man resound in my ears. You raised your eyebrows, Doctor; don't you know you're supposed to be a mirror? Think I'm histrionic, eh? Of course I know that I threw away my freedom, but that wasn't the way it felt then. By the time that elevator door shut, I was quaking inside and probably outside as well. One of the attendants pushed a button and up we went.

The elevator opened and we were on the "floor"; it was dark and gloomy. Once the elevator door closed, I was locked in. For the next month, I did not leave there without an attendant opening that door and escorting me wherever I was going. Have you ever been locked up? If you're writing that the patient suffered a narcissistic wound in being hospitalized, you're right in spades. Four years later, I still shudder at those locked elevators. Yes, you can put down claustrophobia too. I felt bewildered. I couldn't remember how I had gotten there; I didn't know what had happened to the day. It was now night and apparently it was late, since nobody was around. The attendants led me to my room. It was actually a reasonably cheerful and comfortable room, but I didn't notice it then. What I did see were the bars on the windows. A shiver ran down my spine.

The attendants told me that the doctor was coming to examine me in much the same tone they might have used to announce that God was coming to see me. I was told to take a shower to prepare for the examination. That made me feel dirty, and I probably was. I wondered if I smelled. I felt some resentment, but far more fear. The sense of being locked in was fading, and I even felt a little secure behind those locked doors and barred windows, but by then my blood alcohol level must have been falling and I was feeling more and more shaky. Every nerve was screaming for a drink and so was I. I managed to shower and put on the hospital gown I had been given. It was not easy, with rubbery legs and arms that wouldn't work quite smoothly.

"The doctor," who turned out to be two very young residents, arrived. They acted very seriously, as if to make sure that nobody treated them like kids. If you've read Kernberg, you know that I was using devaluation as a defense, just like I'm doing now. Don't you ever smile? Well, I needed to devalue them; they frightened me. At that point everything did. They asked me a seemingly endless series of questions. They weren't exactly great at establishing rapport, and I sure needed some rapport. I must have been in pretty bad shape because I had a hard time answering those questions and I'm a real smart guy. I thought, "Oh shit, I really did it this time; I'm brain damaged." Mercifully, the residents gave me a physical. I found it reassuring. Although I didn't like being poked and jabbed, I guess I felt cared for.

I had been drinking two quarts of rye a day for quite a while, and you might say that I was more than a little worried about my health. You'd better get your eyebrows analyzed, Doctor; they're not under ego control. I wasn't a light case, and two quarts a day it was. The examination ended; I was given some medicine and fell into a sleep of sorts.

I woke feeling like death. A nurse came in and told me to dress and come to the dayroom. By now every nerve in my body was screaming and all I could think of was a drink. I left my room and entered a bustling world of patients and staff. I unsteadily made my way down a seemingly endless corridor and entered the dayroom. I was struck by the fact that the people there didn't look like patients, however patients are supposed to look; they just looked like people. Pretty well-dressed ones at that. I found this reassuring; maybe this wasn't such a bad funny farm after all.

I was taken to see my "regular doctor," a Dr. Kruse. Although he was a resident too, he looked grown up and somehow very medical. He was very authoritarian, or at least that's the way I perceived him. He told me that he was detoxifying me from alcohol and that I would be given pentobarbital in decreasing dosages for five days and then nothing; that I would see him three times a week; and that I could stay in bed and not participate in the floor activities for the next two days. I found him so intimidating that I forced myself to tell him that alcohol strips the body of B vitamins and that I should be given vitamins. I don't even know if that's true. Is it? At any rate, Kruse prescribed the vitamins and I felt a little more in control. Pathetic, isn't it? Still, being able to ask for something and get it helped.

Then I panicked. Five more days and then no alcohol and no medicine. I literally didn't think I would survive. I didn't even have to deal with a drugless state for five more days, yet I was already going up the walls. At that moment I turned to my AA experience and decided that this was going to be tough, very tough, but that I would deal with it a day, an hour, a minute at a time, and I did. My two and a half years in AA were not wasted; I used the program to get through the hospital experience and to get all that I could from it. I also decided not to stay in bed but to participate in the hospital program from the start. This desperate attempt to retain a little dignity in front of Kruse and my decision to use AA's day-at-a-time concept to do what I had to do to face being drug free were important events in my recovery. I know it sounds corny, but it was at that point that I started to fight to get well and somehow, sick as I was, I knew it then. Knowing it was almost as important as doing it, because knowing it changed how I felt about myself a very little, but vital, bit. Nothing like an "observing ego," eh, Doctor? Smiled that time, didn't you? As soon as I was capable of it, I tried to understand what was happening to me as it happened. Sure, this was a defense against feelings, and I can intellectualize forever, but this trying to understand also helped me a great deal. If it did nothing else, even if all the insight was pseudoinsight, it increased my self-esteem. Interesting patient, aren't I?

These vestigial feelings of self-worth and of having a coping strategy didn't last long. In fact, they didn't even last until I left Dr. Kruse's office. As I walked up that endless corridor to the dayroom, I was in a panic, and I mean a *panic*. My skin crawled; my breath came hard and then seemed to come not at all until it started to come all too rapidly and I started to hyperventilate; my palms dripped sweat; my heart pounded wildly; the vessels in my temples pulsed and felt like they would pop; my legs quivered; my hands shook; my vision blurred; the lights seemed to dim. Somehow I reached the nurses' station. Ever have a panic attack, Doctor? Do you know Edvard Munch's painting *The Scream*? I see you do. Well, that's just what it's like. Oh, why am I explaining—you're human, aren't you? "Nothing human is alien to me," eh? I must stop mocking you. It's part of my cool, detached, arrogant, yet proper and polite persona, a facade that I used as a defense in the hospital just like I'm doing now. I didn't tell you about that. In the hospital I was polite and very controlled—under the shaking, that is. I mean, I liked to look in control. Pathetic, wasn't it? But I already said that. I was also superintellectual. Technical terms poured from my lips like I had four PhDs. Back to that word—pathetic—that really was pathetic, and I say that without self-pity. It's repetitious, but it's apt.

At the nurses' station I was given my pentobarbital. It took a little while until it hit, but when it did, it was wonderful. It was like two double-double Seven-and-Sevens. I soon felt drunk, and I loved it. Somewhere I knew that this was but a reprieve which would come to an end, but that didn't matter much. I felt too good.

That pentobarbital hit me hard. Soon I was staggering and slurring my words. Pat, the big, snappish, tough-sounding black nurse who had given me the medicine tried to talk me into going to bed. I said, "No. I want to participate in the hospital program, and the doctor said that I could if I wanted to." She relented and I staggered from the nursing station to the dayroom, literally bouncing off the walls. An alcoholic rehab would have kept me in bed at that point. I'm glad that the hospital took some risk of my injuring myself and let me stagger around for a few days. Like I said, discovering the will to fight, wherever that came from, made the difference.

It's a mystery, isn't it? Why did I choose life instead of death at that point? I don't know, but I did. God? The anabolic forces of the universe? A massive psychic reorganization? Symbiotic union with the hospital? Who knows, but it happened. Somehow I was able to say to myself, "I fucked up, but I'm going to do it differently this time; I'm going to build on bedrock instead of sand, a minute or a second at a time." Somehow, somewhere I knew then that I could, although of course there were many moments of panic and despair in the process. Perhaps I was drawing on a deeply buried repository of all the love I had received in my life. Again, I don't know. But I had decided to fight to build on solid ground this time. To do that I decided to use everything the hospital had to offer and get everything I could from the experience. Kind of goody-goody, eh? Of course, I was also casting myself in a heroic role, and part of me enjoyed it. But so what? Why shouldn't I have given myself some fringe benefits by way of enjoying my private version of the myth of death and rebirth. Funny, I never thought of it that way before—being in therapy does have its uses.

So I bounded and staggered into the dayroom. I was very drugged. Sitting there were a very angry-looking bear of a bearded, middle-aged man and a 70ish, stylishly dressed woman: Bill and Sadie. Bill was slapping down cards from a tarot deck on a table top with great force and looked every bit the conjurer. I wobbled across the room, introduced myself, and said, "Will you overlook my ataxia and dysarthria? They are induced by the medication I'm taking." Sadie looked blank; Bill said, "Sure, kid," and slammed the tarot cards harder. I lunged into a jargon-filled discussion of my condition. Bill said, "Sit down and let me get a reading of your cards." I felt accepted, but I remained standing. You look bemused, Doctor. I told you I was playing the most pleasant of gracious intellectuals who knew more or less everything and was willing to share it with all. "Gladly learn and gladly teach," eh? As they say in AA, I was being a "people pleaser" in my own strange way. Bill and Sadie took it all in stride and again invited me to join them at the card table. This time I did.

I was slurring badly enough that it would have been difficult to understand me even if I was making sense, which I almost certainly wasn't. That didn't seem to bother Bill and Sadie. As we say in AA, we ran our stories. Bill, a lecturer on communications at a local college, was manic-depressive. He said he was in the hospital because his wife was afraid of him. Looking into the almost infinitely deep pools of hatred and rage in his eyes, I understood why, but I was too drugged to feel afraid. Sadie said she was 67 years old and in her third hospitalization for depression. She was very much the lady, and I thought it was funny when she told me that her doctor during her last hospitalization 20 years ago had told her to buy a set of cheap dishes and break them all. I couldn't picture her doing that. That old internalized anger doesn't do much for people. Looking back on it, it almost killed me. I didn't know that then.

Just as Bill, Sadie, and I were getting acquainted, a chime rang. I'll always be able to hear that chime. It rang for meals, for meds, for activities, for bedtime, for everything. Structure for the structureless, I suppose. Comfort in routine. Comfort or not, I got to hate those chimes. This particular chime called us to activities. The dayroom had filled up with about 20 people, but I hadn't noticed. We were lined up and marched—at least, that's the way it felt—to the locked elevators. The attendants were actually kind and friendly, but I still experienced them as prison guards, which in part they were. Being escorted everywhere through locked doors was humiliating. There is just no other word for it. I staggered as the others walked. We were taken up to the top floor, which had a gym, game rooms, and a screened-in roof garden. The younger patients played volleyball while the older patients played in the game room. I didn't feel capable of doing anything, so I went out on the roof garden and looked down at the traffic far below through the wire mesh. At least it's not barbed, I thought, as my depression rose like waves through the waning pentobarbital.

For the next four or five days, I followed the hospital routine, participating in what I could. There was individual therapy with Dr. Kruse, group therapy, recreational therapy, occupational therapy, dance therapy, and community meetings. As the withdrawal medication was titrated down, my anxiety returned and once again moved toward panic proportions. The slurring and staggering gave way to a sort of spasticity. My arms and legs would jump up, much as though I was a dancer in the dance of the toy soldiers. It was embarrassing, although it was hard to feel embarrassed in the totally accepting atmosphere of the floor. It was also disabling.

I remember sitting and playing bridge with Bill, Sadie, and "the Princess," a wealthy, very uptight woman who had gotten herself hooked on pills and had attempted suicide. I had had my last dose of pentobarbital about three hours before. I could feel the drug losing its effect. I was excited about being drug free and terrified at the same time. Suddenly the dayroom grew bright and the objects in it sharply defined. It was as if the lights had gone on in a dark theater. I was fascinated. So this was what the world was supposed to look like. Then I was dealt a hand. As I picked it up, my arm involuntarily snapped over my head and the cards flew. The heightened illumination of the room now seemed sinister. My thoughts raced. I thought, I'm going mad. This is the madhouse. I'm losing my mind. I'll never get out of here. I felt sheer terror. I felt I wasn't going to recover; I felt it was all over. Yet I picked up those cards with those spastic arms and bid one trump. Made the hand, too. I wanted to talk about what was going on inside of me, but I was afraid to. My thoughts kept speeding up and became more and more confused. I jumped up and ran to my room, where I collapsed on the bed in a state of utter despair. I know part of it was physiological, but I must have been close to madness that night.

I finally fell into a deeply troubled sleep. After I don't know how long, I woke to one of the strangest sensations I have ever felt. There were waves of force emanating from the center of my abdomen, traveling through my body, and smashing against my skin. Rhythmic and relentless wave succeeded wave. It felt like I would shatter, that the waves would break me into pieces. The impact of the waves against the surface of my body was so strong that I feared that I would fly off the bed. I reached up and grasped on to the bars of the bed above my head and held on for dear life. Smash, smash, smash, they kept coming, relentlessly, inexorably. I thought of screaming out, but I didn't. Suddenly a thought occurred to me: Holy shit, that's my anger, my rage, *my, my* anger coming out. This is not something happening to me; it is me—it's my rage. I held on to that thought as my last tie to reality. I repeated to myself over and over again, "It's my anger and nothing else." It was my Copernican revolution, though I certainly didn't think of it that way while it was happening. What I mean is that that thought changed the center of things for me. It was I who was doing this thing, not some outside force. This was another pivotal point in my recovery, just as important as my decision to fight. It took a long while for the waves of pressure to stop shattering themselves against my flesh, but the terror was gone. Finally I fell into a deep sleep, from which I awoke exhausted and drained, yet somehow freer than I had felt for a long time. Doctor, I suppose you'd classify what happened to me as a somatic delusion, and I suppose it was, but that doesn't really matter. What did matter was that I was able to use it to own my anger, or at least some of it.

The floor consisted of two long arms connected to a body consisting of the dayroom, the nurses' station, and the dining room. My room was at the end of one arm and Dr. Kruse's office was at the end of the other arm. The total distance was a full city block. During the days following the anger waves, I paced those arms, the corridors, obsessively. Whenever I wasn't in a scheduled activity, I paced. You are probably thinking that I was going in and out of Mother's arms to her breasts, the nurses' station. Perhaps you're right on that, but I sure didn't experience it that way. It's probably of some significance that I forgot to mention that my mother was dying, or at least was supposed to die during my final round-the-clock binge and was still critical when I entered the hospital.

Responded to that one, didn't you, Doctor? As it turned out, Mother unexpectedly survived, but her illness must have had something to do with that final binge. Lost the girlfriend, losing the mother, eh? Let me tell you something strange: One of the things I am most grateful to AA for is that it taught me how to mourn. Maybe that doesn't make much sense, and I don't know how it happened, but after my nine-month slip, when I returned to AA I was somehow able to mourn another loss, that of my father. That was an old loss and I somehow think that my failure to come to terms with my feelings about him and his death was connected to my slip, although the occasion, if not the cause, of that slip was girlfriend trouble. Gratitude for being able to mourn. That's really crazy, isn't it? I don't really believe that; I know it isn't crazy. It's just that I'm embarrassed by the depth of my feelings. AA puts a lot of emphasis on gratitude: gratitude for sobriety; gratitude for the program itself. Sure, sometimes that gratitude is defensive, another form of denial, a reaction formation, but sometimes it's genuine—and that's been an important part of my recovery. Melanie Klein[1] would understand that, wouldn't she? Gratitude for the good breast making possible reparation for spoiling that good breast and turning it into the bad breast—working through the depressive position—that's what AA is all about. Read the Steps. It may sound like I'm intellectualizing again, but I'm not, even if I'm showing off a bit. I really am choked up right now, thinking of all I have to be grateful for.

As the days passed, the spastic jerking of my extremities became less and less frequent. I still paced, but now the focus of my concerns had shifted. I became hypochondriacal and drove Pat, the nurse, crazy demanding blood pressure readings. The ubiquitous chimes summoned us to have our blood pressures taken three times a day, shortly after they had summoned us for meds. Pat did not take kindly to my pestering. She rebuffed me harshly and gruffly. I thought of her as the ogre of the floor.

During my hypochondriacal phase, I was also very aware of my anger. At times it was so intense that I thought it might break me in half, but never after the anger-wave hallucination did I experience it as exter-

---

[1]Melanie Klein is a psychoanalytic theorist who wrote of breast envy being overcome by gratitude.

nal. It was an objectless anger. Is there free-floating rage like there's free-floating anxiety? I guess there is; I had it. So overwhelming was its intensity and the intensity of some of my other feelings, especially my fear, that all I could do was to self-consciously constrict my experience of the world to an instant at a time. More and more constricted did my world become until I was living in a succession of infinitesimal flecks of time, an infinitesimal at a time, so to speak. I did not dare to live even five minutes ahead or look five minutes behind; it engendered too much fear. Similarly, I constricted my spatial world to tiny patches of perceived space. I mean this quite literally; when my anxiety was high enough I could feel my world shrinking toward an instant and a point. It was like a camera in my head was being focused more and more narrowly. This was being in the here-and-now with a vengeance.

I remember being in the gym, totally overwhelmed by rage and fear and something like despair as I stared at the punching bag. Suddenly my visual field narrowed to a patch of pebbly brown; this was about ten percent voluntary and 90 percent involuntary. I tried to open my visual field, but it didn't happen. I thought, well you really did it this time; you're stimulus bound now. Then I thought, so be it; I'll be stimulus bound, and I started pounding that patch of pebbly brown with the pent-up rage of a lifetime. When I stopped, wringing wet and exhausted, my point world gradually expanded to encompass the gym and my fellow patients. That was scope enough for me. I knew that something important had happened, but oddly I didn't feel much relief.

Another way my hypochondria manifested itself was in blinding headaches. They fed my obsessional worry about high blood pressure. I ran from nurse to nurse trying to get aspirin. I tried to manipulate Dr. Kruse into prescribing medicine. Forget it. If I stood on my head, there was no way that hospital was going to give me anything but a vitamin tablet once I was detoxified.

I've often wondered what my experience would have been in an alcoholic rehab unit instead of a psychiatric hospital. Fortunately, the hospital I was in was very "hip" on alcoholism; witness their reluctance to give me drugs. At least half of the patients who came and went during my month-long stay on the floor were drug or alcohol cases, whatever else may have been wrong with them. Popular problem, eh? I worked in an alcohol rehab after I became a counselor, so I know what they're like. I learned the psychoanalytic "lingo" from one of the social workers on the unit. We were the mavericks on that staff. I missed the alcohol education that I would have received in an alcohol rehab, but on the whole my hospitalization really worked. Since I already had AA exposure, the psychiatric hospital was probably best for me. Alcohol rehabs are less humiliating and less frightening, but they are also kind of doctrinaire. I don't like that. My hospital did a terrific job of creating a therapeutic community on the floor. For all of the inevitable aloneness, there was a real feeling of shared adventure and closeness. I also liked the hospital's emphasis on being honest about your feelings and expressing them. It wasn't AA, but its values were similar. I know that I have a lot of negative feelings about that hospital and about being treated like a prisoner. But my positive feelings aren't all a reaction formation or a form of denial either.

Paradoxically, my period of being stimulus bound, as I thought of it, coincided with my increasing involvement in the life of the floor. It was almost cinematic the way my scope of focus would spatially, and to a lesser extent temporally, expand and contract. During my relatively expansive periods, my relationships with Bill, Sadie, and the Princess, Jan, became more important. There was a real bond around the bridge table, a bond not without its conflicts and disturbances. I became increasingly afraid of Bill. He really looked like he might kill everyone on the floor. Sitting across from him at the bridge table was no easy thing. His psychiatrist was trying to get him to take a major tranquilizer. He was threatening to sign himself out if the doctor insisted that he take it. I finally got up my courage and told him I thought he was dangerous and that he should take the medicine. Amazingly, he agreed. After that we became closer, and I was initiated into the tarot card mystique. When I was given a good reading I felt elated. A recovery is made of many tiny steps, like those infinitesimals I spoke of, that accrete into something substantial and solid. Telling Bill he was dangerous was such a step for me.

Sadie was a truly lovely person who had had a lot of loss in her life. I wished so hard that she would break those damn dishes. The Princess could be arrogant, but she was bright and witty. I enjoyed her. She had been in the hospital for a long time and was scheduled for discharge. She went on pass and took an overdose of Valium while she was out. Her suicide gesture greatly upset me; I thought maybe nobody gets out of here intact. I was surprised when the Princess was discharged as planned. I often wonder what happened to her. She was replaced by an overtly psychotic patient. When I told him I was in for alcohol abuse, he said, "Oh, that. I stopped drinking years ago and joined AA. Look at me now." This frightened and discouraged me more than the Princess's suicide attempt. At about the same time, a middle-aged man was brought in on a stretcher. He had also attempted suicide. He turned out to be a physician whose son had been killed in a South American political upheaval. He clearly did not want to live. The sadness in his eyes was as profound as the anger in Bill's. He was a charming and worldly man whose charm and worldliness were automatic and mechanically empty. He insisted on leaving the hospital after a week and was discharged against medical advice. I was sure he was doing to his death.

During my social period in the hospital, I felt a great need for the approbation of my fellow patients. After I confronted Bill, I seemed to regress. He improved on his medicine and was gone from the floor on pass more and more frequently. The Princess was leaving. Although I liked her, Sadie was limited companionship. I felt isolated and alone. I became even more of a people pleaser; I felt that I needed the approval of every person in that hospital. Under my formal, helpful, intellectual, polite facade, I was enraged at the people leaving and distrusted the newcomers. My facade clearly turned some people off, particularly Pat.

The floor held community meetings each evening. Generally I didn't participate much. The night the Princess left and Bill's discharge date was set, I was particularly forlorn. Left behind in the madhouse. At the community meeting some blowhard took the floor and monopolized the meeting in a way that really annoyed me. It seems ridiculous now. I've become quite good at telling people to go fuck themselves, but then I couldn't risk alienating anybody, including that asshole. I should tell you that a psychotic medical student had been brought in that day. She kept repeating "E equals MC squared." In the course of the day, she became more and more disorganized. They put her in the quiet room, an isolation cell used for out-of-control patients. This terrified me. Other patients, particularly Ruth, a provocative streetwise teenager, had been put in the quiet room. But this was for short periods, sort of like sending a kid to her room. The quiet room held a peculiar fascination for me. I was utterly terrified by it. I suppose I was afraid of losing control, but unconsciously wished to at the same time. Fear of confinement permeated every fiber of my being. The quiet room was a prison within a prison. I identified with Julie and her "E equals MC squared," and by that night all of my terrors were focused on the quiet room. So at that community meeting I was not only desperately into people pleasing, but terrified of losing control lest I be put into the quiet room. At one level I knew this was ridiculous, but my terror wouldn't go away.

So there I was, listening to that long-winded asshole ramble on. Suddenly I knew I had to say something. I was slumped down into a couch almost as if I wanted to bury myself in it. It took every bit of strength I had to force myself to sit up. I was sweating and shaking. Finally I managed to say, "I don't like what you're doing. You're taking over this meeting. Sit down and shut up." My body almost convulsed, but I had done it. I relaxed and sank back into the couch. That was one of the most significant accomplishments of my life; it took more courage and there was more fear to go through to say those few words than has been the case in some seemingly much more significant accomplishments. At the end of the meeting, Pat came over and put her arm around me and said, "You did good." I shan't forget that.

Speaking up at the community meeting opened things up to me. Julie, the medical student, grew increasingly agitated. I thought she was reacting to being locked in the quiet room. I would look through the window of her locked door. The staff stopped me from doing this. Julie became more frantic. Finally they "snowed" her, put her out with massive doses of tranquilizers. Now she lay unconscious on the floor of the quiet room, with her arm raised and splinted as intravenous solution dripped into it. I thought, "God, they're killing her." I became totally absorbed in her fate and my identification with it. The quiet room became a symbol for all that I feared and dreaded, yet perhaps secretly wanted—after all, hadn't I rendered myself unconscious with a drug, alcohol? Hadn't I sought death? That day in my session with Kruse, I said, "I'm afraid of you. You have too much power." The reference was to Julie, but I was also thinking of myself.

Another way in which I opened up was by running my story. I had learned to do this in AA, and I had been doing it to some extent since I entered the hospital. But now I ran my story to everybody who would listen and to some who didn't. I did it in group therapy; I did it at the community meetings; I did it with the staff; I did it with my fellow patients. Each time I told my story, I learned something new. I suppose you would call that "working through." I knew that I was boring people and taking advantage of a captive audience, but I didn't care.

I also opened up physically, with my body. I had never been very involved in recreation therapy. I had played volleyball only with the greatest reluctance and only when pushed by the recreation therapist. I played fearfully, self-protectively, holding my body tight and closed. Naturally my playing was awful. A few days after that community meeting, I was cajoled into playing volleyball. This time it was different. I could feel the energy flowing through my body. I became the game. I felt myself leaping into the air. I felt myself coming down hard. I felt myself taking risks. The closeness, the tightness, the self-protectiveness fell away. It was wonderful. They say that how you play the game is a picture of yourself; it's true. I was not self-conscious while it was happening, but afterwards I processed what had occurred, and that helped too; it was part of my changing my self-image.

I had a somewhat similar experience in occupational therapy. At first I was reluctant to do anything because of my physical condition. Besides, I looked upon "arts and crafts," let alone "basket weaving," as I thought of it, with derision. But I said to myself, "Fuck it; I'll do this garbage since I've decided to work the hospital for all it's worth." So commitment won over arrogance. I struggled for weeks to make a mosaic ashtray. At first it was almost impossible to do because my hands shook so both from the withdrawal and from anxiety. I finally finished the thing. I couldn't believe the way I was reacting; I was ecstatic. What was important about this was that it convinced me that I could function in the face of and in spite of anxiety. I told Pat that the ashtray was "an external and visible sign of an internal and invisible grace." She treated this bit of pretension with the contempt it deserved, but the idea behind it was valid enough. I've recalled making that ashtray many times when I thought I couldn't do something because of emotional pain, and sometimes I was then able to do it.

Julie stayed "snowed out" for days, and I kept returning to that window to stare at her prostrate body until a staff member chased me away, much like a child compulsively putting his tongue to a sore loose tooth. Finally, she regained her feet, although she was still very much out of it. One of the staff told me, "It's okay. She needs to regress." I oscillated between thinking that this was a rationalization of what they had done to her and that it reflected a deep empathy. I guess that reflected my ambivalence toward the hospital—mistreated and understood at the same time. A few days later Julie was released from the quiet room. She and Ruth immediately became friends. I remember one exchange between them. Julie asked, "Why is this nuthouse different from all other nuthouses?" Ruth, perfectly seriously, answered, "It's the real McCoy." For some reason, I loved the medical student and the street kid for this exchange.

I was getting better. I was given a pass to leave the hospital. As I walked out of the hospital and tried to walk down the street, I felt a magnetic force drawing me back to the hospital. I don't mean this metaphorically; I mean I actually felt pulled back to the hospital. Another quasipsychotic episode, I suppose. I thought, no, this can't be happening. But it was. It really felt like the force would pull me back. I fought it and succeeded in breaking loose. No doubt a projection of my desire to cling to the mother, eh, Doctor? Or was it the regressive, seductive pull of madness? Whatever it was, it sure was no joke then. A need to regress indeed. I had had enough regression; I feared it as much as I desired it. Fortunately, the fear was stronger than the desire, and I escaped the regressive pull of the hospital and of madness. I started to run and didn't stop until I ran out of breath several blocks away. The pull was gone.

I felt a surge of joy. I was free. I bounded toward the park. I felt as if I had springs in my heels. It was a little like being on speed. Looking back on it, I was more than a little manic. I ran toward the polar bears in the zoo. They seemed glad to see me. We spoke for a while; at least I spoke to them. I felt a great sense of communion with the polar bears. My social worker friend told me that one of the psychoanalytic theorists had spoken of the toddler's "love affair with the world" when he starts separating from his mother. I suppose my feelings in the park were like that. Later that day I stubbed my toe, so to speak, and ran crying back to my mother-hospital. You know, AA's like that—a safe home base from which one can go into the world to take his lumps and return to be comforted.

Rapprochement—that's what they call that stage. But we all need that, don't we? Funny, I never thought of AA that way before. After a while, I left the park and went to my girlfriend's. Our relationship had just begun to get close when I started to avoid her during my heavy drinking, yet she had come to visit me several times in the hospital. Like most of those places, they strictly regulated phone calls and visits. It took a while to get phone privileges and even longer to be allowed visitors. They wanted us to "act in," to work out our shit right there in the hospital. When she was finally allowed to see me, Ann was very supportive and that meant a lot to me. I shared as much of the hospital experience with her as I was able to. I had an overwhelming fear of being impotent sober. If you've been to many AA meetings, Doctor, you know that's a very common fear. At her last visit, I had spent an hour explaining to Ann that we couldn't make love for at least a year after I left the hospital because I couldn't afford to jeopardize my sobriety by putting any pressure on myself. I was perfectly serious. Five minutes after I arrived in her apartment, we were in bed. Everything went fine.

Several hours later, I left Ann to go to an AA meeting. I had come down off my "pink cloud," but I was still feeling good. I was excited about going back to my old group. I had bounced in and out of that meeting during my nine months of drinking. Now I was sober and hopeful. I walked into the meeting and immediately felt estranged. I couldn't connect with anything or anybody. It was horrible. I sat through the meeting, but I wasn't really there. I felt very far away. It was as if a thick, viscous fluid surrounded me and isolated me from the group. Again I do not speak metaphorically. I could feel that viscous medium intruding between me and the people in that room. It prevented me from making human contact. It was a little like being in an underwater movie. I must have been distancing, but I sure didn't know it then. I left in a state of deep despair. Whatever my ambivalence toward the hospital, I felt warmth and concern, something like loving care there. I had counted on finding that at my AA meeting, but I didn't. I have never felt as alone as I did on my return to the hospital. I felt defeated and profoundly depressed. I wanted to give up.

During the following days, I went through the hospital routine mechanically. My friends had been discharged, which made me feel even more forlorn and abandoned. For some reason I didn't talk about my experience at the AA meeting back at the hospital. My discharge was approaching. I was given another pass. I didn't want to use it, but I did. With great reluctance, I decided to try a new AA group. This one was a few blocks from the hospital and met, as it turned out, fittingly at the Church of the Epiphany. I was very shaky as I walked into that meeting. I didn't really expect anything good to happen, but I felt that I had to try to get back to AA anyway. The meeting started with the preamble, "Alcoholics Anonymous is a fellowship of men and women who share their experience, faith, and hope with each other. . . ." Something was happening. Those words sounded like pure poetry to me. The speaker was a beautiful young woman, intensely and vibrantly alive. Her vivacity and sparkle certainly facilitated what was to happen to me. Eros, I'll take all the help I can get from you. She spoke of her years of drugging and drinking, of her progressive spiritual and emotional death. Finally she said, "I got to the point that I couldn't feel anything. For no particular reason, I went on a trip across the country with some drinking buddies. As we crossed the country my feelings became more and more frozen. We arrived at the Grand Canyon. I looked at it and felt nothing. I knew that I should be responding with awe and wonder to the sight before me, but I couldn't. I had always loved nature; now that love, like everything else about me, was dead. I decided to take a picture of the magnificence spread before me, so that if I ever melted I could look at the picture and feel what I couldn't feel then."

At that moment, something incredible happened to me. I completely identified with the speaker. I understood her frozen feelings; they were mine. I understood her wish to preserve a precious moment in the hope that some day she could adequately respond with feelings of awe and wonder to it. Something welled up in me. I began to sob, deep, strong, powerful sobs; they did not stop for the hour and a half that the meeting lasted. As the speaker told her story—how she had managed to stop drugging and drinking and how her feelings had become unfrozen—my feelings became unfrozen. I was still crying when I shook her hand and thanked her. I walked out of that meeting feeling happy. I couldn't even remember feeling happy.

As I walked down the street toward the hospital, the tears were still flowing. Now they were tears of happiness and gratitude. I, who had been so formal and controlled and concerned to impress, walked past staring strollers with tears streaming, completely indifferent, indeed oblivious, to their reactions. Doctor, do you know Edna St. Vincent Millay's poem *Renascence*? It tells of a young woman who has been buried; then the rain comes, washing her grave away and returning her to life. She becomes aware of "A fragrance such as never clings/To aught save happy living things. . . ." I had always loved that poem; now I truly understood it. My tears were like that rain in the poem; they, like the rain, washed me out of the grave I had dug for myself with alcohol and emotional repression. I too smelled the fragrance that never clings to aught save happy living things.

I walked onto the floor feeling buoyant. As I joined the perpetual rap session in the dayroom, a thought came to me: God is in the quiet room. I didn't know where it came from nor what I meant by it, but I vocalized it. I think it had something to do with feeling loved and connected and potentially loving myself. It seemed that whatever I had experienced at that AA meeting was also present in the quiet room. That's as close as I can get to understanding what I was trying to express in that phrase. What had happened at the meeting had something to do with receptivity, with being open and being able to hear. That part of it was a gift, from whom I do not know. When I left the hospital a week later, I was given a goodbye party, as all about-to-be-discharged patients were. At the party, I was given a pastel drawing of my saying, "God is in the quiet room." I still have it.

I'm not much on theodicies and I can't do much with a young girl going mad as a manifestation of divine grace. I don't know who or what, if anything, is out there, and I haven't become religious in any formal sense—I don't belong to a church. So when I said, "God is in the quiet room," I must have meant it in some metaphorical sense. But I did mean it. There was certainly denial in that statement, denial of evil and pain and sorrow, denial of all I hated about the hospital, denial of my rage at the waste my life had been, but there was something else in it too, something that liberated me to engage in the long, slow, up-and-down struggle for health. In AA, we say that sobriety is an adventure; it certainly has been for me.

Well, Doctor, now that I've told you my story, let me tell you about why I came here. My fucking job is driving me crazy; I hate it. . . .

John, the recovering alcoholic whose hospital experience we have been sharing, tells his story with such an observing ego that I cannot add much to his self-analysis. The central point of his story is that he hit bottom in the hospital and that both the empathic "holding environment" and the limit-setting of the hospital facilitated that happening. What saved John was his capacity, under all of the intellectualization and narcissistic and histrionic defenses he constantly used, to *feel* deeply and sincerely. Clearly, whoever works with him needs to go for the affect—to elicit emotion. John's self-hatred and prevailing feelings of worthlessness and failure desperately need to be expressed.

Even though he slipped, John's AA experience clearly served him well. Many clients don't make it the first (or second or third) time, yet the treatment they receive is not wasted. If they are as fortunate as John, they can use what they learned along the way when they finally turn the corner to stable recovery.

Since this story says nothing of John's childhood or drinking career, it is hard to know what brought him to the sorry pass he was in when he entered the hospital. But I invite you to speculate on what role his personality and defensive style played in his addiction. He worked as a counselor; what kind of counselor do you think he was? If you were his vocational counselor, what direction do you think you might point him in? What do you think of the notion of hitting bottom? Is it necessary to recovery? John's is very much an AA story. What is your impression of the program from what John has said? What answers did you come up with for the questions that preceded John's narrative? Rethink them and see if you have changed your mind.

Chapter 12

Treatment Settings, Programs, and New Modalities for Alcoholism

As research into the etiology, physiology, and psychology of alcoholism has burgeoned, treatment alternatives also have evolved and even taken on daring new forms. This final chapter explores some of these developments.

REHABILITATION PROGRAMS

During the past 15 years inpatient rehabilitation programs for alcoholics and other substance abusers have grown in number. Most programs are privately run. They usually last 28 days, since that is what most insurance policies have covered. With the advent of managed care, however, insurance companies have cut back their coverage and the average length of stay in rehabilitation units has been shrinking. Although the future of inpatient rehabs is in doubt, most units will probably survive and learn to work under the new, more restrictive conditions. For some alcoholics, recovery is not possible without inpatient treatment. Fortunately, there are also public programs, usually administered by state mental hospitals, that offer the benefits of low cost and the possibility of more extended treatment.

Inpatient rehabilitation programs have several functions: (a) they buy time for sobriety to take hold by providing external controls until internal ones can be established; (b) they provide an opportunity for intensive education on the nature of alcoholism, emphasizing the disease concept of alcoholism, since belief in this concept reduces guilt and facilitates recovery, even if it should turn out to be a metaphor or a beneficent myth; (c) they provide a safe environment for the alcoholic to experience and express intense affects that have been anesthetized and repressed; (d) they create a therapeutic community in which patients have an opportunity to overcome isolation and gain self-esteem through a sense of common adventure; and (e) they introduce patients to and require attendance at AA meetings. Alcoholic rehabilitation programs also provide many models of both illness and recovery with which the patient can identify.

Inpatient programs are multimodal, utilizing didactic lectures; films; informal discussion groups; therapy groups; psychiatric evaluation and, if appropriate, treatment; nutrition counseling; recreational therapy; occupational therapy; family therapy; individual counseling; structured self-evaluative formats that the patient works on and then discusses with his or her counselor; and participation in AA and other twelve-step programs such as Adult Children of Alcoholics (ACOA) and Narcotics Anonymous (NA). Twelve-step programs promote growth and "lock in" sobriety. Patients are strongly urged to join an *after-care group* when they are discharged. Participation in the rehabilitation after care program, which is usually a weekly group session, is seen as an important, indeed vital, tool for recovery. After care groups concentrate on alcohol and the problems of early sobriety, especially recognizing drink signals before they are acted on.

Although scientific outcome studies are rare and we don't really know how well these programs work or for whom, they have a large number of enthusiastic recovering alumni. Inpatient rehabilitation units see themselves as, and sometimes are, safe places to "let it all hang out." They often use treatment modalities that encourage a great deal of affective arousal and release. The most common is the *psychodrama* group. Led by a skilled facilitator, these groups are indeed effective forums for "decompression," allowing the barely sober alcoholic to discharge long-repressed emotions, which makes maintenance of sobriety immediately after discharge more likely. Conflicts are enacted instead of acted out. Psychodrama is also said to increase participants' empathy for their significant others by promoting identification with each of the actors in the psychodrama.

Although at present all the inpatient alcohol rehab programs with which I am familiar are AA, twelve-step oriented, programs of the future may offer alternate treatment options. I see this as highly desirable since many people find the AA ideology unpalatable and many are too schizoid or borderline to benefit from it. To mandate that a client attend AA or an AA oriented rehab, as happens fairly commonly, is rather like mandating that somebody attend church. Although AA is a nondenominational "spiritual" rather than religious program, one of its central tenets is the "higher power" and much is made of the members' relationship to that higher power. To mandate that a person affiliate with a program with that much spiritual, or if you regard that as a fudge, religious content, seems to me to be a dangerous violation of that person's civil liberties. I say this even though I am in full agreement with the intuitive understanding of the dynamics of alcoholism that is incarnated in the AA Program and fully believe that AA affiliation vastly increases the likelihood of remaining sober.

STRUCTURED DAY PROGRAMS
AND HALFWAY HOUSES

Some alcoholics are too damaged by their disease or were so impaired premorbidly that they cannot sustain a recovery in the community after discharge from inpatient rehab with only the support of AA and outpatient counseling. They need a structured day program that provides on an ongoing basis much of what an inpatient rehabilitation program provides. Day programs are looser and more informal. They serve as a place to hang out when structured activities are not scheduled.

Halfway houses are residences for recovering alcoholics and usually offer some form of treatment as well as providing for the basic needs of the residents. The contents of the programs provided vary widely, but almost all offer guidance, support, and structure in addition to food and shelter. Recreational activities are commonly offered. The residents either go to a day program or have jobs. Antabuse and other medications are usually dispensed to residents if indicated. Many of these facilities are run by charitable agencies or religious groups.

With the cutbacks in third-party reimbursements, many inpatient alcohol and drug rehabilitation programs have started four-evenings-a-week intensive treatment programs aimed at employed alcoholics who would, in all probability, have been treated as inpatients a few years ago. If a patient relapses while in such a program, the rehab can then argue to the insurance company that that particular alcoholic really needs inpatient treatment. Frequently the strategy works and the patient is admitted. These evening programs differ from the structured day programs discussed above in that they are aimed at a different, more functional population. They do not target profoundly damaged alcoholics and are far less global in their approach. They offer a combination of educational didactic programs that teach the disease model of alcoholism and intensive group psychotherapy aimed at the breakdown of denial and the teaching of coping skills. They are Twelve Step oriented and push AA attendance hard. They are still too new for there to be any real sense of their efficacy, let alone rigorous outcome studies. In spite of this, they are said to be cost-effective and may well be the wave of the future.

TREATING CROSS-ADDICTION

Today it is rare to encounter an alcoholic who is not cross-addicted. This is especially true of patients under 35 years of age. Alcoholics are particularly prone to using other sedative drugs, such as barbiturates and tranquilizers. Alcohol and cocaine is also a popular combination, and marijuana smoking is all but ubiquitous among the young. Cocaine addicts frequently use alcohol to "come down" and become hooked on it also. Conversely, it is not uncommon for alcoholics to self-medicate the depression that is a consequence of alcohol abuse with cocaine. Speed (amphetamine) is used for the same purpose, and hallucinogens also are in widespread use. More rarely the counselor will encounter alcoholics cross-addicted to heroin or morphine, which are also sedating drugs, or to methadone, the synthetic used to wean addicts off heroin. It is not possible to use any drug safely once addiction to another drug is established. Therefore, alcoholics must be educated to the fact that the use of any mood-altering drug, with the exception of properly prescribed psychotropic medications, will sooner or later result in a resumption of active alcoholism. Cross-addicted alcoholics are treated in much the same ways as non-cross-addicted alcoholics. After detoxification from all drugs, educational and psychological interventions are used to build ego strength and to help the patient deal with feelings without resorting to drugs of any kind. Participation in a self-help group is also strongly encouraged.

SELF-HELP GROUPS

Twelve-Step Programs

Alcoholics Anonymous (AA) was the first of the self-help groups. Founded during the Depression by Bill Wilson, a stockbroker, and Bob Smith, a surgeon, both of whom were alcoholics, it has become enormously influential. Its basic concept—that there is something uniquely healing in their sharing of their "experience, strength, and hope" by people who are suffering from a common problem—has been widely imitated, to the benefit of people with diverse other problems. Members are enjoined to "identify, don't compare." The commonality of the alcoholic experience, which cuts across age, social class, gender, occupation, and race, is stressed. When a speaker "qualifies" (that is, tells his or her story), members are asked to identify with the feelings of the alcoholic speaker, not with the circumstances of his or her addiction. At some meetings, the evening's activity consists of speakers telling their stories to the group. Usually these meetings are open and nonalcoholics are welcome. Other meetings use a different format in which a brief qualification is followed by a discussion, often of a topic such as "dealing with tension" or "gratitude for recovery." These meetings are closed (that is, restricted to those "who have a desire to stop drinking"). Closed meetings are more like traditional group therapy than are open meetings, but they discourage "cross-talk," (lengthy interchanges between members) so again, identification with the story-teller is emphasized. Members are encouraged to have a "sponsor," a member with "time" (who has been sober for a while) and "quality sobriety" who acts as a guide and mentor, and to follow AA's Twelve Steps of spiritual growth. Many different things occur in the process of AA participation, but the most important are cognitive restructuring (changing one's beliefs about alcohol and self) and unconditional acceptance, with its concomitant emotional support by the group as a whole and by individual members, including the sponsor.

Counselors and others working with alcoholics need knowledge by acquaintance with as well as knowledge about AA. They should attend open meetings. Reading AA's literature, especially *Alcoholics Anonymous* (known as the "Big Book") and *Twelve Steps and Twelve Traditions* (known as "the 12 and 12") (Alcoholics Anonymous World Services, 1952, 1976) is also a good idea. By reading this literature, one can learn the steps and slogans of AA, which are useful in relating both to stably sober and to active alcoholics. The AA concepts of "one day at a time" and "the first drink gets you drunk" are particularly useful in helping active alcoholics deal with their addiction. Although participation in AA is not every problem drinker's route to sobriety, it remains the single best way for most alcoholics to achieve and maintain sobriety. Some will reject AA, and others will become true believers. In general, the more emotionally disturbed the drinker, the less likely that AA will work. Nevertheless, an AA referral is always worth a try with active alcoholics.

AA talks about a higher power, and this spiritual side of AA turns some drinkers off. Of course, such a turnoff can be in the service of denial. AA sees alcoholism as a misguided quest for spirituality ("spirits instead of the spiritual") and actively encourages its members to "come to believe." For those who dislike AA's spiritual side, it is sometimes helpful for counselors to translate it into more secular terms. For example, AA's third step, "make a decision to turn our will and our lives over to the care of God *as we understand him*," can be secularized into "let it happen." AA's higher power can be interpreted as the AA group itself. AA stresses relinquishing control and can be seen as a group cognitive behavioral treatment for pathological narcissism with its concomitant need for omnipotent control.

There are other self-help groups that model themselves after AA and adapt its Twelve Steps. *Alanon* works with the alcoholic's significant others, and *Alateen* works with the teenage children of alcoholics. The populations serviced by *Narcotics Anonymous* (NA), *Overeaters Anonymous* (OA), and *Adult Children of Alcoholics* (ACOA) are apparent by their names. Like AA, these groups publish pamphlets listing the time and place of meetings. Meeting books are available for cities and most rural areas across the country.

Double Recovery Anonymous (DRA) is a twelve-step program with a difference. It is for dual-diagnosed patients and although it is a peer organization, its leaders receive training and guidance from mental health professionals. It is reported to be effective with a population whose prognosis is usually regarded as poor.

There are also non-twelve-step self-help groups. The two most important are *Rational Recovery* (RR) and *Women for Sobriety.*

Rational Recovery

Rational Recovery (RR) is a self-help group founded by a disaffected AA member named Jack Trimpey. RR is based on the principles of *rational-emotive therapy* (RET), a cognitive-behavioral approach to the treatment of psychopathology developed by Albert Ellis (1962, 1988). RET teaches that psychopathology, including addiction to alcohol, is the result of irrational thinking. RET challenges—or as its adherents say, "disputes"—false beliefs and tries to replace them with more "rational" beliefs. Ellis, who started as an analyst, says that he was inspired by the stoic philosopher Epictetus who taught that nothing could hurt the wise man. Ellis and Trimpey believe that alcoholics have a rigid, absolutistic, commanding approach to life and that they are addicted to *"must*urbation" (Ellis is much in favor of masturbation). They must be liked, loved, and do well, none of which are necessary (although they may be desirable) for adult happiness. Becoming frustrated when these goods are not forthcoming, they drink. Pharmacology does the rest. Ellis's style is abrasive and encountering, but there are gentler cognitive therapeutic approaches (such as Beck, 1976) that share Ellis's basic assumptions about psychopathology and its treatment.

RR does not regard alcoholism as a disease; rather, it sees it as a behavioral disorder resulting from faulty learning and irrational beliefs. It does not see alcoholism as progressive, believes that there is no such thing as loss of control, and that drinking (except perhaps in severe withdrawal) is a choice, and that no higher power is necessary for recovery. In fact, RR regards belief in the higher power and in most of the rest of the AA ideology as itself irrational. It takes particular exception to the AA notion that one is always recovering, rather than recovered, and requires lifelong treatment (in the form of participation in AA) in order to sustain recovery. RR sees its function as short-term education, support, and cognitive restructuring. It self-consciously teaches the exact opposite of AA, particularly in regard to the notion of powerlessness. The first of the Twelve Steps is "We realized that we were powerless over alcohol and that our lives had become unmanageable." RR's one and only step is, "We made a fearless evaluation of our most personal beliefs and chose the recovery program that made the most sense." (This mocks AA's fourth Step, "We made a fearless moral inventory"). RR teaches its members that they do have power over their drinking (not in the sense that they can drink with impunity but in the sense that they don't have to drink) and over their lives. In counterdistinction to the AA surrender and acceptance of dependency needs, RR inculcates self-sufficiency and seeks to enhance self-efficacy. It teaches its members to dispute "The Beast," the inner voice that would lead them back to irrational, self-destructive behavior usually taking the form of picking up a drink. (Note, how close this is to the AA admonition, "That's your disease talking.")

RR rejects AA's view of itself as a spiritual program, seeing it as clearly a religion. It rejects such religiosity as a prerequisite to recovery. The principles of RR are set forth in *The Small Book* (Trimpey, 1989); its title is of course a self-conscious contrast with that of the AA *Big Book,* as *Alcoholics Anonymous* (Alcoholics Anonymous World Services, 1976) is usually called by Program members.

RR meetings are group therapy sessions that, although they are self-help groups in terms of ideology and ethos, have a leader who is an RET therapist and donates his or her time to lead the group. (Presumably they get referrals in return.) The members discuss their vicissitudes with alcohol during the past week and the ways in which The Beast led them toward irrational thinking or even to a drink. More rational thinking is encouraged and supported. There are RR groups in most major cities and some rural areas.

Women for Sobriety

Jean Kirkpatrick, another disaffected AA member, founded a self-help group for women, *Women for Sobriety*. Less angry than Trimpey at AA, she sees much that is good in it and acknowledges that it helped her. However, she sees AA as a predominantly male organization whose treatment is right on target for male alcoholics, but somewhat off-center as a treatment for female alcoholism. Seeing the central issue in female alcoholism as low self-esteem, she too questions the AA admission of powerlessness as the only route to stable sobriety. She tells of the experiences that led her to found Women for Sobriety and explains the principles on which it operates in *Turnabout: Help for a New Life* (Kirkpatrick, 1977). Women For Sobriety has not caught on as well as RR has, but meetings can be found in the larger urban areas and some smaller ones. Kirkpatrick saw Women For Sobriety as meeting female needs not met by AA, not as antithetical to it. Many Women For Sobriety members also attend AA. Nevertheless, Kirkpatrick advocates exclusively female professional treatment programs, feeling that women get lost and are undertreated in the standard co-ed rehab.

OUTPATIENT TREATMENT

Outpatient treatment of alcoholism is conducted in clinics, social agencies, hospital and rehabilitation after care programs, and the offices of private practitioners. It is delivered by physicians, nurses, psychologists, social workers, and alcoholism counselors. Sometimes *Employee Assistance Program* (EAP) counselors are involved. EAPs are short-term counseling and referral departments located in businesses, industries, labor unions, and government agencies. They assist employees with many kinds of problems, but their focus is usually on alcohol and drug abuse. Aside from medical interventions, outpatient treatment takes three main forms: individual counseling, group therapy, and family therapy.

This is not a book on counseling technique and reading and studying it will not make you an alcoholism counselor. Rather, it is a prolegomena— that is, a critical, interpretive introduction—to counseling. Counseling is best learned in a clinically supervised field placement. Notwithstanding this disclaimer, it will be useful to be introduced to some counseling approaches and techniques.

Individual Counseling

The essence of individual counseling is the building of a relationship. It is the emotional bond between client and counselor or patient and therapist that gives impetus to the treatment. It is what makes information conveyed by the counselor credible to and capable of being heard by the client. Individual counseling can be used to convey information about alcohol and alcoholism; to teach clients to recognize and abort drink sig-

nals; to help clients build affect tolerance, the ability to sta'
feelings, and ego strength; and to help clients explore the
feelings, thoughts, memories, aspirations, and values. Ther'
ferent ways to do this. Some counselors work behaviorally, doing ...
training, teaching relaxation techniques, and using reinforcement to encourage sobriety. Other counselors work in a more cognitive behavioral
way, endeavoring to change clients' belief systems (such as by challeng-
ing the belief that drinking is manly or the belief that other people's
approval is always necessary). Still other counselors work more in the
gestalt tradition, using confrontation to arouse feelings. Existential counselors focus on ultimate or ontological issues (that is, those intrinsic to the
human condition) such as mortality, finitude and meaninglessness. Non-
directive or client centered therapy reflects back the client's feelings in an
atmosphere of unconditional positive regard. Counselors working in the
psychodynamic tradition focus on the relationship (its transferential and
its realistic aspects) to help a client understand his or her inner world,
defenses, manner of relating, and the degree to which his or her past
influences present behavior. Transference, as discussed earlier, is the
reenactment of early relationships in a present one, for instance, experiencing the counselor as rejecting regardless of the counselor's actual behavior, because one or both parents were rejecting. Counselors interpret
the transference to demonstrate how the client distorts his or her interpersonal perceptions.[1]

Alcoholism counseling has evolved out of all of the major counseling
traditions into, it is hoped, an integrated and not merely random, eclectic
specialty that draws on the scientific research of recent years in formulat-
ing a treatment approach uniquely suited to its client population. Different
alcoholics have different needs and the same alcoholic will have different
needs at different times. The newly sober person who is barely clinging to
sobriety does not need to learn about his unconscious wish to murder his
father, at least not yet. The stably sober client who cannot figure out why
he keeps provoking each new boss until he is fired—an occurrence that
always makes him think of drinking, thereby endangering his hard-won
sobriety—may very much need to know that he is simultaneously trying
to murder his father and punish himself for that forbidden wish. Treatment deals first with maintaining sobriety and only later, if at all, with
unconscious motivations.

---

[1]The reader interested in a more detailed discussion of the counseling process and
counseling techniques is referred to *Treatment of Alcoholism and Other Addictions: A
Self-Psychology Approach* (Levin, 1987). Since the literature on each of the counseling
traditions is so voluminous and many excellent counseling texts are available, I have
otherwise omitted references or recommendations from this section.

Group Therapy

Group therapy is a popular modality in alcoholism treatment. Active alcoholics are usually treated in inpatient groups. Outpatient groups can be effective, however, with active alcoholics if their alcoholism is relatively mild and they are capable of and willing to abstain on the days the group meets. Such a group can be used to teach members about alcohol and its effects. The group can also be used to teach the disease concept of alcoholism. However important the conveyance of such information is, especially because it reduces guilt, it is not enough. The group must also be used to confront denial and to help members recognize, correctly label, appropriately express, and deal with feelings. The goal with all members of a Stage 1 group (a group for active or very recently active alcoholics) is sobriety.

There are several reasons why group therapy is a very popular form of treatment. The use of a group is believed to dilute and make manageable the intensity of the alcoholic transference so that all too powerful feelings of love and hate do not get acted out by drinking or quitting treatment. Also guilt can be shared. The curative power of this sharing cannot be overemphasized, since alcoholics punish themselves for sins real or imagined, including their alcoholism, by drinking more. Another reason that groups are thought to be effective is that "it takes one to know one," which makes stage 1 groups extremely powerful devices to confront denial and unmask bullshit. At the same time, the sharing of a common problem makes relinquishing denial less painful. The sharing of painful experiences and humiliations acts as a balm for the narcissistic wounds that are an ineluctable concomitant of an alcoholic career.

Stage 2 groups focus on alcohol and the problems of early sobriety. They alter their members responses to drink signals, provide support and mutual identification, and serve as a safe place to express feelings. They are settings in which maladaptive defenses quickly manifest themselves. In a Stage 2 group these defenses can be confronted and interpreted or they can be supported in such a way that they protect the alcoholic without being overly destructive until the alcoholic is strong enough to relinquish them.

The Stage 3 group is a group of stably sober alcoholics usually with "time" (that is, sobriety of considerable duration). Such groups are homogeneous; all of their members are alcoholic. However, they do not focus on alcoholism per se. Rather, they seek to uncover and modify maladaptive defenses. They work far more psychodynamically than do Stage 1 and Stage 2 groups, using the group process in much the same way that transference is used in psychodynamic individual treatment. As an alternative to a Stage 3 alcoholism group, the stably sober alcoholic can join a heterogeneous, psychodynamically oriented outpatient group. If such a choice is made, something of the potential for identification found in the homogeneous alcoholism group is lost, but the possibility of identification with a broader range of human experience is gained.

Special population groups are also commonly used in alcoholism treatment. Examples would be a group for women alcoholics, a group for alcoholic cops, and a group for teenage substance abusers. Sometimes special interest groups are effective when more mixed groups are not. Homogeneity versus heterogeneity in group membership is an important treatment decision. Many clients benefit from participation in both types of groups.

Family Therapy

Family therapy is another popular form of alcoholism treatment. In fact, alcoholism is said to be a family disease, in that one family member's alcoholism powerfully affects the other family members. The children of alcoholics are often tragically affected and afflicted by their parents' alcoholism. Despite the drinker's pernicious effect on them, other family members often come to have an investment in the alcoholic's drinking, although they usually do not know it. Family systems theory looks at the way in which a family maintains its homeostasis, its equilibrium, be that equilibrium benign or malignant. Systems theory postulates that inertia causes any family system to resist change. Since an alcoholic's becoming sober is a profound change, it follows that the change will be resisted by family members. Family systems therapists look at who has the power, who has what effect on whom, who has what role, and how the role incarnations affect other family members and their roles. This thinking has been applied to the alcoholic family to describe a set of typical roles, one of which is the *parentified child*, or *hero*, defined as the child who takes care of the alcoholic parent. Other identified roles of children in alcoholic homes are the *scapegoat*, the *lost child*, and the *mascot*.

Family therapists see the family members together, and their interactions and interdependencies are worked with in various ways, depending on the therapist's theoretical orientation. An alcoholic family member's becoming sober will affect the entire system, and a readjustment of roles and relationships—which may be far from welcome although this is almost always denied—will take place. Family therapy sessions help the family understand the ways in which the alcoholic family member's drinking affected it and the impact that sobriety has on the family. Family therapy often makes the family members aware of their *codependency* and of their denial of both that codependency and the alcoholic's alcoholism. (In its original meaning, a codependent was somebody who remained in a relationship with an active alcoholic because doing so met unconscious needs of their own. Codependents were said to *enable* the alcoholic to continue drinking. Unfortunately, the term has become so overgeneralized as to lose meaning. Today, if you say hello to your spouse, you may be labeled codependent.) In the case of the adolescent substance abuser, family therapy is considered highly desirable and often necessary for successful treatment.

Network Therapy

Marc Galanter (1993) of New York University Medical School has developed an intriguing treatment modality called *network therapy*. Since it is a recent development, there is no outcome study as yet (although there is a grant proposal for such a study); nevertheless, Galanter reports encouraging results. An outgrowth in some ways of family therapy, there are important differences. In family therapy, the family system and all of its members (who theoretically, although not necessarily in practice, are not focused on as individuals apart from the system) are the targets of intervention. Not so in network therapy, where the entire system (family or otherwise) is involved in the treatment, but the alcoholic or substance abuser is the only patient. In family therapy, the identified patient is seen as the repository of all of the pathology in the system, and family therapy seeks to elucidate and make manifest the multifaceted ways in which the system and its members project their dysfunctionality onto the patient. In network therapy, the dysfunction—pathology in the system—is ignored and the "network" is exclusively used to assist the identified patient, the user or drinker, in achieving and maintaining sobriety.

This modality is most effectively used with patients who are motivated, however ambivalently, to stop drinking, but who have difficulties resisting cravings. They might be said to be the motivated impulse ridden. In that way, they resemble the population who benefits the most from disulfiram therapy; in fact, network therapy might be seen as interpersonal Antabuse. There is, however, an important difference. Antabuse patients have often destroyed their social networks or been affiliated with highly pathological ones, while the network candidate must either have an intact network or be able to create one that is sufficiently healthly and able to support and not undermine the patient from a stance of nonjudgmental positive regard. That is not easy to come by, so network therapy candidates, in spite of their ego and self deficits, may be assumed to have at least a modicum of ego strength.

In network therapy, the counselor is quite directive. Network is an abstinence therapy; no attempt is made to construct or evoke a network until the client has made a commitment to sobriety. At that point, the counselor explores whether the client can achieve sobriety on his or her own, even with program support (if the client is willing to affiliate with AA). If the answer is no, the counselor suggests eliciting the help of family, friends, teachers, bosses, and clergy to create a support network. Explicit danger points or situations are probed for and the counselor suggests ways in which the network can be used to get by these rough spots. For example, Bill always got drunk Friday night and gets very strong drink signals on Friday afternoons. He arranges with Uncle Henry to meet Fridays after work to play basketball which he enjoys. Sally always drank when she felt sad. She arranges with her friend Joan to call her whenever she feels sad and with Aunt Sadie to go shopping which cheers her up, when she's down.

The counselor meets regularly with the network, although less frequently than with the client. There are no secrets or privileged communications and everything pertaining to the client's sobriety is discussed. Galanter recommends that network therapy be used as one component of a multimodal comprehensive treatment program.

Neurobiofeedback

There have been reports (Peniston & Kulkosky, 1989; Peniston & Kulkosky, 1990) of high rates of recovery (prolonged abstinence and improved scores on psychometric tests) in chronic alcoholic patients with long histories of relapse using neurobiofeedback training. Peniston and Kulkosky first worked with Veterans' Administration Hospital patients who were long-standing alcoholics for whom no previous therapy had provided any sustained benefit. They were trained in *temperature* or *thermal biofeedback*, that is, to relax using skin temperature as an external cue. Once they had mastered the use of thermal biofeedback to increase relaxation, they were given *brain wave training* (BWT) in which *electroencephalograph* (EEG) measures were used to provide feedback so that an alpha and later a theta rhythm could be achieved. The EEG feedback was also used to teach the patients to increase the amplitude of their alpha waves. Alpha states are "serenity" states and the greater the amplitude and synchronicity of the alpha waves, the greater the serenity. Alpha is experienced subjectively as peace, calm, and deep relaxation. It is a pleasurable state. Theta rhythms are characteristic of deep meditation states.

Alpha BWT was suggested by the studies (Schuckit & Gold, 1988) reviewed in chapter 6 that show children of alcoholics to have low amplitude, poorly synchronized alpha waves that are improved by drinking, and by the studies (Porjesz & Begleiter, 1983) that show that Cloninger Type 1 alcoholics suffer deficiencies in alpha activity. It is also known that clinical alcoholics manifest impaired alpha rhythms far into sobriety. The degree to which these findings are consequent or antecedent to the

alcoholism is debated. The widespread use of relaxation training and meditation groups in alcoholic rehabilitation may also have suggested that BWT
aimed at optimizing alpha and theta states would be an effective treatment modality for alcoholism.

The original protocol called for fifteen 30-minute sessions of alpha-
theta BWT and no other treatment. The patients were first given *autogenic
training* (Jacobson, 1938) a method of attaining a state of deep relaxation
utilizing alternating tension and relaxation of body parts. ("Now tense the
fingers on your left hand. Make them as tense as possible. Now let go and
feel the tension leave your hand. Your hand is becoming more and more
relaxed," and so forth until the entire body is brought to a state of deep
relaxation.) The alcoholics were then given the pretraining in thermal biofeedback discussed above. Using their autogenic training to achieve deep
relaxation, these patients become able to raise their external body temperature (measured by a finger device) to 95 degrees, the raised temperatures
were used as feedback cues of relaxation. After their pretraining, the
chronic alcoholics received alpha-theta brain wave training. EEG electrodes were attached to their scalps and the electrical activity picked up
was used to provide aural and visual feedback. A hum signaled alpha
activity. While in the alpha state the subjects were instructed to imagine
themselves refusing drinks or getting through a situation of "temptation"
without drinking.

In the Peniston and Kulkosky (1989) study, eight of ten chronic alcoholics were stably sober 13 months later as well as maintaining improved
scores on psychometric instruments of various sorts. Interestingly, the subjects' serum beta-endorphin levels were not elevated by the alpha-theta
BWT, while the beta-endorphin levels of patients receiving traditional
alcoholism treatment became elevated, a condition correlated with high
levels of stress. Peniston and Kulkosky concluded that traditional alcoholism treatment (such as group therapy) may increase stress to the point
where chronic alcoholics drink (their patients had multiple admissions for
alcoholism), while alpha-theta BWT lowers stress and facilitates the maintenance of sobriety.

This treatment model, often modified by the addition of sessions of
cognitive behavior therapy and guided imagery, has been promoted by the
Menninger Clinic and by biofeedback institutes. Two unexplained phenomena have been reported associated with neurobiofeedback treatment
of alcoholism. Some patients spontaneously recover repressed traumatic
memories, often with intense emotional upset. Others become ill if they
drink; for them, BWT serves as a permanent Antabuse.

Although further study of outcomes is clearly needed, the equipment
used is expensive, and the unexpected effects are disconcerting, neurobiofeedback appears to be a useful addition to our armamentarium of techniques to treat alcoholism.

Acupuncture

Acupuncture (Smith, 1989) has been used to reduce craving for alcohol and drugs. This technique, pioneered by Lincoln Hospital in the Bronx, is structured as an on-demand walk-in protocol so that "non-traditional" patients, many of whom are homeless or stylistically street people, can avail themselves of treatment which they could not do if acupuncture were to be offered on a by-appointment set-time basis. Lincoln reports that many of these patients, who are schizoid, paranoid, or realistically leery of the "establishment," are able to develop rapport and connection in this minimally threatening environment and go on to more structured counseling experiences.

Drawing on traditional Chinese medicine, which believes that there are special relations between strategic points on the skin and various bodily functions, addiction acupuncture has established four points on the ear (see Figure 12.1) that reduce craving. The same points are used to reduce withdrawal symptoms and are sometimes the only treatment used. Although acupuncture has more often been used with drug users, it appears to hold promise in the treatment of alcoholism. Its use is spreading and it has been introduced as an adjunctive treatment in some alcohol rehabs treating middle-class patients.

Treatment of Shame-Based Behavior

John Bradshaw is former priest who is a recovering alcoholic who has had a tremendous impact on the community of recovering persons. He writes for the general public, and his popular books, and seminars have had wide influence. Although a "pop" psychologist, he has something important to say. His basic position is that addiction (including alcoholism) is the result of the repression of childhood shame experiences (Bradshaw, 1988). He calls this *toxic shame*. Bradshaw is not referring here to the shame that comes from or with addiction; rather, he is talking about the kind of shame that comes from having been abused as a child or from growing up in an alcoholic home particularly if the shame is anesthetized, denied, repressed, or acted out. One suspects that Bradshaw is primarily speaking to and about those alcoholics whose parents were alcoholic. Like all single factor theories, his is overly simplistic and his writings tend to be repetitious. They do however have the virtue of highlighting the centrality of shame in the dynamics of alcoholism. His treatment recommendations are a synthesis of the psychodynamic (such as recovery of repressed memories and dream work) and the cognitive behavioral (for instance, cognitive restructuring and self-efficacy training). He stresses work with the "inner child."

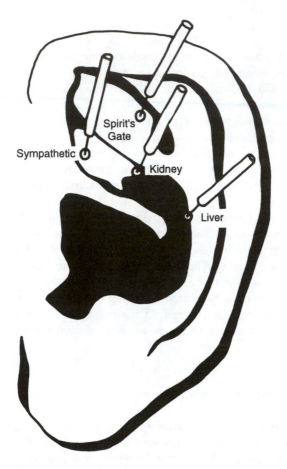

Figure 12.1 Acupuncture Points Reported to Reduce Craving for Alcohol and Drugs (Courtesy of Lincoln Hospital, Bronx, New York). "Spirits gate and "sympathetic" needles are inserted as shown to relax the body and adjust its chemical balance. "Kidney" and "liver" needles are inserted as shown to strengthen the function of the two organs, key body systems in the processing of drugs and alcohol.

Bradshaw's formats of workshops and video presentations make for high states of emotional arousal and sometimes for intense feelings of connectedness. Like the marathon therapy groups of the 1960s and 1970s, people leave feeling good; however, the degree to which they change and maintain that change is unknown. Of course, a great meal or an orgasm does not last forever either, yet may be an intrinsically positive experience. Perhaps that is also the case with participation in Bradshaw or Bradshaw-style workshops.

Relapse Prevention

Relapse prevention has always been a part of alcoholism counseling. After care groups have long focused on making conscious or increasing awareness of drink signals, as well as on teaching alternative coping skills to replace drinking as a way of dealing with dysphoria of various sorts. And AA has long taught that "people, places, and things" can get you drunk, with its implied admonition to change or avoid those people, places, and things. Like the character in the Moliere's play *Le Bourgeois gentilhomme*, we are learning that we have "spoken prose all our lives." However, in recent years *relapse prevention* has been formalized by G. Alan Marlatt and Judith R. Gordon (1985). Using a social learning model of addiction and relapse, they have highlighted five causes of relapse: feeling controlled by or unable to resist the influence of others; low self-efficacy (feelings of powerlessness, fatalism, and learned helplessness); availability of alcohol, particularly in social situations that encourage its use; lack of adequate alternate coping responses; and high expectancy that drinking enhances coping. They found that negative emotional states (frustration, anger, anxiety, and fear) caused 38% of relapses, craving and triggers 16%, and social context or conflict 20%, while drinking to achieve positive affect (euphoria) accounted for only 3% of slips. In my experience most slips are rage reactions, the rage often being unconscious. The "fuck you martini" gets an awful lot of people drunk (again).

Marlatt and Gordon have devised protocols for dealing with each of these vulnerabilities to relapse using modeling (such as seeing a model refuse a drink), teaching new coping skills (for instance, assertiveness training), changing expectancies through *cognitive restructuring* (if we approve of changing someone's thoughts and values we call it cognitive restructuring; if we do not, we call it brainwashing); and suggesting environmental changes. In short, the entire range of cognitive behavior therapy technique is brought to bear on the prevention of relapse.

The abstinence violation effect (AVE), "if I drink, I won't be able to stop and I will have to hate myself for doing so" (see discussion of AVE under criticisms of the disease model in chapter 5), is circumvented by teaching that drinking is a choice, that the taking of a drink does not compel you to take another, and that there are reasons for relapse, so that rather than taking the abstinence violation as a reason for self-hatred, its causes can be analyzed so that the slip becomes a learning experience. Thus, for example, if the slip resulted from social influence, the client could learn to say no or to change his or her associates. Although this conceptualization of slips as both freely chosen and as determined seems self-contradictory, it clearly has clinical utility (as Emerson said, "consistency is the hobgoblin of little minds"). So does the Marlett and Gordon approach as a whole. Relapse prevention techniques are applicable to both abstinence and controlled drinking treatment models.

CONCLUSION

The techniques and modalities available to counselors are Stage 1 group therapy, Stage 2 group therapy, family therapy, network therapy, informational and educational interventions, behavioral counseling, cognitive restructuring, relapse prevention, gestalt therapy and psychodrama (with their emotional arousal and discharge of affect as well as opportunity to establish empathy with others), and psychodynamically oriented counseling. All of these have a place in the treatment of alcoholism. The trick is to know when to do what. The alcoholism counselor needs to ask: What does this alcoholic most need to know, learn, or experience now, and how can I facilitate that knowing, learning, or experiencing? The name of the game is to replace rum with relationship and then to use this relationship between client and counselor to assist the alcoholic in growing in such a way that alcohol (or other drugs) is no longer necessary to deal with feelings, maintain self-esteem, or reduce anxiety.

A Possible Bridge
Between the Neurochemistry
of Dreaming and Blackouts

In this appendix I would like to explore and suggest a possible link between the neurochemistry of dreaming, the pharmacology of alcohol, the
disruptive effect of alcohol on REM sleep, and palimpsets (blackouts).
The theory of dreaming I am drawing on is Jonathan Winson's (1990),
summarized in his article "The Meaning of Dreams." (See also Winson,
1985.)

There are a number of competing theories about the function and
mechanisms of dreams. The best known of these are Freud's theory of the
psychological meaningfulness of dreams as compromise formations, which
give disguised expression to repressed, forbidden wishes and drives; the
Hobson-McCarley activation-synthesis hypothesis that dreams are the
cortex's best fit interpretation of random stimulation from the brain stem
and are inherently psychologically meaningless; and the Crick-Mitcheson
reverse learning theory that holds that information overload from the day's
experiences prevents orderly storage of relevant information into memory
and that REM sleep with its concomitant dreaming erases spurious associations allowing the coding and storage of information to proceed. The
later theory has been summarized as "We dream to forget." The trouble

with this theory is that the dreamer has to "know" what to forget and what to retain for processing, and the theory provides no criterion for, nor mechanism of, such a discrimination. Hobson has abandoned the position that dreams are psychologically meaningless and now holds that the order imposed on the random spikes from the brain stem is a function of the personal view of the world and of remote (childhood) memories of the dreamer.

Winson believes that dreams are meaningful and that they play a vital role in the processing of memory. He bases his theory partly on evolutionary evidence and partly on studies of the hippocampus, REM sleep, and theta rhythms. The hippocampus is a subcortical brain structure importantly involved in learning and in memory; REM sleep is the sleep stage during which dreaming occurs; and theta rhythms are brain waves that occur during survival behavior and during dreaming in most mammals. According to this theory, dreams are a nightly record basic to the mammalian memory process, and a means by which animals form strategies for survival by evaluating current experience.

Sleep in healthy human adults normally follows a pattern of stages from hyponogogic to slow wave to rapid eye movement (REM) to slow wave to REM to slow wave to REM to slow wave to REM. A similar pattern prevails in all marsupial and placental mammals. REM sleep is under the control of the brain stem. Pontine-geniculate-occipital (PGO) electrical spikes go from the pons in the brain stem to the visual processing center in the occipital lobe of the cortex demonstrating electrochemical transmission along this path. At the same time, theta wave activity can be measured.

Theta waves are 6 cycles per second (CPS) brain waves found in the hippocampus of animals during survival behavior: predation in the cat, apprehension of danger in the rabbit, and exploration in the rat. Each of these behaviors is not rigidly genetically controlled and requires response to changing environmental conditions. Theta waves accompany the REM sleep of all of these species. They can be measured in the hippocampus where they probably play a vital role in memory processing. Egg laying mammals (montremes) do not have REM sleep, nor do they dream. This evolutionary evidence suggests that REM sleep has survival value for higher mammals. Winson argues that theta waves reflect neural processes whereby information essential for survival (Freud's "day residues") are reprocessed into memory during REM sleep.

The basic mechanism of memory is believed to involve *Long-Term-Potentiation* (LTP), a process in which relatively enduring changes in nerve cells are induced by intense electrical stimulation. After tetanic (high frequency electrical) stimulation of the pathway from the cortex to the granule cells of the hippocampus, a single electrical pulse causes rapid firing, far above baseline, of the granule cell neurons. The potentiation of these neurons is considered a model for memory, a mechanism by which neural structure and function is altered. LTP is induced by activity of the N-methyl-D-aspartate (NMDA) receptor. This receptor molecule is embedded in the dentrites of the neurons of all of the above mentioned structures and circuits. The NMDA receptor is activated by a neurotransmitter, the amino acid, glutamate. Glutamate opens a non-NMDA channel that permits the entry of sodium ions from the intracellular space depolarizing the neuron. NMDA is unique among receptor molecules because it can be further activated by glutamate opening a second channel that allows the influx of calcium ions (Ca^{2+}). Ca^{2+} serves as a "second messenger"; its presence in the cell provides additional electric stimulation eventuating in LTP. LTP is caused naturally by theta waves activating NMDA receptors. Thus, NMDA in the presence of theta waves provides the neurochemical basis for long-term storage of biologically significant information.

It has been demonstrated that hippocampal neurons that fire during neural mapping of survival information also fire during REM sleep, which suggests that re-mapping or re-processing is occurring. Non-REM mammals (metromes) have a large amount of neo-cortex; REM mammals have proportionately less; they do not need it to interpret, integrate, and re-process survival information. The information being re-processed is both motor and visual, and inhibition of motor, but not eye, activity is required if REM is not to be interrupted. And, indeed, motor inhibition is characteristic of REM states.

So each species processes information vital to its survival: location of food, means of predation, or escape strategies. In REM sleep this information is re-accessed and integrated with past experience to form a survival strategy for the future. Since animals don't have language their dreams are visual, so are those of humans. This suggests that human dreams reflect individual strategies for survival. Experiments have demonstrated that people dream about current crises and try to work out strategies for dealing with them in their dreams. Dreams are hard to interpret because the associations the neocortex brings to them are complex. These associations tend to reflect childhood experiences. Dreams give us access to and themselves constitute an infrastructure by which new experience is compared to past and integrated.

This brings us to alcohol. The pharmacology of ethanol is still poorly understood but two types of mechanisms have been demonstrated (see chapter 1). The classical theory holds that alcohol asserts its effect by disorganizing the fatty material in the cell membrane of the neuron, which in turn disorganizes and disrupts the functioning of the receptor protein molecules embedded in those fatty layers. The trouble with this theory is that effects of alcohol on these phenomena, particularly in low doses, is too small to account for the subjective and behavioral consequences of drinking. More recent theories have demonstrated and highlighted ethanol's direct effects on nerve cell receptors, particularly on the NMDA receptor (the recognition site for glutamate that activates the second messenger system by opening a channel for Ca^{2+}). The response of the neuron to glutamate is greatly reduced by alcohol. (The effects of alcohol on the GABA receptor also plays an important role in intoxication.) But, as we saw above, the glutamate-NMDA-Ca^{2+} second messenger system is the basis of LTP which in turn is the basis of memory. Further, it is well known that alcohol disrupts and disturbs REM sleep, in fact, reducing it; and that REM rebound occurs when drinking ceases. NMDA plays a vital role in the hippocampal-neocortex re-processing that occurs during REM. If alcohol blocks NMDA functioning, preventing LTP during REM, this may be the mechanism of blackouts. The kind of blackouts where there is no recall at all may be due to the lack of REM re-processing that results from alcohol's blockage of LTP by the NMDA-glutamate-Ca^{2+} mechanism; while the kind of blackout that the drinker comes out of while still drinking may be due to blockage of primary memory processing by the same mechanism in the hippocampus during awakeness.

Further, if Winson's dream theory is correct, we have another instance of an attempt at self-cure through the use of alcohol not only failing, but making things worse. If some people drink because they have difficulty coping, and dreaming is an important coping mechanism through which current information is fixed in memory and integrated with past experience, excessive drinking disrupts and diminishes this process. The heavy drinker is depriving himself of an important coping response and a vicious cycle is set up. A fundamental resource for understanding self and world is lost, and the anxiety engenders by that loss may well set up the next drinking episode.

References

Abraham, K. (1979). The psychological relations between sexuality and alcoholism. In *Selected papers on psychoanalysis* (pp. 80–90). New York: Brunner/Mazel. (Original work published 1908)

Alcoholics Anonymous World Services. (1952). *Twelve steps and twelve traditions.* New York: Author.

Alcoholics Anonymous World Services. (1976). *Alcoholics anonymous* (3rd ed.). New York: Author.

Alexopoulos, G. S., Lieberman, K. W., & Frances, R. J. (1983). Platelet MOA activity in alcoholic patients and their first-degree relatives. *American Journal of Psychiatry, 140*(11), 1501–1503.

Amark, C. (1951). A study in alcoholism: Clinical, social, psychiatric, and genetic investigations. *Acta Psychiatrica Neurologica Scandinavica, 70,* 1–283.

American Psychiatric Association. (1980). *Diagnostic and statistical manual of mental disorders* (3rd ed.). Washington, DC: Author.

American Psychiatric Association. (1987). *Diagnostic and statistical manual of mental disorders* (3rd ed. rev.). Washington, DC: Author.

American Psychiatric Association. (1994). *Diagnostic and statistical manual of mental disorders* (4th ed.). Washington, DC: Author.

Babor, T. F., Wolfson, A., Boivan, D., Padouco-Thomas, S., & Clark, W. (1992). Alcoholism, culture, and psychopathology: A comparative study of French, French-Canadian, and American alcoholics. In J. E. Helzer & G. J. Canino (Eds.), *Alcoholism in North America, Europe, and Asia* (pp. 182–195). New York: Oxford University Press.

Bales, R. F. (1959). Cultural differences in rates of alcoholism. In G. McCarthy (Ed.), *Drinking and intoxication.* Glencoe, IL: Free Press.

Balint, M. (1968). *The basic fault.* London: Tavistock.

Bandura, A., & Walters, R. H. (1963). *Social learning and personality development.* New York: Holt, Rinehart & Winston.

Barnes, G. E. (1979). The alcoholic personality: A reanalysis of the literature. *Journal of Studies on Alcohol, 40,* 571–634.

Barnes, G. E. (1983). Clinical and prealcoholic personality characteristics, In B. Kissin & H. Begleiter (Eds.), *The biology of alcoholism, Vol. 6. The pathogenesis of alcoholism: Psychosocial factors* (pp. 113–196). New York: Plenum.

Bateson, G. (1971). The cybernetics of "self": A theory of alcoholism. *Psychiatry, 34,* 1–18.

Bateson, G., & Ruesch, J. (1951). *Communication: The social matrix of psychiatry.* New York: W. W. Norton.

Beck, A. T. (1976). *Cognitive therapy and the emotional disorders.* New York: International Universities Press.

Begleiter, H., Porjesz, B., Bihari, B., & Kissen, B. (1984). Event-related brain potentials in boys at risk for alcoholism. *Science, 225,* 1493–1495.

Bentham, J. (1939). An introduction to the principles of morals and legislation. In E. A. Burtt (Ed.), *The English Philosophers from Bacon to Mill* (pp. 791–852). New York: The Modern Library. (Original work published 1789)

Berglas, S. (1985). Self-handicapping and self-handicappers: A cognitive/attributional model of interpersonal self-protective behavior. In R. Hogan and W. H. Jones (Eds.), *Perspectives in personality theory: Theory, measurement and interpersonal dynamics.* Greenwich, CT: JAI Press.

Blane, H. T. (1968). *The personality of the alcoholic: Guises of dependency.* New York: Harper & Row.

Bleuler, M. (1955). Familial and personal background of chronic alcoholics. In O. Drethelm (Ed.), *Etiology of chronic alcoholism* (pp. 110–166). Springfield, IL: Charles C. Thomas.

Bohman, M. (1978). Some genetic aspects of alcoholism and criminality: A population of adoptees. *Archives of General Psychiatry, 35,* 269–276.

Bradshaw, J. (1988). *Healing the shame that binds you.* Deerfield Beach, FL: Health Communications.

Bunzel, A. (1940). The role of alcoholism in two Central American cultures. *Psychiatry, 3,* 361–387.

Butzel, R. (1982). Intoxication and withdrawal. In N.J. Estes & M. E. Heinemann (Eds.), *Alcoholism: Developments, consequences, and interventions* (2nd ed., pp. 102–108). St. Louis: Mosby.

Cadoret, R. J., O'Gorman, T. W., Troughton, E., & Heywood, L. (1984). Alcoholism and antisocial personality: Interrelationshps, genetic and environmental factors. *Archives of General Psychiatry, 42,* 161–167.

Cahalan, D., Cisin, H., & Crossley, H. (1969). *American drinking practices: A national survey of behavior and attitudes* (Monograph 6). New Brunswick, NJ: Rutgers Center for Alcohol Studies.

Cappell, H. & Herman, C. P. (1972). Alcohol and tension reduction: A review, *Journal of Studies on Alcohol, 33,* 33–64.

Child, I., Bacon, M., & Barry, H. (1965). A cross-cultural study of drinking. *Quarterly Journal of Studies on Alcohol* (Suppl. 3), 5–96.

Clark, W. B. & Cahalan, D. (1976). Changes in problem drinking over a four-year span. *Addictive Behaviors, 1,* 251–259.

Clark, W. B., & Midanik, L. (1982). Alcohol use and alcohol problems among U.S. adults. Results of the 1979 national survey. In *Alcohol consumption and related problems* (Alcohol and Health Monograph No. 1, DHHS Publication No. ADM 82-1190). Washington, DC: U.S. Government Printing Office.

Cloninger, C. R. (1983). Genetic and environmental factors in the development of alcoholism. *Journal of Psychiatric Treatment and Evaluation, 5,* 487–496.

Cloninger, C. R. (1987a). A systematic method for clinical description and classification of personality variants: A proposal. *Archives of General Psychiatry, 44,* 573–588.

Cloninger, C. R. (1987b). Neurogenetic adaptive mechanisms in alcoholism. *Science, 236,* 410–416.

Cloninger, C. R., Bohman, M., & Sigvardsson, S. (1981). Cross-fostering analysis of adopted men. *Archives of General Psychiatry, 36,* 861–868.

Cloninger, C. R., Sigvardsson, S., & Bohman, M. (1988). Childhood personality predicts alcohol abuse in young adults. *Alcoholism: Clinical and Experimental Research, 12,* 494–505.

Conger, J. J. (1956). Reinforcement and the dynamics of alcoholism, *Quarterly Journal of Studies on Alcohol, 13,* 296–305.

Conner, R. (1962). The self-concepts of alcoholics. In D. Pittman & C. Snyder (Eds.), *Society, culture and drinking patterns* (pp. 455–467). Carbondale: Southern Illinois University Press.

Cox, W. M. (1985). Personality correlatives of substance abuse. In M. Galizio & S. A. Mausto (Eds.), *Determinants of substance abuse: Biological, psychological, and environmental factors* (pp. 209–246). New York: Plenum.

Cox, W. M. (1987). Personality theory and research. In H. Blane and K. Leonard (Eds.), *Psychological theories of drinking and alcoholism* (pp. 55–89). New York: Guilford Press.

Cruz-Coke, R., & Varela, A. (1966). Inheritance of alcoholism: Its association with colour-blindness. *Lancet, ii,* 1282–1284.

DeLuca, J., & Wallace, J. (1981). *The fourth special report to the U.S. Congress on alcohol and health* [DHHS Publication No. (ADM)81-1291]. Washington, DC: U.S. Government Printing Office.

Deutsch, H. (1965). Some forms of emotional disturbance and their relationship to schizo-phrenia. In *Neuroses and character types* (pp. 262–281). New York: International Universities Press.

Durkheim, E. (1987). *Suicide.* Glencoe, IL: Free Press.

Ellis, A. (1962). *Reason and emotion in psychotherapy.* Seacaucus, NJ: Citadel.

Ellis, A. (1988). *Rational-emotive therapy with alcoholics and substance abusers.* Oxford: Pergamon Press.

Fenichel, O. (1945). *The psychoanalytic theory of the neurosis.* New York: W. W. Norton.

Field, P. (1962). A new cross-cultural study of drunkenness. In D. Pittman & C. Snyder (Eds.), *Society, culture, and drinking patterns* (pp. 48–74). Carbondale: Southern Illinois University Press.

Fingarette, H. (1988). *Heavy drinking: The myth of alcoholism as a disease.* Berkeley, CA: University of California Press.

Freud, S. (1953). Interpretation of dreams. In J. Strachey (Ed. and Trans.), *Standard edition of the complete psychological works of Sigmund Freud* (Vols. 4 & 5, pp. 1–628). London: Hogarth Press (original work published 1900).

Freud, S. (1955). Beyond the pleasure principle. In J. Strachey (Ed. and Trans.), *Standard edition of the complete psychological works of Sigmund Freud* (Vol. 18, pp. 1–64). London: Hogarth Press (original work published 1920).

Freud, S. (1956). The ego and the id. In J. Strachey (Ed. and Trans.), *Standard edition of the complete psychological works of Sigmund Freud* (Vol. 19, pp. 1–66). London: Hogarth Press (original work published 1923).

Freud, S. (1957). On narcissism: an introduction. In J. Strachey (Ed. and Trans.), *Standard edition of the complete psychological works of Sigmund Freud* (Vol. 14, pp. 67–104). London: Hogarth Press (original work published 1914).

Freud, S. (1961). Dostoevsky and parricide. In J. Strachey (Ed. and Trans.), *Standard edition of the complete psychological works of Sigmund Freud* (Vol. 21, pp. 173–194). London: Hogarth Press (original work published 1928).

Freud, S. (1974). *Cocaine papers* (B. Byck, Ed.). New York: New American Library.

Freud, S. (1985). *The complete letters of Sigmund Freud to Wilhelm Fleiss* (J. M. Mason, Ed. and Trans.) Cambridge, MA: Harvard University Press. (Originally written 1897).

Fromm, E. (1941). *Escape from freedom.* New York: Rinehart.

Fromm, E. (1964). *The heart of man.* New York: Harper & Row.

Galanter, M. (1993). *Network therapy for alcohol and drug abuse: A new approach in practice.* New York: Basic Books.

Gay, P. (1988). *Freud: A life for our time.* New York: W. W. Norton.

Gilman, A. G., Goodman, L. S., & Gilman, A. (Eds.). (1985). *Goodman and Gilman's The pharmacological bases of therapeutics* (7th ed.). New York: Macmillan.

Glover, E. (1928). The etiology of alcoholism. *Proceedings of the Royal Society of Medicine, 21,* 1351–1355.

Goldstein, G. (1976). Perceptual and cognitive deficit in alcoholics. In G. Goldstein & C. Neuringer (Eds.), *Empirical studies of alcoholism* (pp. 115–152). Cambridge, MA: Bollinger.

Goodwin, D. W. (1988). *Is alcoholism hereditary?* New York: Ballantine Books.

Goodwin, D.W., Schulsinger, F., Hermansen, L., Guze, S. B., & Winokur, G. (1973). Alcohol problems in adoptees raised apart from alcoholic biological parents. *Archives of General Psychiatry, 28,* 283–343.

Hall, T. (1989, March 15). A new temperance is taking root in America. *The New York Times,* pp. A1, A6.

Harris, L., and Associates, Inc. (1971). *American attitudes toward alcohol and alcoholism* (Study no. 2188). A survey of public opinion prepared for the National Institute on Alcohol Abuse and Alcoholism. New York: Louis Harris.

Hartocollis, P., & Hartocollis, P. (1980). Alcoholism, borderline and narcissistic disorders: A psychoanalytic overview. In W. Fann, I. Karacon, A. Pokorny, & R. Williams (Eds.), *Phenomenology and treatment of alcoholism* (pp. 93–110). New York: Spectrum.

Hartocollis, P. (1968). A dynamic view of alcoholism: drinking in the service of denial. *Dynamic Psychiatry, 2,* 173–182.

Heath, D. B. (1958). Drinking patterns of the Bolivian Camba. *Quarterly Journal of Studies on Alcohol, 19,* 491–508.

Heath, D.B. (1991). Continuity and change in drinking patterns of the Bolivian Camba. In D. Pittman & H. A. White (Eds.), *Society, culture, and drinking patterns reexamined* (pp. 78–86). New Brunswick, NJ: Rutgers Center of Alcohol Studies

Hewitt, C. C. (1943). A personality study of alcohol addiction. *Quarterly Journal of Studies on Alcohol, 4,* 368–386.

Horton, D. (1943). The functions of alcohol in primitive societies: A cross-cultural study. *Quarterly Journal of Studies on Alcohol, 4,* 199–320.

Hull, J. G. (1981). A self-awareness model of the causes and effects of alcohol consumption. *Journal of Abnormal Psychology, 90,* 586–600.

Huxley, A. (1954). *The doors of perception.* New York: Harper & Row.

Irgens-Jensen, O. (1971). *Problem drinking and personality: A study based on the Draw-a-Person Test.* New Brunswick, NJ: Rutgers Center for Alcohol Studies.

Jacobson, E. (1938). *Progressive relaxation.* Chicago: University of Chicago Press.

James, W. (1902). *Varieties of religious experience.* New York: Longmans.

Jellinek, E. M. (1952). Phases of alcohol addiction. *Quarterly Journal of Studies on Alcohol, 13,* 673–684.

Jellinek, E. M. (1960). *The disease concept of alcoholism.* New Haven, CT: College and University Press.

Jellinek, E. M. (1962). Cultural differences in the meaning of alcoholism. In D. J. Pittman and C. R. Snyder (Eds.), *Society, culture, and drinking patterns* (pp. 382–388). Carbondale: Southern Illinois University Press.

Jellinek, G. (1994). Heredity and premature weaning: A discussion of the work of Thomas Trotter, British Naval Physician. In J. Levin & R. Weiss (Eds.), *The dynamics and treatment of alcoholism: Essential papers* (pp. 28–34). Northvale, NJ: Jason Aronson. (Trotter's original work published 1804, Jellinek's article, 1943)

Jessor, R. (1987). Problem-behavior theory, psychosocial development, and adolescent problem drinking. *British Journal of Addictions, 82,* 331–342.

Jessor, R., Graves, T. D., Hanson, R. C. & Jessor, S. L. (1968). *Society, personality, behavior: A study of a tri-ethnic community.* New York: Hold, Rinehart & Winston.

Jones, K. L., Smith, D. W., Ulleland, C. N., & Streissguth, A. P. (1973). Pattern of malformation in offspring in chronic alcoholic women. *Lancet, i,* 1267–1271.

Jones, M. C. (1968). Personal correlates of antecedents of drinking patterns in adult males, *Journal of Consulting and Clinical Psychology, 32,* 2–12.

Jones, M. C. (1971). Personality antecedents and correlates of drinking patterns in women, *Journal of Consulting and Clinical Psychology, 36,* 61–69.

Julien, R. M. (1991). *A primer of drug action* (6th ed.). San Francisco: W. H. Freeman.

Jung, C. G. (1973). In G. Adler (Ed.), *C.G. Jung: Letters, Vol. II, 1951–1961* (pp. 623–625). Princeton, NJ: Princeton University Press. (Originally written 1961)

Kaij, L. (1960). *Alcoholism in twins: Studies on the etiology and sequels of abuse of alcohol.* Stockholm: Almquist & Wiksell.

Kaminer, W. (1993). *I'm dysfunctional, you're dysfunctional: The recovery movement and other self-help fashions.* New York: Vintage.

Kandel, D. B. (1975). Stages in adolescent involvement in drug use. *Science, 190,* 912–914.

Kandel, D. B., Yamaguchi, K., & Chen, K. (1992). Stages of progression in drug involvement from adolescence to adulthood: Further evidence for the gateway theory. *Journal of Studies on Alcohol, 53,* 447–457.

Kant, I. (1929). *The critique of pure reason* (2nd Ed., M. K. Smith, trans.). London: MacMillan. (Original work published 1787)

Kazin, A. (1976, March). 'The giant killer': Drink and the american writer. *Commentary, 61*(3), 44–50.

Keller, M. (1958). Alcoholism: Nature and extent of the problem. *Annals of the American Academy of Political and Social Science, 315,* 1–11.

Kernberg, O. (1975). *Borderline conditions and pathological narcissism.* New York: Jason Aronson.

Khantzian, E.J. (1981). Some treatment implications of ego and self-disturbances in alcoholism. In M. H. Bean & N. E. Zinberg (Eds.), *Dynamic approaches to the understanding and treatment of alcoholism* (pp. 163–188). New York: Free Press.

Kierkegaard, S. (1944). *The concept of dread* (W. Lowrie, Trans.). Princeton, NJ: Princeton University Press. (Original work published 1849)

Kirkpatrick, J. (1977). *Turnabout: Help for a new life.* New York: Doubleday.

Klausner, S. (1964). Sacred and profane meanings of blood and alcohol. *The Journal of Social Psychology, 64,* 27–43.

Knight, R. P. (1937). The dynamics and treatment of chronic alcohol addiction. *Bulletin of the Menninger Clinic, 1,* 233–250.

Knight, R. P. (1938). The psychoanalytic treatment in a sanitarium of chronic addiction to alcohol. *Journal of the American Medical Association, 111,* 1443–1448.

Kohut, H. (1971). *The analysis of the self: A systematic approach to the psychoanalytic treatment of narcissistic personality disorders.* New York: International Universities Press.

Kohut, H. (1977a). *The restoration of the self.* New York: International Universities Press.

Kohut, H. (1977b). *Psychodynamics of drug dependence* (National Institute on Drug Abuse Monograph 12, pp. vii–ix). Washington, DC: U.S. Government Printing Office.

Krystal, H., & Raskin, H. (1970). *Drug dependence: Aspects of ego function.* Detroit: Wayne State University Press.

Levin, J. D. (1981). A study of social role conflict in chronic alcoholic men affiliated with Alcoholics Anonymous (Doctoral dissertation, New York University, 1981). *Dissertation Abstracts International, 42-12B,* 4970. (University Microfilms No. 8210924)

Levin, J. D. (1987). *Treatment of alcoholism and other addictions: A self-psychology approach.* Northvale, NJ: Jason Aronson.

Levin, J. D. (1991). *Recovery from alcoholism: Beyond your wildest dreams.* Northvale, NJ: Jason Aronson.

Levin, J. D. (1993). *Slings and arrows: narcissistic injury and its treatment.* Northvale, NJ: Jason Aronson.

Levin, J. D. & Weiss, R. H. (Eds.) (1994). *The dynamics and treatment of alcoholism: Essential papers.* Northvale, NJ: Jason Aronson.

Lex, B. (1985). Alcohol problems in special populations. In J. H. Mendelson & N. K. Mello (Eds.), *The diagnosis and treatment of alcoholism* (2nd ed., pp. 89–188). New York: McGraw-Hill.

Lipscomb, T. R., Carpenter, J. A., & Nathan, P. E. (1980). Static ataxia: A predictor of alcoholism? *British Journal of Addictions, 74,* 289–294.

London, W. P. (1990). Left-handedness and alcoholism. In S. Coren (Ed.), *Left-handedness: Behavioral implications and anomalies,* pp. 457–484. New York: Elsevier Science.

Loper, R. G., Kammeier, M. L., & Hoffman, H. (1973). MMPI characteristics of college freshmen males who later became alcoholics. *Journal of Abnormal Psychology, 82,* 159–162.

MacAndrew, C. (1965). The differentiation of male alcoholic outpatients from non-alcoholic psychiatric outpatients by means of the MMPI. *Quarterly Journal of Studies on Alcohol, 26,* 238–246.

MacAndrew, C. & Edgerton, R. B. (1969). *Drunken comportment.* Chicago: Aldine.

MacAndrew, C., & Geertsma, R.H. (1963). Analysis of responses of alcoholics to Scale 4 of the MMPI. *Quarterly Journal of Studies on Alcohol, 26,* 23–38.

Maccoby, M. (1977). Alcoholism in a Mexican village. In McClelland, D., Davis, W. N., Kalin, R., & Wanner, E. (Eds.). *The drinking man,* pp. 232–260. New York: Free Press.

Mahler, M., Pine F., & Bergman, A. (1975). *The psychological birth of the human infant: Symbiosis and individuation.* New York: Basic Books.

Marlatt, G. A. & Gordon, J. R. (1985). *Relapse prevention: Maintenance strategies in the treatment of addictive behaviors.* New York: Guilford Press.

Masserman, J., & Yum, K. (1946). An analysis of the influence of alcohol in experimental neurosis in cats. *Psychosomatic Medicine, 8,* 36–52.

Masters, W. H., & Johnson, V. E. (1970). *Human sexual inadequacy.* Boston: Little, Brown.

McClelland, D. C., Davis, W., Kalin, R., & Wanner, E. (1972). *The drinking man: Alcohol and human motivation.* New York: Free Press.

McCord, W., & McCord, J., with Gudeman, J. (1960). *Origins of Alcoholism.* Stanford, CA: Stanford University Press.

McCord, W., & McCord, J. (1962). A longitudinal study of the personality of alcoholics. In D. J. Pittman and C. R. Synder (Eds.), *Society, culture and drinking patterns* (pp. 413–430). Carbondale, Ill.: Southern Illinois University Press.

Mello, N.K., & Mendelson, J.H. (1970). Experimentally induced intoxication in alcoholics: A comparison between programmed and spontaneous drinking. *Journal of Pharmacology and Experimental Therapeutics, 173,* 101–116.

Mello, N. K. & Mendelson, J. H. (1972). Drinking patterns during work-contingent and noncontingent alcohol acquisition. *Psychosomatic Medicine, 34,* 139–164.

Menninger, K. (1938). *Man against himself.* New York: Harcourt Brace.

Meyerson, A. (1940). Alcohol: A study of social ambivalence. *Quarterly Journal of Studies on Alcohol, 1,* 13–20.

Murray, H. A. (1938). *Explorations in personality.* New York: Oxford University Press.

National Institute on Alcohol Abuse and Alcoholism (1983). *Fifth special report to the U.S. Congress on Alcohol and Health from the Secretary of Health and Human Services* (DHHS Publication No. 84-1291). Rockville, MD: Author.

National Institute on Alcohol Abuse and Alcoholism (NIAAA) (1988). *Sixth special report to the U.S. Congress on alcohol and health from the Secretary of Health and Human Services* (DHHS Publication No. 85-0009). Rockville, MD: Author.

National Institute on Alcohol Abuse and Alcoholism. (1990). *Seventh Special Report to the U.S. Congress on Alcohol and Health from the Secretary of Health and Human Services* (DHHS Publication No. 90-1656). Rockville, MD: Author.

National Institute of Alcohol Abuse and Alcoholism (1994). *Eighth special report to the U.S. Congress on alcohol and health from the Secretary of Health and Human Services* (NIH Publication No. 94-3699). Rockville, MD: Author.

Park, P. (1973). Developmental ordering of experiences in alcoholism. *Quarterly Journal of Studies on Alcohol, 34,* 473–488.

Pavlov, I. (1927). *Conditioned reflexes.* Oxford, England: Oxford University Press.

Peninston, E. G. & Kulkosky, P. J. (1989). Brainwave training and B-endorphin levels in alcoholics. *Alcoholism: Clinical and Experimental Research, 13,* 271–279.

Peninston, E. G., & Kulkosky, P. J. (1990). Alcoholic personality and alpha-theta brainwave training. *Medical Psychotherapy, 3,* 37–55.

Petrie, A. (1978). *Individuality in pain and suffering* (2nd ed.). Chicago: University of Chicago Press.

Pitts, F. N., Jr., & Winokur, G. (1966). Affective disorder—VII: Alcoholism and affective disorder. *Journal of Psychiatric Research, 4,* 37–50.

Polich, J., Armor, D., & Brainer, H. (1981). *The course of alcoholism.* New York: Wiley.

Polich, J., & Bloom, F. E. (1987). P300 from normals and adult children of alcoholics. *Alcohol, 4,* 301–307.

Pollock, V. E., Volavka, J., Goodwin, D. W., Mednick, S. A., Gabrielli, W. F., Knop, J., & Schulsinger, F. (1983). The EEG after alcohol administration in men at risk of alcoholism. *Archives of General Psychiatry, 40,* 857–861.

Porjesz, B., & Begleiter, H. (Eds.). (1983). *The biology of alcoholism, vol. VII: The pathogenesis of alcoholism, biological factors* (pp. 415–483). New York: Plenum Press.

Prochaska, J., & DiClemente, C. C. (1984). *The transtheoretical approach: Crossing the traditional boundaries of therapy.* Homewood, IL: Dow-Jones/Irwin.

Prochaska, J. V., DiClemente, C. C., & Norcross, J. C. (1992). In search of how people change: Applications to addictive behaviors. *American Psychologist, 47,* 1102–1114.

Propping, P., Kruger, J., & Mark, N. (1981). Genetic disposition to alcoholism: An EEG study in alcoholics and their relatives. *Human Genetics, 35,* 51–59.

Rado, S. (1933). The psychoanalysis of pharmacothymia. *Psychoanalytic Quarterly, 2,* 2–23.

Richards, H. J. (1993). *Therapy of the substance abuse syndromes.* Northvale, NJ: Jason Aronson.

Robbins, L. N., Bates, W. N., & O'Neal, P. (1962). Adult drinking patterns of former problem children. In D. J. Pittman & C. R. Snyder (Eds.), *Society, culture and drinking patterns* (pp. 395–412). Carbondale: Southern Illinois University Press.

Robbins, L. R., & Smith, E. M. (1980). Longitudinal studies of alcohol and drug problems: sex differences. In O. J. Kalant (Ed.), *Alcohol and drug problems in women.* New York: Plenum Press.

Roe, A. (1945). The adult adjustment of children of alcoholic parents raised in foster homes. *Quarterly Journal of Studies on Alcohol, 5,* 378–393.

Rohsenow, D. J. (1983). Alcoholics' perceptions of control. In W. M. Cox (Ed.), *Identifying and measuring alcoholic personality characteristics* (pp. 37–48). San Francisco: Jossey-Bass.

Rooney, J. F. (1991). Patterns of alcohol use in Spanish society. In. D. Pittman & H. R. White (Eds.), *Society, culture, and drinking patterns reexamined* (pp. 78–86). New Brunswick, NJ: Rutgers Center of Alcohol Studies.

Rotter, J. B. (1966). Generalized expectancies for internal versus external control of reinforcement. *Psychological Monographs, 80.*

Rush, B. (1994). An inquiry into the effects of ardent spirits upon the human body and mind. In J. Levin & R. Weiss (Eds.), *The dynamics and treatment of alcoholism: Essential papers* (pp. 11–27). Northvale, NJ: Jason Aronson. (Original work published 1785)

Sandor, S. (1968). The influence of ethyl alcohol on the development of the chick embryo. *Revue du-Embryologie et de-Cytologie, Serie Embryologie, 5*, 51–76.

Schuckit, M. A., & Gold, F. O. (1988). A simultaneous evaluation of multiple markers of ethanol/placebo challenges in sons of alcoholics and controls. *Archives of General Psychiatry, 45*, 211–216.

Shaffer, H. J. (1992). The psychology of stage change: The transition from addiction to recovery. In J. H. Lowinson, P. Ruiz, & R. B. Millman (Eds.), *Comprehensive textbook of substance abuse* (2nd ed., pp. 100–105). Baltimore: Williams & Wilkins.

Shaffer, H. J. (1994). Denial, ambivalence, and countertransferential hate. In J. D. Levin & R. H. Weiss (Eds.), *The dynamics and treatment of alcoholism: Essential papers*, pp. 421–437. Northvale, NJ: Jason Aronson.

Sher, K.J . (1987). Stress response dampening. In H. T. Blane & K. E. Leonard (Eds.), *Psychological theories of drinking and alcoholism* (pp. 227–271). New York: Guilford Press.

Shipley, T. E., Jr. (1982). Alcohol withdrawal and its treatment: Some conjectures in the context of the opponent-process theory. *Journal of Studies on Alcohol, 43*, 548–569.

Simmel, E. (1948). Alcoholism and addiction. *Psychoanalytic Quarterly, 17*, 6–31.

Skinner, B. F. (1938). *The behavior of organisms.* New York: Appleton-Century-Crofts.

Smith, M. O. (1989). *The Lincoln Hospital acupuncture drug treatment program.* Testimony presented to the Select Committee on Narcotics of the U.S. House of Representatives, July 25, 1989.

Sobell, M. B. & Sobell, L. C. (1978). *Behavioral treatment of alcohol problems: Individualized therapy and controlled drinking.* New York: Plenum Press.

Sobell, M. B., & Sobell, L. C. (1993). *Problem drinkers: Guided self-change treatment.* New York: Guilford Press.

Solomon, R. L. (1977). An opponent process theory of acquired motivation: The affective dynamics of addiction. In J. D. Maser & M.E.P. Seligman (Eds.), *Psychopathology: Experimental Models* (pp. 66–103). San Francisco: W. H. Freeman.

Spitz, H. I., & Rosecan, J. S. (1987). *Cocaine abuse.* New York: Brunner/Mazel.

Szasz, T. (1958). The role of the counterphobic mechanism in addiction. *Journal of the American Psychoanalytic Association, 6*, 309–325.

Tabakoff, B., Hoffman, P. L., Lee, J. M., Saito, T., Willard, B., & Deleon-Jones, F. (1988). Differences in platelet enzyme activity between alcoholics and nonalcoholics. *New England Journal of Medicine, 318*, 134–139.

Tarter, R. E. (1981). Minimal brain dysfunction as an etiological disposition to alcoholism. In R. E. Meyer (Eds.), *Evaluation of the alcoholic: Implications for research, theory, and treatment* (NIAAA Monograph Series). Washington, DC: National Institute on Alcohol Abuse and Alcoholism.

Tarter, R. E. & Alterman, A. I. (1989). Neurobehavioral theory of alcoholism etiology. In C. D. Choudron & D. A. Wilkinson (Eds.), *Theories of alcoholism.* Toronto: Addiction Research Foundation.

Tillich, P. (1952). *The courage to be.* New Haven, CT: Yale University Press.

Trimpey, J. (1989). *Rational recovery from alcoholism: The small book* (3rd ed.). Lotus, CA: Lotus Press.

Vaillant, G. E. (1983). *The natural history of alcoholism: Causes, patterns and paths to recovery.* Cambridge, MA: Harvard University Press.

Varela, A., Rivera, L., Mardones, J., & Cruz-Coke, R. (1969). Color vision defects in non-alcoholic relatives of alcoholic patients. *British Journal of the Addictions, 64*, 67–71.

von Knorring, A.-L., Bohman, M., von Knorring, L., & Oreland, L. (1985). Platelet MAO activity as a biological marker in subgroups of alcoholism. *Acta Psychiatrica Scandinavica, 72*, 51–58.

Williams, G. D. & DeBakey, S. F. (1992). Changes in levels of alcohol consumption: United States 1983 to 1988. *British Journal of Addictions, 87 (4),* 643–648.

Wilsnack, S. C. (1973). Sex role identity in female alcoholism. *Journal of Abnormal Psychology, 82,* 253–261.

Wilsnack, S. C. (1984). Drinking, sexuality, and sexual dysfunction in women. In S. C. Wilsnack & L. J. Beckman (Eds.), *Alcohol problems in women: Antecedents, consequences, and interventions,* pp. 189–228. New York: Guilford Press.

Wilsnack, S. C. & Beckman, L. J. (Eds.) (1984). *Alcohol problems in women: Antecedents, consequences, and intervention.* New York: Guilford Press.

Wilsnack, S.C. (1991). Sexuality and women's drinking: Findings from a U.S. national study. *Alcohol and Health Research World, 15*(2), 147–150.

Wilson, G., & Lawson, D. (1978). Expectancies, alcohol, and sexual arousal in women. *Abnormal Psychology, 85,* 358–367.

Winnicott, D. W. (1958). The capacity to be alone. In *The maturational processes and the facilitating environment* (pp. 29–36). New York: International Universities Press, 1965.

Winnicott, D. W. (1960). Ego distortion in terms of true and false self. In *The maturational processes and the facilitating environment* (pp. 140–152). New York: International Universities Press, 1965.

Winokur, G. (1974). The division of depressive illness into depressive-spectrum disease and pure depressive disease. *International Pharmaco-psychiatry, 9,* 5–13.

Winokur, G., Rimmer, J., & Reich, T. (1971). Alcoholism IV: Is there more than one type of alcoholism? *British Journal of Psychiatry, 18,* 525–531.

Winson, J. (1985). *Brain and Psyche: The Biology of the Unconscious.* New York: Anchor Press, Doubleday.

Winson, J. (1990). The Meaning of Dreams. *Scientific American,* November 1990. 86–96.

Wise, R. A. (1987). Psychomotor stimulant properties of addictive drugs. *Pharmacological Therapy, 35,* 227–263.

Witkin, H. A., & Oltman, P. K. (1967). Cognitive style. *International Journal of Neurology, 6,* 119–137.

Witkin, H. A., Karp, S. A., & Goodenough, D. R. (1959). Dependence in alcoholics. *Quarterly Journal of Studies on Alcohol, 20,* 493–504.

Wurmser, L. (1978). *The hidden dimension: Psychodynamics in compulsive drug use.* New York: Jason Aronson.

Zucker, R. A. & Gomberg, E. S. L. (1986). Etiology of alcoholism reconsidered: The case for a biopsychosocial process. *American Psychologist, 41,* 783–793.

Zuckerman, M. (1979). *Sensation seeking: Beyond the optimal level of arousal.* New York: Wiley.

Index